BOMBAY LONDON NEW YORK

AMITAVA KUMAR

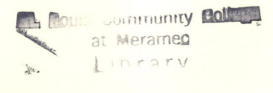

New York Routledge London

Published in 2002 by
Routledge
29 West 35th Street
New York, NY 10001
www.routledge-ny.com

Published in Great Britain by
Routledge
11 New Fetter Lane
London EC4P 4EE
www.routledge.co.uk

Routledge is an imprint of the Taylor & Francis Group.
Printed in the United States of America on acid-free paper.

Library of Congress Cataloging-in-Publication Data

Kumar, Amitava, 1963–
    Bombay—London—New York / Amitava Kumar.
        p. cm.
    Includes index.
    ISBN 0-415-94210-1 (acid-free paper) — ISBN 0-415-94211-X
    (pbk. : acid-free paper)
        1. Indic fiction (English)—20th century—History and criti-
    cism. 2. East Indians—Great Britain—Intellectual life. 3. East
    Indian Americans—Intellectual life. 4. American fiction—Indic
    influences. 5. English fiction—Indic influences. 6. East Indians
    in literature. 7. India—In literature. I. Title.
    PR9492.5 .K86 2002
    823′.9109954—dc21   2002004589

In some of Abhi's books, Sandeep found the following written on the first page:

Abhijit Das
17 Vivekananda Road
Calcutta (South)
West Bengal
India
Asia
Earth
The Solar System
The Universe.

Amit Chaudhuri,
A Strange and Sublime Address

Our generation has been exposed to so much. You have many more influences; you can think beyond your village, your town, your country. I read the Bible, I read American books, I read European books. Now my favorite writers are Indian.

Moses Isegawa, in an interview
in *Transition*

And if you simply must read a book about India, buy the *Lonely Planet* guide.

Kai Friese,
Voice Literary Supplement

For Mona

Tum na aaye the to har cheez wahi thi ke jo hai
Aasman haddad-e-nazar, raahguzar raahguzar,
sheesha-e-maye, sheesha-e-maye

CONTENTS

1

This book is about recent Indian fiction in English, but it is also, I have found out, about how and why we read.

In my childhood home, paper, of any kind, was to be touched only by hand. If you stepped on a book by accident, you were to pick it up and raise it respectfully to your forehead. I am not from a culture, although that seems the wrong word here for any number of reasons, where you rubbed paper on your arse.

I did not know what to write on the notebooks I first bought as a child when I visited my birthplace, Ara. The nibs we were given were of wood. We dipped them in ink. My cousins and I sat in a row near our elderly aunt who had become crippled with grief after her husband died young. His blood had turned black before his death; when he died, my aunt didn't move for months. Her legs swelled up and she could no longer walk. That is what at least I had heard my mother and others say. When she lay on her back in bed, my aunt couldn't sit up or raise herself without help. Through most of the day, she would sit with her legs immobile on the side of the bed that faced the door. Her son was studying to be a doctor. We were told that he wanted to be a doctor because his father had died of an incurable disease, *kalaazar*. And his mother was waiting to be able to walk again. There was reverence and also a faintly morbid, perhaps dread, expectation in that house. My aunt told me not to buy notebooks that had the pictures of Bombay film stars on them, and to always remember to touch the notebook with my forehead if I stepped on it. Her crippled hand gave to the alphabets she wrote out for me a larger, rounder form. I remember her as being neat and very strict, this aunt who wore a widow's white sari. Her room smelled of Dettol. In her presence, I wrote my first letters on the plain sheets of my notebook, always afraid that I would make mistakes. I always made mistakes and as soon as I had made one, I didn't want to use that notebook anymore.

It was in that same house in Ara, where my aunt lived, in which Naniji, my grandmother on my mother's side, died a few days short of my seventh birthday. When Naniji died, her sons' wives tore out the blank pages from our notebooks. The women rubbed clarified butter—"pure ghee"—on my grandmother's feet and then placed the sheets of paper against her soles. In the months that followed, these oily prints were filled with heavy embroidery and hung on the walls of the houses of all the relatives on my mother's side, including my old aunt. This is what remains of my earliest lessons in writing: the red footprints of my dead grandmother pointing toward eternity. On those sheets of the notebooks that I used to so quickly tire of when I made mistakes, the creases on Naniji's soles were stitched stiff with green silk.

Paper was to be worshipped, like money or the Gita. This freed you from the burden of doing any reading. My maternal

uncles worked in the prison bureaucracy. I looked up to cousins who, on the flimsy wooden doors of the rooms that they shared, wrote down in chalk their names with fancy titles. There were notebooks around, and some textbooks with their covers wrapped in pages taken from newspapers or magazines, but I do not remember any books. There was certainly no library. The comfortable ritual that I enter into now — a part of the privilege of living in a place like the United States — of choosing and reading books from the shelves that line my study, could not have been imagined at that time. The rituals in my grand-mother's house, in that small town in India's most backward province, had more to do with cleaning your teeth with tooth powders that had tobacco in them or concentrating on a cure for constipation.

2

There is a short story I like in which a young man comes to the United States from India and becomes obsessed with the desire to know everything about the Indian tradition. The story was written in Kannada by A. K. Ramanujan, who taught for many years at the University of Chicago. In the story, the young man named Annayya is amazed at how, unlike him, the American anthropologists knew so much about Indian culture. Annayya begins to read books on India: "On the second floor of the Chicago library were stacks and stacks of those books which had to be reached by climbing the ladders and holding on to the wooden railings. Library call number PK 321. The East had at last found a niche in the West."

The number PK 321 is tied, in my mind, with another code or number, a cryptic marker of mid–twentieth century globalization. It is PL 480, short for Public Law 480, 83rd Congress. Beginning in 1951, the United States provided wheat to India and other newly independent nations and accepted payment for the grain in local currency. The money that was "interest payable by the Government of India on the Wheat Loan of 1951" was used to fund "cultural exchange." In other words, monies to buy Indian books for American libraries in return for the regulated disposal of wheat from the American Midwest. The PL 480 library program for India and Pakistan began in January 1962. The library at the University of Chicago was selected by the Library of Congress as one of the top beneficiaries of the program. The books about ancient Hindu traditions that Ramanujan's Annayya was reading concealed a more contemporary exchange involving, among other things, the regulation on the open market of the price of thousands of tons of wheat from places like Kansas.

It was after coming to America as a foreign student that I read "Annayya's Anthropology" for the first time. For me, there was even a glimmer of self-recognition in Ramanujan's description of Annayya in America: "He read the *Gita*. In Mysore, he had made his father angry by refusing to read it. Here he drank beer and whisky, ate beef, used toilet paper instead of washing himself with water, lapped up the *Playboy* magazines with their pictures of naked breasts, thighs, and some navels as big as rupee coins." But what caught my attention during a subsequent reading was a detail in Ramanujan's story: the American anthropologist whose book Annayya was reading in the Chicago library stacks was a Ford Foundation fellow in India. In this fact hides the repetition of the link with PL 480.

Under the National Defense Education Act of 1958, a South Asia Language and Area Center was started at Chicago; as a result, the university received substantial Ford Foundation long-term grants. The same Ford Foundation was, of course, also interested in grains. India, with help from the Americans, was trying to succeed at launching the Green Revolution, which was to later make grain transfer to India unnecessary. But that was not the only aim of the Green Revolution. The environmental scientist Vandana Shiva has written that under the Ford Foundation program in India, "agriculture was transformed from being based on internal inputs to being dependent on external purchased inputs for which credits become necessary." The creditor was going to be America. We begin to see the further irony hidden in Ramanujan's remark that the East had found a niche in the West under the call number PK 321: the ghost that lurks beside that call number is the PL 480 program and the story of American grains and even gain. As Shiva points out, "The social and political planning that went into the Green Revolution aimed at engineering not just seeds but social relations as well."

In Ramanujan's story, however, it is in a different way that Annayya brushes against the grain of history. The book that he is reading in the library stacks contains photographs that reveal to Annayya scenes that appear familiar. When looking at the photograph showing a Hindu cremation, Annayya recognizes his cousin Sundararaya, who owned a photography studio in their hometown. Annayya reads the foreword and finds mention of his cousin's name. He returns to the photograph of the funeral. He realizes that the picture was taken in his own home. He looks at the corpse. Now the truth dawns on him: this is a photograph of his father's funeral. His father is dead.

I had only recently left my home in India when I read this story and was drawn by the drama of Annayya's loss. There was a lesson there, too, about books and libraries. I saw that the book is not removed from the world, from the realities of trade and profits and power. There was certainly a lesson there also about travel and what it grants in terms of awareness that results from displacement. The act of opening a book or entering a library also produces results akin to travel. All of this was present in Annayya's experience. And also in mine, when I read Ramanujan's story.

This lesson about the worldliness of books and libraries, and the reality or even illusion of travel, pervades those pages of Raj Kamal Jha's novel *The Blue Bedspread*, where he describes a visit to the American Center Library in Calcutta. The chapter is entitled "American Dream." People step in carefully in ones or twos, shuffling past the metal detectors and the uniformed guards, and enter another world. The visitors leave sweat marks on the glass-top counters. These visitors, Jha writes, wipe away carefully, surreptitiously, those marks with their shirt sleeves. And then, the visitors sit down. "The sweat begins to evaporate; outside, the wind continues to blow across the desert, the waves continue to churn in the ocean, through the Venetian blinds in the window, they can see the air shimmer as if in a mirage."

This memory shimmers for me through the mirage of time. It returns me to my youth when I would go to the American Center Library near Connaught Place in Delhi. It was one of those libraries that granted students like me entry whereas Indian libraries, controlled by the regulations of the bureaucracy and the elite intelligentsia, barred their doors to us. We would need letters of attestation from two "gazetted officers" to get admission to the Indian government libraries. The U.S. library or the British library, even if they made you feel more alien in your own land, allowed easier entrance. Apart from the freedom of entry, there were also other distinct, sensual pleasures that appeared wholly luxurious. I recognize Jha's description of the civic comforts offered by the library: in the bathroom, "the cold faucet is blue, the warm is red, they wash their faces, pour out the liquid soap that floats, like cool green jelly, in their palms. They tear out the tissue paper for the first time in their lives, watch it stain dark in patches as it soaks in the water from their washed hands." In Jha's narrative, the visitors pick up last week's *New York Times Sunday Magazine*, and look at the haute couture ads. They peel off the perfume strips and rub the smell on their wrists. Such smells are a prelude to a reverie. They flip back to the ads for expensive houses near Central Park West that are available for sale. They even manage to fall asleep, for half an hour.

That detail stops me. The half an hour nap. It is statement about limits. It reminds one of the duration of a fantasy and, therefore, of the material conditions of the real world. Perhaps what stirs in me is the memory of a desire to fall asleep in the American Center Library, the cool metal of the chair on which I was sitting in touch with my skin. The desire, at that point of my life, might have had a name: America. But as with Annayya, to come to America means to discover anew what had till now been home. The scrutiny takes banal forms. Why doesn't liquid soap float, "like cool green jelly," in the bathrooms in the town in which I was born? I return to a childhood memory of the home in Ara where I was learning to write alphabets during my visits to the town with my mother. In the corner of the house was the toilet: it had a hole in the floor and underneath it a bucket that was removed by an "untouchable" each morning. The bucket, foul and always tilting, was visible from the narrow back street that ran past the house. A bucket stood under each house on the street. When you were inside in the toilet, you could watch through the hole under you the *mohallah*'s pigs that had wandered in from the street. You would see them grunting over the bucket, fighting among themselves to eat your waste.

The sight fascinated me as a boy. I return to that memory now when I read in a book by an Indian novelist a description of a bathroom in a library run by the U.S. government in India. The contrasting images that arise in my mind make me reflect on the strange process through which books—and libraries— help you mark and discover the stations of your displacement. Books narrate history, and not simply by what they tell you between their pages. It is the same with libraries, as the narrator of Jha's novel finds during his visit to the bathroom of the American Center Library. In this process of discovery of the divided world, and the motion within it, lies nothing as narrow as a static lesson about inequality, undeniable as it may be. Rather, I ask myself whether there isn't an invitation to come close to the insight shared in that wonderful memoir *Beyond a Boundary*, by C. L. R. James: "Time would pass, old empires would fall and new ones take their place. The relations of classes had to change before I discovered that it's not the quality of goods and utility that matter, but movement, not where you are or what you have, but where you come from, where you are going and the rate at which you are getting there."

3

The movement I am most conscious of now is the movement of memory, shuttling between places. One place is home, the other the world. In one place, paper is worshipped; in the other, there is reading. But this is a false distinction. The two divided zones enter each other. There was such worldliness in the use of paper at home. I am suddenly reminded of Hindi newspapers being read in the trains that ran between Ara and Patna. For twenty paise, someone sitting around me would buy a newspaper like the *Indian Nation* or *Aryavarta*. A man on the adjoining berth, a complete stranger, would ask for a page from the paper. The newspaper would circulate among readers in the compartment, its individual pages sometimes torn and separated for easy reading by all. The news would incite conversation and debate. The one who had originally bought the newspaper could very well choose to be less generous and, spreading out the newspaper on the upper berth like a bedsheet, promptly go to sleep under the ineffectual railway fan screwed to the compartment's ceiling. When peanuts and puffed rice would be eaten, the pages from the newspaper would serve as makeshift plates. Outside, rain would begin to fall and people would roll up their newspapers to be unfurled later and used to cover their heads as they rushed to their homes or offices. The newspaper could also serve other ends. Sometimes, the toilets in the train would have no water. On those occasions, the newspaper would be put to more uncustomary use.

When I think of Annayya in the library at the University of Chicago, I also think that what he was beginning to learn, in some complex sense, was that you do not know love or death's loss except through language. And that language is changing. It dies. This sense of weighted mortality was perhaps not Annayya's, but it certainly is mine when I think about language. Unlike Annayya, who had learned about the death of his father, I have experienced in slow and small ways the death, in at least my own private universe, of my mother tongue. For the past fifteen years, I wrote in Hindi only when I bought the pale blue aerograms to post letters to my old grandmother living in a village in Bihar. My grandmother died two years ago. I seldom use Hindi anymore in my writing. All the news I get from India, either on the web or in print, is in English. The loss that Annayya was feeling is experienced by me as the loss also of the language in which that loss would first be felt and communicated. I discover myself as stranded at a distance. I am united with the people I am no longer among only by the dispossession of a common tongue.

There is a moment in a short story by a contemporary Hindi writer, Uday Prakash, where in the loss of a language what is also seen is the arrival of the triumphalist West. The protagonist of Prakash's tale is a Hindi poet, Paul Gomra. His real name is Ram Gopal Saksena, but upon witnessing the popularity of foreign brands in the market, "names like Maruti, Cielo, Zen, Sierra, Sumo, Honda, Kawasaki, Suzuki and whatnot," Ram Gopal reverses his name and comes up with Paul Gomra.

Standing at the turbulent borders of a changing age, the Hindi poet feels bewildered. Gomra has seen nations like Yugoslavia and East Germany and superpowers like the Soviet Union vanish from the political map of the world. With the demise of socialism in Europe, people have been waiting with great anticipation for its disappearance from Asia and the Third World. Prakash writes: "If matters had stopped there, Paul Gomra would not have been too much worried. But he could see that with the same speed with which socialism had been wiped out of Eastern Europe, now all the Hindi magazines and newspapers were being wiped out in Delhi." When I think about the transformation that Uday Prakash is describing, I am struck by another fact. It is only in books and in language that the disappearance of books and languages is to be mourned. And also fought.

In my hometown, Patna, there is a general consensus that culture, like the surrounding economy, lies in ruins. And yet a visit to the Khudabaksh Library reveals another world, distant from the cramped, dusty streets outside filled with rickshaws and cars with loud, blasting horns. A librarian, his right hand shaky, pulls out a book on medicine that was written two thousand years ago. The book is titled *Kitab-ul-Hashaish*. The edition the librarian holds in his hands is from the thirteenth century A.D. The book was translated from Greek to Arabic by the order of Haroun-ul-Rashid; it carries beautiful illustrations painted with herbal and mineral colors that still appear clean and bright. The librarian is old; his spectacles sit crookedly over his bulging eyes. He wants to show you ancient paintings of war scenes where, he says, "no two faces are alike." He keeps using the phrase "hidden treasures." There are 22,000 handwritten books in this library; about five thousand to seven thousand of them are rare manuscripts.

A well-known historian, Surendra Gopal, accompanies me on my visit to this library. Gopal tells me that the library was gifted to the government in 1891 and is today "the richest manuscript library on Islam in the world." When I hear this, I am only conscious of the wretchedness on the streets outside. A stone's throw away is the Patna Medical College and Hospital, where I had been treated and operated upon when I was a boy. My mother, too, was a patient there. Later, my sister worked in its wards as a doctor. Medical procedures in the hospital were sometimes performed in the light of lanterns and torches: when it was raining, flying ants would crowd in and settle down on the open wounds during operations. Even during the day, stray dogs pulled away at bandages on patients. Patna is a place where rats carried away my mother's dentures.

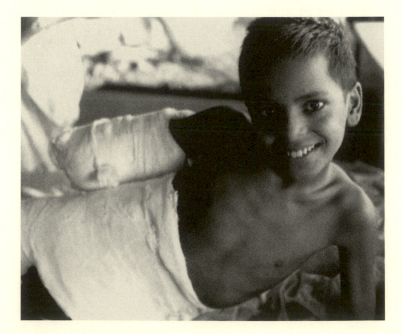

The librarian at the Khudabaksh has taken out from his safe another book. He tells me that it is a priceless book of poems by the Persian poet Hafiz. The book was presented to the Mogul ruler Humanyun by the emperor of Iran. The Mogul rulers used the book to read omens, or "shakun": they would turn to a page and try to foretell the future from the words on the page that was open before them. Akbar was emperor when his son Jahangir, banished to Allahabad for his philandering, sought the help of the book to divine his future. The lines that the young prince came across were *"Gham-e-garibi wa mehnat chun bar-namitabun / bashar-e khud rawam washaher yaar khud bashan"* (If it is intolerable for you to live in the foreign land, Then you should return home. You will be emperor). In the margins of the book, Jahangir had written that he was in Allahabad and had been perplexed; he returned home to Fatehpur-Sikri on read-ing the augury and a few days later, following Akbar's death, was crowned emperor.

The librarian's dark finger hovers over the lines that the emperor had inscribed. The page is filigreed in gold, the bare portions stained with age. I want to touch the page myself. I ask the librarian's permission, and when he says yes, I gently place my index finger where the emperor has signed his name.

The librarian and the historian talk for a long time. I do not want to leave the library. It is hot outside. The temperature has exceeded 110 degrees Fahrenheit. The librarian, who knows Urdu, Arabic, and Persian, is reciting poetry. The words were written by the last Mogul governor of Bihar. The historian, Gopal, mentions his name. I ask the librarian to repeat the lines. The poet was addressing the deer in the forest, saying to them what they know, that Majnun, the lover, has died. But what the poet wants to know from the deer is what has passed over the wilderness, how the forest has suffered. The librarian is a man of courtesy, what is called *tahzeeb* in Urdu. When I am leaving his office, he gestures toward Gopal and says, "He is a museum of knowledge. There are very few people left like this in Patna." Patna is the wilderness; people like the librarian recall Majnun, who has departed.

Gopal has been affected by the conversation about Patna and the loss of cultural institutions. He says that there is a complete absence now of those kinds of conversations that he felt were essential to civilized life. He is nostalgic about his youth in a young India. We pass Patna's Gandhi Maidan, only a mile or so from the Khudabaksh library; this is the place where the most important political gatherings have taken place in Patna's history. Gopal repeats the two lines of poetry that he had heard the poet Sahir Ludhianvi recite at a socialist meeting there in the 1950s: *"Har cheez yahan bikti hai, har cheez ko bikte dekha hai"* (Everything here is for sale, I have seen everything being sold here). The historian is burdened by his memories. He talks about the lack of funds, the theft of public money, the closing of colleges and libraries.

I think of the librarian with his unsteady hand, lovingly laying out the volume that was brought to India by Humayun *badshah*. The acquisition of those books was also a part of a process of trade and conquest. It was tied to commerce and, indeed, to the sale of both precious and ordinary goods. But this was not all. There are other truths too, like the words written by a reader in the margins of the text, about hopes, and fears, and the unknown. There are auguries of the future and a melancholia about the past. Libraries are haunted by the marketplace—but, it can be hoped, the opposite is true as well. At the same time, there is the enormous tussle of memory and desire that cannot all be neatly or fully regulated by the market or, for that matter,

Paper

the rulers of nations and corporations. Writers bear witness to this uneven battle too: it is part of the reality of the writer's work, of struggling every day with the worldliness of the word. Writers are caught in the contradictory tasks of building imaginary worlds that are removed from the everyday life and, at the same time, establishing how the imagination is not detached from the quotidian world and very much a vital part of it. To realize the truth of this condition is to know that books not only offer refuge from the world, they also return you *to* it. When I had understood this truth, I had stopped worshipping paper and become a reader.

This book is a record of my reading practice. It bears witness to my struggle to become a writer. I view the pages that follow only as marginal entries in a book written by others. Again and again, I have put my finger on the place where a writer has signed his or her name. This book tells the story of the many times that I have opened the thick book of Indian writing in order to divine signs for the journey I was about to undertake. The name I have given this literary journey is *Bombay-London-New York*.

1

What I am always going back to is the moment when I was going away. I want to write:

Only one plane flew out from Patna during the afternoon. Through the small window in the plane, I watched the rest of my family standing far back from the tarmac. It was hot outside. My grandmother, who had been brought from her village, and my parents and others from the family, stood in the shadow of a small aircraft that was parked about fifty meters away.

Although they were unable to see me, one or two of my relatives would raise their hand and wave. When the plane started moving, a cousin took off her long, scarflike *dupatta* and held it up with both hands so that an elegant span of bright orange unfurled in the strong breeze.

Then we were in the air. I removed from my hair the marigold leaves and grains of rice that my mother had sprinkled on me for good luck. Using the tip of her ring finger, my mother had put a spot of curd and red *sindoor* in the center of my forehead. I scrubbed it off as I watched the attendant, young and smartly clad in a sari, slowly making her way down the aisle toward me.

I cannot go much further with this writing before I stop. I was trying to describe a beginning: the moment of my departure from my hometown in India for the United States. But after putting down those words, I realize that my beginning was also a repetition.

On the last page of *Miguel Street*, one of the earliest books by V. S. Naipaul, the narrator leaves his tropical home to travel abroad to the West in pursuit of a degree: "I left them all and walked briskly towards the aeroplane, not looking back, looking only at my shadow before me, a dancing dwarf on the tarmac." My choice of the airport as the place to mark the beginning had come from Naipaul. It wasn't just the writing, I was also *experiencing* my own departure as an echo of what I had discovered as a student in the pages of a writer with whom I felt I shared my past and my origins in rural life. There is no beginning that is a blank page.

At that time, I hadn't read *The Enigma of Arrival*, an autobiographical novel in which Naipaul described his journey from Trinidad, first to America and then England. His family had given him a roasted chicken in a bag. He had no knife, no fork, no plate. The meal was eaten in his hotel room over the wastepaper basket. The chicken smelled. Naipaul had brought a diary. He thought he was getting to be a writer but he was aware that he was ending the day like a peasant.

On my first day in America, I ate beef and drank beer. And I think because of an exaggerated consciousness of the momentous shift in my life, I thought it proper to think of Mohandas Gandhi.

It began with my remembering the story my mother had told me of Gandhi's struggle with meat in his youth. An older friend told Gandhi in high school that many of their teachers were secretly eating meat and drinking wine. In the state of Gujarat, because of the influence of Jainism in particular, there is an abhorrence of meat among Hindus. But Gandhi wanted to be strong and free of the fear of thieves and darkness.

He had been told that if he ate meat he would gain physical and psychological strength. In his autobiography, *The Story of My Experiments With Truth*, Gandhi tells us that there was even a doggerel of the Gujarati poet Narmad that was popular among boys: "Behold the mighty Englishman/He rules the Indian small/Because being a meat-eater/He is five cubits tall."

A day was chosen by Gandhi and his friend. On a lonely spot by the river, Gandhi ate goat meat for the first time. He felt wretched and was unable to complete the meal. That night he was wracked by nightmares and remorse. Still, neither his friend nor Gandhi himself was willing to give up the experiment. Their surreptitious meals continued for over a year. Then, Gandhi decided he had no stomach for lying constantly to his mother about his meals. He gave up meat, saying to himself that he wouldn't take it as long as his parents lived. He never ate meat again.

I had never eaten beef before in my life. Only once, on a visit to the southern Indian city of Hyderabad as a schoolboy, I had seen cow's meat being sold in the open. I was in a car with my parents and sisters. I turned to look at a large hunk of meat hanging in front of a butcher's kiosk. The driver, trying to per-haps make common cause—among Hindus—where none was needed, said, "This is a Muslim area. They wouldn't dare to sell beef anywhere else in the city."

I had turned my eyes away at the remark as if I needed to quickly erase the evidence my eyes had seen. I knew that reli-gious riots between Hindus and Muslims often began with the killing of a cow or a pig and the carcass getting thrown into a temple or a mosque to provoke a response. In my young mind, it was the possibility of religious violence that I was turning away from if I straightened my gaze and looked instead at the road ahead.

Now I was in America and it didn't matter. I remember thinking of my mother's story about Gandhi, but felt no overwhelming sense of guilt.

My companion was a friend who was also from Patna. We had both gone to college in Delhi and now he too had been admitted to the same university in Syracuse, New York. Two blocks from the apartment that we had found with the help of the International Students Office, was a sandwich place that sold gyros and beef subs. I ordered beef because I wanted to know how it tasted. I had also decided I wasn't going to pretend I was still in India. I then asked for Heineken beer because I had seen it advertised in *Time* magazine in India.

I had no dreams that night of bleating animals that Gandhi was plagued by. If there was anything terrifying for me that first night in this country, it was the fear of failure, of never being able to become the scholar and writer that I wanted to be. I was quite convinced in my heart that although I had left home, even now the INS could send me home if I wrote terrible sentences.

Anyone could have told me that first night that I was indeed a failure. I was announcing to myself that I was free. But how? By drinking a bottle of Heineken!

If I wanted to console myself, I could have told myself that my failure was like Gandhi's. Not because I didn't like the meat I was served, but because I was finding out how I was defined by my past. It was another form of going back. I was also only rehearsing earlier breaks and repeating other departures.

The simpler truth was that I wanted desperately to believe that I belonged elsewhere. When I now think of that first day

in this country, I am reminded of the time when I left Patna
to join secondary school in Delhi. I had recently won a scholarship. I took one of my mother's small steel trunks to the New
Market a few miles from our house and got it painted a shiny
black. In bold white letters in the right-hand corner, I had the
painter carefully write: A. KUMAR, NEW DELHI.

To this day, some of my relatives call me by that whole
"name." I was only sixteen then. The move had been made, I
felt, from the provinces to the capital city. Suddenly, I wanted
to be better at English and would write in a notebook all the
unfamiliar words I encountered. The first entry in my notebook
was the word "lambent." I had come across it, if memory serves
me correctly, in Hardy's *Tess*.

Now, in America, I wanted to drink Heineken. That too
was a debt to my past. The magazines in which I had seen
the beer advertised were used copies of *Time* and *Newsweek*.
Those magazines were available for fifty paise in the *chor*

bazaar, a flea market behind Delhi's Red Fort. I took the magazines home to my parents in Patna to show them that I was now a citizen of the world. Those magazines as well as the blue-gray school uniform in which I traveled back in the train to Patna were, for me, my own distinctive signs of modernity.

Two more years passed in Delhi, and I cannot say exactly how, but those markers changed. I got interested in poetry, Marxism, the Indian New Wave films. I was increasingly drawn by street plays and theater at the National School of Drama, the paintings of ordinary life that I saw coming out of Baroda, and the authors whose books I found in the Sahitya Akademi Library, books that I would later recognize among the imports to the United States under the PL 480 program.

That was nearly twenty years ago. Most of those interests have stayed with me, and as I think back, they give my life some continuity. One thing has changed, however. Now, when I walk on Delhi's streets, men walk up to me and ask me if I have any dollars to sell. I am recognized as an N.R.I., a nonresident Indian.

Who is an N.R.I.? The one who goes back—with many suitcases instead of that single one that he or she had brought on the first journey. The tourist citizen. In Pankaj Mishra's *Butter Chicken in Ludhiana,* an account of his travels through small-town India, the writer describes a conversation in a hotel where an N.R.I. family "had arrived some time back, filling the silent empty courtyard behind us with their twangy American accents and voluminous suitcases." Mr. Tomar, the hotel owner, and Mishra were talking when a boy from the N.R.I. family came to speak to Mr. Tomar—and as I now read the details Mishra provides, I wonder whether I have not begun to occupy a new species of stereotype, one in which, uneasily, I recognize myself:

Halfway through his spiel, Mr. Tomar was interrupted. It was the teenaged boy from the Indian-American family that had arrived some time ago. 'Excuse me,' he said, 'may I have a boddle of Bissleri wadder?' A nonplussed Mr. Tomar looked at us first, and then, at him. 'Sorry,' he said, shaking his head in apology, 'I didn't hear you.' The boy repeated: 'May I have a boddle of Bissleri wadder?' Mr. Tomar heard him attentively; then lunged at the only word he could guess at. 'Oh, Bisleri!' he cried, 'Yes, of course! How many bottles?'

2

Naipaul had once impressed Paul Theroux with the critical observation that Columbus never mentioned that it was hot in the New World.

Then, or so goes Theroux's claim, Naipaul made the same mistake in *India: A Million Mutinies Now.* In Naipaul's book, Theroux writes, "there is little landscape and hardly any weather." The list goes on a little longer: "There is no smell, no heat or dust, no sweating men, no lisping saris, no honking traffic, nothing except the sound of yakking Indians." There was no going back to the real India for Theroux if he could not also have his sweating but silent subalterns.

Unfortunately for Theroux, there are a billion yakking Indians now. Those who write in English in India—in fact, those who even read English—add up to no more than 2 percent of the population according to official counts, though others argue that the more realistic estimate should be around 15 percent. This is still a small percentage but it translates into a lot of human beings—as Nirad C. Chaudhuri once commented, "In a country like India, so vast and populous, the individuals who form the exceptions may well run into millions."

Indian writers in the West, no doubt with what has been called the surplus visibility of minorities, are now seen everywhere. It has become more and more common in the last few years for people to strike up a conversation with me about Indian writers in English. I am speaking, of course, of people in the West, mostly in the United States. We can be at a party, or in the bus, or in the airport bookstore. The conversation so often begins or ends with my interlocutor asking me if I am Indian. Yes? Are you a doctor? No. You are in computers? No, I teach English. Oh! . . . I love Salman Rushdie! Or Vikram Seth, Arundhati Roy, Hanif Kureishi, Amitav Ghosh, Rohinton Mistry, Anita Desai, Jhumpa Lahiri. Once, I was asked if I was related to Hari Kumar in *The Jewel in the Crown* playing on PBS's *Masterpiece Theater*.

In my first few years in this country, I was incessantly quizzed about arranged marriages and bride burning. Suddenly it is more common now to be asked about novels. I guess one could regard that as a change for the better.

Except, it is important to remind oneself that Indian writers actually form a very small group, the better known among them number fewer than a dozen, with the majority of the established ones now based in the West. Most crucially, those so loosely identified as "Indian writers" are all writing in only one language, English. But India has seventeen languages recognized by the constitution; people write books and letters, make films, produce plays, print newspapers, talk, teach, preach, fight, make love, and dream in all those languages; there are more than thirty-five languages that are used by more than a million people who do all or some or more of the tasks mentioned above; the number of dialects that are spoken in India is estimated to be around 22,000. At a writers' conference in Connecticut, I heard an editor from a major commercial publishing house in New York explain what kind of books she didn't want. "I don't do homeopathy self-help books," she said. And added, "And male Indian novelists. I mean, I don't know what I'll do if I get yet another book by a male Indian novelist." What would this editor do if confronted by the vast amount of writing done in India in languages other than the one in which Barnes and Noble prints its catalogs?

In India, the phrase "Indian writer in English" seems to have been easily adopted as a name. But there is nothing natural in this naming. A well-known critic, Meenakshi Mukherjee, has commented, "If I were to write a novel in Marathi, I would not be called an Indian writer in Marathi, but simply a Marathi novelist, the epithet Marathi referring only to the language. . . . No one would write a doctoral dissertation on the Indianness of my Marathi novel." Is there any reason why, when it comes to any fiction in English, there should be an obsession with the issue of its Indianness? For Mukherjee, the "complicating factor" is that "English is not just any language — it was the language of our colonial rulers and continues even now to be the language of power and privilege." Mukherjee is right. And yet, as she herself points out, "the issues are far more complex, entangled with questions of class, mobility and readership." In such circumstances, Mukherjee argues that it is perhaps futile to establish a fixed opposition between the use of English and the vernaculars, or to use this opposition to flagellate the writers who choose English, as if it was always a matter of choice.

I am also reminded of an episode in Vikram Seth's *A Suitable Boy*. In the novel, the writer Amit Chatterjee has just finished doing a reading at a literary meeting. A challenging voice asks Chatterjee, "Why is that you do not write in Bengali, your mother tongue?" The writer answers that it wasn't for him a question of choice. Someone who has been trained all his life to play the sitar could not become a sarangi player because his ideology or conscience told him to. " 'Besides,' Amit added, 'we are all accidents of history and must do what we are best at without fretting too much about it. Even Sanskrit came to India from outside.' "

Arguing from what seems a similar position, Mukherjee recommends the following course: "It may be more useful for us to understand the circumstances that lead to the loss of the mother tongue than to charge these writers for capitalizing on their loss." I would not necessarily disagree, but we can also go in another direction. In some ways, English is very much a mother tongue for many Indians; of course, it is an English that is informed by other Indian languages and literatures. More important, what I would like to try to understand is what the emergence of a prominent number of Indian writers in English means for a young Indian who is beginning to write in English—whether this be in a city in India, or even in England and America.

In a long essay published recently, Naipaul reminisces about his early formation in Trinidad. "There was a further world," he writes, "of which our colonial world was only a shadow." It was this outside world that sent to the Caribbean islands their governors and their goods: smoked herring, salted cod, condensed milk, Dr. Sloan's liniment, the tonic called Six Sixty-Six, and all the books that were so crucial in Naipaul's making as a writer. But the books didn't permit easy entry into their imaginative world. Naipaul explains why: "Such a social knowledge as I had—a faint remembered village India and a mixed colonial world seen from the outside—didn't help with the literature of the metropolis. I was two worlds away." It is difficult not to think of this distance when one reads the writers from India who employ English. Today, a young writer in Trinidad can read Naipaul or Sam Selvon, one in Nigeria can read Buchi Emecheta or Ben Okri, and in India, Rushdie, Seth, Ghosh, Roy, and any of the others. Those who remain several worlds away are those who live and write, in those places, in languages other than English. And we must remind ourselves that this is happening even while in the world today there is a greater movement, across the global divide, of workers, students, tourists, bombs, software, arms, and even books. Inequality reigns in horrifying ways, and not everyone can read, but the world of media and advertising withholds very little from the imagination of the dispossessed.

In the diaspora, the gaps between the classes might be narrower, though even that is doubtful. Yet the example of the established writer can once again be a great consolation. To the extent that much of Indian fiction in English is also diasporic and reflects that experience, this writing also brings other satisfactions to the immigrant community. Because here, in the diaspora, there is a different hunger. For the well-to-do Indian immigrants, the excitement of reading new Indian fiction is almost palpable because they have not had the stories of their lives told except through the stamps and signatures in the pages of their passports. In the pages of this new fiction, they find flags for their hitherto unrecognized identities. They also make passionate, eager readers. Are these the kind of readers an Indian writer could not have had twenty years ago in the West?

There is an account of Naipaul talking to an editor about himself and his brother, Shiva:

If we were addressing audiences of people like ourselves, we would have been different writers. I am always aware of writing in a vacuum, almost always for myself, and almost not having an audience. That wonderful relationship that I felt an American writer would always have with his American readers, or a French writer with his French readers—I was always writing for people who were indifferent to my material.

Ah, readers. . . . To think that a critical mass of the right kind of readers could have saved us from the truth of those words, and also, given the fact that Naipaul has often been accused of cultivating a Western audience, their self-tormenting irony. That an audience of "ourselves" would have relieved us not only of the mannerisms, but also the desperate grasping for authenticity, which produces, as Theroux would want it, the mistress of spices, the heat and dust, sweating men and women in lisping saris, brought together in arranged marriages, yes, the honking traffic, and the whole hullabaloo in the guava orchard. In short, the sound of yakking Indians.

3

When I came to the United States, I had thought I was going to go back to India after two years. Then, I went to Minneapolis to join a doctoral program. Two years became five. And then, the question never came up in the same way anymore.

In Minneapolis it used to be bitterly cold outside. I never got used to the snow. I was living in a small, attic apartment—through the sloping roof close above my head, I heard the scurrying of animal feet as I slept—and would come down at rigidly prescribed hours to cook my meals. My landlady, who allowed me the use of her kitchen, was a recently divorced woman in her fifties. She lived alone, playing the piano and drinking martinis at night, and I was struck by the fact that she never ate the green olives she put in her drink. Before I moved to Minnesota, I had never seen an olive. Now, each morning, there were two or three plump olives lying discarded in the kitchen sink. On Saturdays, a Native American woman would come to clean the house. I cleaned my room myself, and I was permitted to do my laundry in the basement on weekdays.

One evening, I descended from the attic to cook supper after my landlady had eaten, as was my custom: rice and Progresso lentil soup, disguised with a few basic spices to taste a bit like dal. When I sat down at the kitchen table, I saw that the landlady—I had not thought of her until I started writing this, but I believe her name was Meg—had left the day's *New York Times* for me, with a blue arrow pointing to an article. The headline read: "Street Dramatist in India Slain Over Play." The story began: "A leftist who was one of India's most popular street theater directors was beaten to death by thugs last weekend after he refused a politician's demand to stop a drama in support of an opposing candidate, witnesses said."

The slain theater activist's name was Safdar Hashmi. I had watched his plays with great interest in India, before I came to this country; in the two years prior to his death, I had written poems in which I hoped to emulate the didacticism and the wit that were the hallmark of Hashmi's plays. I sat looking at the *Times*'s photograph of his corpse. Around him, illuminated by the light of the Delhi morning, stood many progressive intellectuals whose faces I recognized. I do not think I had ever felt as alone as I did that evening in my landlady's kitchen.

I will not claim that Safdar was a friend of mine, although I had exchanged greetings with him at the bus stop, or at his street performances at Delhi University. He had an easy charm and a handsome face, and his talent was legendary. He was only nine years older than I, and he had provided me a model for the writer I wanted to become in the future. Even in faraway Minneapolis, in the brief obituary, I caught a glimpse of what had made him so inspiring: "Mr. Hashmi was popular for brief, biting satires that made fun of corrupt politicians, policemen and businessmen, which drew laughter and cheers from large audiences of industrial workers. . . . His plays . . . moved from the propagandist dramas of the early 1970s to subtler themes." A month later that year, Khomeini was to place the *fatwa* on Rushdie's head, and I could only think of Safdar being bludgeoned to death on a road in Sahibabad outside Delhi. He was thirty-four years old—I remember noticing even in my shock that the *Times* reporter had got his age wrong—and now he was dead.

Safdar's killing unleashed a wave of grief and rage in India. The funeral procession was a nine-mile-long line of artists, workers, students—people from every fragment of a fragmented nation. The play that had been interrupted by Safdar's murder was performed a few days later at the site where the actors had been attacked by thugs. Safdar's widow, Moloyashree, acted in it. The play was also staged on the first anniversary of Safdar's death in towns and cities throughout India.

It was not till a few years later that I was made to think of all this again in a new way. In 1997, Qamar Azad Hashmi published *The Fifth Flame*, an account of the life of her murdered son. The book's epigraph reads "Four flames eternal burn at the shrine / I've come to set the fifth alight." Reading the book from the distance of a migrant's self-inflicted isolation, I found that *The Fifth Flame* also made me nostalgic. This feeling was not the familiar yearning for the land of my birth or its people, but for a return to the social and political organizations that help literature transcend fantasy. I had just taken my first job in the United States, teaching literature at a university. As a writer, I began thinking of my differences from the one who was in some sense my hero.

Safdar Hashmi received his mail in the offices of the Communist Party of India (Marxist) in Delhi; most Indian writers in the West have addresses only in the creative writing programs of American universities. Safdar thought of theater as that which "brings people closer to fighting organizations." Will the West's favorite Indian writers ever find institutions that can mobilize the South Asian community in the United States? Will the AFL-CIO come looking for the immigrant scribes to write about those who toil as cabdrivers, nannies, garment workers, and noncontract laborers in cities like New York and San Francisco? When will Safdar Hashmi come to America?

I am not distrustful of my nostalgia—I think nostalgia can be a weapon in a cultural milieu where you are expected to feel only shame for what you have left behind—but I do want to ask what it means to remember. Clearly, there is more than merely the calculus of loss in what one can call, borrowing a phrase from Rushdie, the business of "nostalgia economics." I am disturbed that the "soft" emotion of nostalgia in the diaspora is turned into the "hard" emotion of fundamentalism. The right-wing ultranationalist party in power in New Delhi gets its greatest support from Indians settled abroad. During his September 2000 visit to the United States, Atal Behari Vajpayee, the head of the government of what is supposedly the world's largest secular democracy, felt bold enough to say at a meeting of his supporters on Staten Island: "Today I am the Prime Minister, tomorrow I won't be. There are plenty of such examples in Delhi. But nobody can take away my right to remain a *swayamsevak.*" In proclaiming his fundamental identity as a member of the ultra-right-wing Rashtriya Swayamsewak Sangh, Vajpayee was removing his moderate mask. But he was also revealing a significant fact about his audience. The Indian prime minister was confident that the crowd of expatriate Indians would cheer his pledge of allegiance to the party that had supplied Gandhi's killer soon after India's independence and that has had a hand in every pogrom against Muslims and other minorities before and since. Indeed, the media reported that Vajpayee's remark was met with "thunderous applause." I have nothing to say to Vajpayee. But I have a question for the large group of his supporters among the immigrants. Is it impossible to use the memories of our loss, our not too burdensome displacement, and even our sometimes huge gains to reflect not only on our past but also on the processes through which we *create* our pasts? Why do we so easily replace our material past with a mythical one, pure and glorious—and then shed blood, ours and that of others, to protect that unreal, entirely illusory sense of ourselves? After all, the India of our pasts has historically been a place of cultural mixing. This process has continued in the diaspora, where our roots have given way to routes.

As the fiction of so many contemporary Indian writers reveals, our memories as Indians are also memories of movements across different countries and continents. We have built our homes in Britain, in Burma, in Africa, in South America, in the Caribbean, and in North America. If our past was all these places, can we be nostalgic for only one place? Can we be nostalgic for a place that never was?

This book has been written with the conviction that all the cities mentioned on our tickets actually hide secrets of other places, small towns and villages, and of people who are perpetually being lost to history. The story of that loss is the true subject here, even if I do not have any illusions of our ever having enjoyed a wholeness or a movie-set perfection that is now forever lost. *Bombay-London-New York* records a movement away from any pure, mythical origin: what it takes even as its starting point is a place that is populated by a mass of shared memories and patterns of forgetting.

4

Against Nostalgia

They will not come back.
The smile on the lips of Safdar Hashmi.
The mornings
on the days just after the Emergency had ended.
My first green kite.
My sister's childhood.
The glitter of her diamond nose-ring
when Begum Akhtar sang.
The red *paan* she put in her mouth.
Bharat Coffee House on Fraser Road in Patna
where we ate masala dosa after watching *Sholay*.
The December afternoon when the last exams

were finally over and every geometry set was now
forever useless.
The cricket commentary about G. R. Vishwanath's
wristy century at Chepauk.
In the summer afternoons
of Delhi when I was eighteen
the meeting of the New Wave
and the heat wave.
The flicker of anger on the screen of Om Puri's face.
A young snake taut
in the middle of the yellow dirt-road at noon.

They will not come back
even if you call them.
Not even the one whose leaving turned
all the leaves sere and brought winter to a barred
    door.

They will not come back.
The minute before Salman Rushdie
learned that there was a fatwa on his head.
The minute after
he had heard
that he was the winner of the Booker Prize.

They will not come back.
Your elder brother who died in a car accident.
Your younger sister only nineteen
who was too young to do much
much less to have taken her own life.
If they will not come back
we will have to take them in our hands
and place our thoughts of them
with great care near the open window
that faces the morning sun.

The mangoes
that were cheap and delicious
even though your father remembered them
being cheaper and more delicious still
in those days

that will not come back.
In those days before asthma and Cortisone
had changed the way your mother looked
at photographs of herself
holding you.

But I have never heard my mother
talk about the days
that she must know will never come back.
What sticks in her throat when she thinks about
    those days?

Calling
out to one
part of us from those days
in which before he became famous
people say Nusrat sang
at the roadside with *surma* in his eyes?

They were never there. Those days
that will never come back.
The days before television.
When there was only one Communist Party.
When you died in the house you were born in.
When you knew who was a Hindu and who a Muslim
and it did not matter.
They were never there. Those days.
Or even if they were
they were there only in the pages of history books.

Like the days when Megasthenes wrote
in his diary in 303 B.C.
that in Pataliputra
people left their doors unlocked.
He was writing in the light
of the oil lamp that left on the gold ceiling
adorned with nude sculptures
a layer of soot as black
as the kohl
in the eyes of the slave woman attending on him.

Going Back

Those were the days
when people left their doors unlocked.
It is only the thieves today
who most loudly repeat the tale
of the Greek traveler in ancient India.

Those were the days
Megasthenes had written in his journal
as he lay in bed
gathering the kohl from the black eyes
of the slave woman
sent to him one night
in Pataliputra which is present-day Patna
where my mother cannot leave her doors unlocked.

Those were the days
that are not going to come back
when people left
the doors of their homes unlocked
    —and those who didn't
    have houses to lock
    were never around to remind you
    that those days will not come back.
What will come back
will be the yellow flowers of *amaltas*
stained with fresh dew.
What will come back are the times we will meet
at the end of long journeys.
What will come back
will come back with new possibilities
of hard defeat and hard-won victories.
What will come back
will be the songs of the striking fisherfolk
in a film by Anand Patwardhan.
What will come back will be the words
you had forgotten though you had always
    remembered the song.
What will come back again
is the need to cry

for that which never came back.
What will come back is the one who never left.

What will come back
among those who have left their homes
will be the new sounds of mutiny
among Asian bands in London.
What will come back are the posters
"In defence of our secular tradition"
brought from the Rafi Marg office of Sahmat.
What will come back even here
is rice and fish in mustard curry.
And stepping out of the dark skyscraper
into light a long-haired woman in a green sari.

What will come back are the promises
you pressed into the hands of those whose shadows
framed the doorways of your departure.
What will come back during evenings
like this one to haunt you are the poems
like friends who helped you understand
that there was no going back for any one of you.

Going Back

PART I

1

By the time I had learned to read, I had become aware that the smartest person in modern India was a man in Bombay called Homi Bhabha. Of course, that isn't how he was described in the history books that I later read in school; in textbooks and the pages of national newspapers, he was called "the father of India's nuclear program."

Homi Jehangir Bhabha was a physicist but he played Beethoven and Chopin. He liked to paint. They said that Bhabha always wore double-breasted suits, even when he launched his cosmic ray balloons in the swamps of southern India. Like Nehru, who had died a year after my birth, Bhabha was described as a man of letters. Both men loved roses. The knowledge of science and this openness to art and to modernity, this attitude toward the larger world that I associated with men like Bhabha, would come to me later as a challenge when I was in my late teens. In 1966, when I had just begun to write alphabets on my own, Bhabha died tragically in a plane crash on Mount Blanc.

Bhabha's name must have entered our household as a result of his untimely death. I would have learned then that he was a brilliant scientist and close to Jawaharlal Nehru. I knew that Nehru, India's first prime minister, had studied at Harrow and Cambridge. At those places, he went by the name Joe. As a boy, in 1909, Nehru had traveled with his father to Berlin to see Count Zeppelin arrive in his airship from Friedrichshafen and be welcomed by the kaiser. This must have meant to me that Nehru was a man in touch with the wider world and with what was modern.

What made the century modern was also to be found in Bombay. It was the city of the Tatas, including J. R. D. Tata, who had pioneered aviation in India. It was Tata who had given Nehru his plane in 1937 to conduct the first Indian political campaign by air. Tata belonged to one of the more powerful Parsi families of Bombay. The advanced physics studies center that Bhabha founded in Bombay was called the Tata Institute of Fundamental Research. The Tatas had also founded a steel factory in Bihar in Jamshedpur, where I had lived when I was a boy. The Parsis in Jamshedpur, surrounded by the less developed Bihar of which I felt myself to be a part, were highly educated and rich. They spoke English and visited clubs. Bhabha, the leading scientist in independent India, was also a Parsi. All of this, repeated more as rumor or gossip than as history in our household, must have produced in a boy's mind a mix of exciting emotions: about Bhabha, about Bombay, and also about India's rise to a position of power and greatness in the world.

There was talk in our house of a conspiracy when the plane carrying Indian investigators to Switzerland also crashed in the Alps. Bhabha and death *together* made infinite sense in my surroundings, but not for any of the reasons I speculate about above. In the middle-class Hindu ethos in which I grew up, there was undeniable reverence for learning, but it was indistinguishable from reverence for death. Even a newspaper could not have so much reminded you of the world outside, as of the threat of the sudden, cataclysmic power of the unknown. Bhabha's name filled me with awe, but it must also have been a harbinger of that awful, threatening world that was immense and distant.

In recent times, I have returned to that world, to Bombay and to Bhabha, because of the reports I have been reading in the newspapers. In 1998, a year after having celebrated fifty years of independence, India conducted nuclear tests in the Thar desert. There was widespread jubilation on the streets of Indian cities, but also strong protest by thousands of people in India and outside. In a brief, inspired polemic entitled "The End of Imagination," Arundhati Roy protested the slide toward nuclearization in a country where even the basic necessities for hundreds of millions of people were only as real as a mirage. The previous year Roy had won fame and the Booker Prize for her debut novel, *The God of Small Things*. In her essay, she wrote: "India's nuclear bomb is the final act of betrayal by a ruling class that has failed its people." As an example of the lunacy of the rulers, Roy cited the words of an official who had declared that India would have no problem surviving a nuclear war. People could take iodine pills, the official had said. They could remain indoors, consume only stored water and food, and also try to avoid milk. This official was the head of the Health, Environment and Safety Group of the Bhabha Atomic Research Centre in Bombay.

My eye stumbled over that one name that had shone so brightly in my childhood. The legacy that Bhabha represented had now melded into the official Indian history of progress:

from the past of the bullock cart into the future of the nuclear age. It was a legacy of development that, sadly enough, the ultranationalist party in power, the government led by the Bharatiya Janata Party, has come to own. In 1955, in Geneva, Bhabha had been the president of the United Nations Conference on the Peaceful Uses of Atomic Energy. But there was nothing peaceful about the deployment of nuclear might now or perhaps ever. Bhabha had wanted India to step confidently into modernity, on equal terms with the West, with technology functioning as a part of our civilizational growth. Or so I had believed. Bhabha's foundational work was now held hostage by those zealots with saffron flags who, even as they attacked Coca Cola for being Western, jingoistically embraced the nuclear bomb as somehow utterly indigenous! The nuclear bomb, for the followers of the ruling party and many others in India, was a way of militantly asserting superiority not only against the neighboring state of Pakistan but also against all those minorities within India who fell outside the dominant Hindu fold: Muslims, Christians, women, homosexuals, the untouchables, and the communists.

After the Indian nuclear tests, the Shiv Sena leader, Bal Thackeray, had declared in Bombay: "We have proved that we are not eunuchs anymore." Thackeray's party—also responsible for renaming the city Mumbai—came to being in the mid-1960s on an anti-immigrant platform. The Sena wanted all the people from other parts of India, most prominently South Indians, to be thrown out of Bombay. Since the 1980s, acting largely out of electoral greed, the Shiv Sena has turned its focus on the demonization of Muslims. In 1984, it entered into national alliance with the BJP. Thackeray has cited Hitler among his heroes. He is also widely reported to have masterminded the Bombay riots after the Babri mosque demolition in north India in 1992; during those periods of rioting, the Sena members went on a rampage, killing Muslims, identifying their homes by using government electoral rolls. Of the 900 officially reported dead in the riots, 575 were Muslims. The result of the government inquiry into the riots, called the Srikrishna Report, states: "For five days in December 1992 and fifteen days in January 1993, Bombay, *prima urbs* of this country, was rocked by riots and violence unprecedented in magnitude and ferocity, as though the forces of Satan were let loose, destroying all human values and civilized behavior. . . . From January 8, 1993, at least, there is no doubt that the Shiv Sena and Shiv Sainiks took the lead in organizing attacks on Muslims and their properties. . . ." The report was released in 1998 but Bal Thackeray has so far gone unpunished.

A few months ago, I went to the Tata Institute of Fundamental Research that Bhabha had founded in Bombay. I was not allowed in. But in the small office outside, in which the guards spoke to me, there was a black-and-white formal portrait of Homi Bhabha wearing a suit. A garland now hung around the picture, and on Bhabha's forehead a red *tilak* had been freshly smeared. I waited under the portrait, suddenly unsure why I was there. An official from inside the institute, who spoke to me on the phone, gave the date for the institute's foundation, the date when the current building had been occupied, and then there was no further talk between us. Standing in that room, the guards looking at me with uncomprehending interest, I didn't feel I could reasonably tell the voice at the other end what Bhabha had meant to me in my childhood. This was clearly not the right place or time to engage a stranger in a conversation about India's garbled modernity.

2

U. R. Anantha Murthy, the noted Kannada writer, once wrote a short story in which a poor villager, who has been abandoned by his family, tells a visitor: "Your son might know my son, Dr Subramanya Shastri. Studied in London. He's an engineer in Bombay. You know the place where they make the atom bomb—there." Anantha Murthy is here attacking our modernity—our modernity that has been given degrees by the West—but he is also mocking the city and its indifference. In the story, the old, dying man's statement underlines his isolation. We are also being told that Bombay has planned the destruction of the small town and the village. Such a conclusion might appear extreme in any other situation, but is it not a fair assessment in the context of the bomb? In his essay entitled "Countdown," Amitav Ghosh describes a visit to the village of Khetolai, close to the site where the Indian government had carried out the nuclear tests. The first nuclear test was conducted in the same place in 1974. Ghosh listened to the villagers there who complained of contracting cancer and strange skin diseases. When it rained, people sprouted sores on their skins. The cattle in the village had developed deformities. One young man told the visiting writer that it was only the politicians in the city who benefited from the bomb. No one else in the country gained anything. "The bomb-cult," Ghosh wrote, "represents the uprising of those who find themselves being pushed back from this table: it is the rebellion of the rebelled-against, the insurrection of an elite." The essay concluded with an unambiguous condemnation: "The pursuit of nuclear weapons in the subcontinent is the moral equivalent of civil war: the targets the rulers have in mind for these weapons are, in the end, none other than their own people."

Ghosh made one particularly chilling observation in "Countdown." A nuclear catastrophe in South Asia, a cataclysmic conflict between India and Pakistan, was likely also because the production and storage of nuclear warheads in both these poor nations is concentrated in a few facilities. "Both sides can therefore," Ghosh noted, "realistically hope to destroy each other's production and storage capacities with a single strike." India's nuclear arsenal is believed to be stored at the Bhabha Atomic Research Centre in Bombay. What would happen in the event of a nuclear attack on that city?

After the 1998 nuclear tests in the Thar desert, an Indian physicist at M.I.T. wrote a paper in which he presented his calculations about the consequences of a hypothetical nuclear detonation over Bombay. The name of that physicist was M. V. Ramana. Ghosh had mentioned Ramana's paper in his essay. I contacted Ramana after reading "Countdown," and he sent me a slim, letter-sized orange book in the mail. Ramana's paper had been published as a book by International Physicians for the Prevention of Nuclear War (IPPNW). Ramana had titled it *Bombing Bombay?* The language of Ramana's tract was scientific in a slow and meticulous way. The catastrophe of a nuclear explosion was imagined as a series of physical and chemical changes, and Ramana had set down mathematical equations to explain the degrees of radiation or changes in pressure that would result from the explosion. But his sentiments about the bomb were made clear by the photographs from Japan, as well as quotes from survivors of the bombing in Hiroshima and Nagasaki, that accompanied Ramana's presentation of data about the hypothetical scenario in Bombay. A bomb of the kind that was dropped on Hiroshima—which produced an explosion that was equivalent to 15 kilotons (or 15,000,000 kilograms) of high-energy chemical explosive—would kill anywhere from 160,000 to 866,000 people in Bombay. A 150-kiloton hydrogen bomb, more typical of modern nuclear arsenals, would cause somewhere between 736,000 and 8,660,000 deaths.

Ramana explained that the initial energy released from the nuclear explosion is in the form of high-energy X rays. When the surrounding air absorbs this energy, the temperature can rise to millions of degrees. A fireball is formed, which expands outward at a tremendous rate, cooling by emitting radiation. The blast from this fireball travels outward as a shock wave, crushing human bodies, damaging lungs, rupturing eardrums. The blast also sets into motion winds that turn objects in their path into missiles. Pieces of glass from a window shattered by the blast, for example, would fly at a hundred miles per hour.

The nuclear reactions that cause the explosion also produce neutron and gamma radiation. Those not shielded from this radiation within a radius of about three-quarters of a mile would be subject to sufficient radiation that would, if one went by the experience of Hiroshima and Nagasaki, cause radiation sickness. They would experience nausea, vomiting, and loss of appetite, diarrhea with blood in their stool, bleeding from the gums and other places, purple spots from hypodermal bleeding, and loss of hair and extremely low white blood cell counts. About 50 to 70 percent of these victims would die within a couple of months.

The heat generated by the explosion is so intense that sand explodes like popcorn. In Hiroshima ceramic tiles and even the granite stone close to ground zero had melted. Everything inflammable would burn owing to the heat and light from the fireball. Buildings with inflammable material would catch fire. Clothes would burst into flames. Fuel tanks and cooking-gas cylinders would also explode. Within fifteen to twenty minutes, cars, trees, buildings, and the furniture inside them, even the rubbish on Bombay's streets, would coalesce into a huge, consuming fire.

Some weeks after the September 11 attacks on the World Trade Center, I wrote to Ramana to ask him about the explosion that brought down the twin towers and killed thousands of people. How does the experience compare with a nuclear explosion? Ramana began his reply by saying that the process of a jet slamming into a building is actually quite complicated and still being studied. Then, he set down his cautious judgment. He said that it seemed reasonable to conclude that the explosion that followed the impact of the jet would have been "the equivalent of a really small nuclear bomb, with perhaps about a thousandth of the explosive energy of the bomb that exploded over Hiroshima or my hypothetical scenario over Bombay." Ramana estimated the temperature close to the center of the explosion to be several thousand degrees. The fireball that we saw burst on our television sets over and over again on September 11 had set a chain of fires inside the towers within minutes. The fire that burnt for a long time was fed by the fuel from the aircraft; the temperature there would have been about 1,000–2,000 degrees. This intense heat explained why so many bodies were never found. And why the steel that held up the twin towers melted and crashed to the ground. Or why, before this happened, people thought it better to step out of the windows, eighty or ninety floors high, and give themselves up to the empty but cool air.

In his paper, Ramana had mentioned that if the explosion targeted Bombay's Fort Area, centered around Hutatma Chowk, then, even with a small yield, the city's financial district as well as the secretariat would be destroyed. In Churchgate

Station, which is the city's busy train terminus, the teeming thousands would be instantly incinerated. Rohinton Mistry's Firozsha Baag, near Chowpatty, would be set aflame. So, too, would Salman Rushdie's Methwold Estate on Warden Road. Saleem Sinai's Cathedral and Connon Boys' High School would be close to the epicenter and its walls would melt instantly. Even to the north, on Juhu Beach, where Ardashir Vakil's Cyrus Readymoney ran out to swim in the sea and where movie stars gathered at the Sun 'n' Sand Hotel, the moisture hanging in the air would condense around radioactive particles and turn to black rain.

Ramana reminded me that his calculations were conservative. The actual density of Bombay's population was higher than the assumed density. If the bombing took place by day, in order to maximize visibility, the number of commuters from places like Pune would be substantial. Bombay is also home to many industries. According to Ramana, India's "highest concentration of chemical industries" is in the Trans-Thane creek area. There are over two thousand factories there. These would cause additional fires, explosions, and the spreading of toxic substances. A chemical disaster of the kind seen in the 1984 Union Carbide accident in Bhopal could be only one of the by-products of a nuclear explosion in Bombay. If the Bhabha Atomic Research Centre, on the outskirts of Bombay, were affected or hit, then all of the above effects would be multiplied. Ramana told me that if the bomb were exploded at ground level and the reactor core were damaged, then its radioactive products would rise into the radioactive cloud, adding to the fallout resulting from the nuclear explosion itself. The radiation dose from this fallout could lead to the deaths of 50 to 70 percent of all those exposed up to fifteen square miles. And since the contents of a reactor core have long half-lives, there would also be a significantly higher occurrence of cancer among the survivors in the decades that followed.

How much of this is known and understood by the people or, for that matter, even by the experts? After India's nuclear tests, the right-wing Vishwa Hindu Parishad had wanted to "distribute radioactive sand from the Pokhran desert" as holy "prasad" to the people all across India. And the scientist at the Bhabha Atomic Research Centre had, of course, suggested his own, easy safeguard. We return to Arundhati Roy:

> Deterrence will not and cannot work given the levels of ignorance and illiteracy that hang over our two countries like dense, impene-trable veils. . . . The Theory of Deterrence is nothing but a perilous joke in a world where iodine pills are prescribed as prophylactic for nuclear irradiation.

3

The Bombay of my childhood did not only mean Bhabha, it also meant Bollywood films. The film industry in India pro-duces—commentators often use the term "churns out"—close to eight hundred films every year. Bombay, or Bollywood, is the principal hub of this production. The Hindi films, even with their formulaic plots and elaborate song-and-dance routines, are technically sophisticated, but most of these films demand no more from their viewers than that they suspend their disbelief. By the time the three-hour film comes to an end, love and valor has limped home safe. And the audience, like a sigh escaping tired lips, exits the theater.

I find myself still enthralled by the magic of Hindi films. They are popular with audiences also in other parts of the world like Turkey, Egypt, Nigeria, and areas of the former Soviet Union. After the Taliban fled Kabul during the recent war in Afghanistan, the *New York Times* ran photographs of Afghan women with uncovered faces. There were photographs also of the men getting their beards shaved—and looking at picture postcards of Bombay film stars.

I wonder if my boyhood admiration for Bhabha, or for Nehru, wasn't, in true Bollywood fashion, a search for heroes and for the victor who would vanquish all. Today, of course, the destructiveness of the nuclear bomb makes a mockery of any such grand victory. But it is also possible that I am being unfair to Bombay films. The classic Hindi films offered criticism of the nationalist project and its skewed modernity. In the 1950s, when Nehru reigned in New Delhi, a string of films called attention to the systematic inequalities of the new democracy: Bimal Roy's *Do Bigha Zameen* (1953), Rajinder Singh Bedi's *Garam Coat* (1955), Sombhu Mitra's *Jagte Raho* (1956), Guru Dutt's *Pyaasa* (1957), and Ramesh Saigal's *Phir Subah Hogi* (1958). These films, I want to say today, were a real part of our experience of becoming modern. The oppressions of class and gender, or the divisions between the city and the country, or the pathos of the poor—I think these films were saying that all this was a part of our new modernity. And that this modernity was not always the same as that of the state and our rulers. I am certain, of course, that this did not occur to me when I was a boy, growing up in a provincial town in the sixties and seventies. I was not aware that these films carried hints of the humble modernity that I inhabited in my daily life. Instead, I believed that there was only one model of modernity, one that was not only urban but also urbane. My eyes were turned to Bombay, to

Bhabha, and I wanted to be a man of science, at ease with English, and able to eat my food in restaurants while someone played the piano. I wanted to learn to use a fork and knife.

I am using a very simplified language here, the language that conveys boyhood desires. A starker division, one that more dramatically captures a sense of opposed modernities in India, was articulated recently by Arundhati Roy at a talk she gave during a visit to a liberal arts college in Massachusetts: "In the lane behind my house, every night I walk past road gangs of emaciated laborers digging a trench to lay fiber-optic cables to speed up our digital revolution. In the bitter winter cold, they work by the light of a few candles." The illogic of development that Roy is protesting against here has been elaborated in greater detail by her in essays that address the specific contexts of nuclearization, big-dam construction, and globalization. The French sociologist and philosopher Pierre Bourdieu once wrote: "Who would link a riot in a suburb of Lyon to a political decision of 1970? Crimes go unpunished because people forget. All the critical forces in society need to insist on the inclusion of social costs of economic decisions in economic calculations." Although she is not alone in doing this and certainly not the first, Roy belongs to the more uncommon breed of writers who have undertaken the important political task of measuring the costs of the decisions made to benefit the powerful few.

Roy's criticism of the nuclear bomb was followed by her essay on the fight against the building of the big dams that Nehru had famously called "the temples of modern India." The writer donated her proceeds from the Booker Prize to the Narmada Bachao Andolan, the group that has been leading the protest against the construction of dams on the Narmada. India is the third-largest dam-building nation in the world.

The whole Narmada Valley Project involves a plan to build 3,200 dams on the Narmada. Citing an independent study, Roy says that fifty-six million people have been displaced by big dams, most of them Dalits and Adivasis, "the poorest of the poor." In another recent essay, focusing on the more avaricious aspects of what one could call "globalization from above," Roy has criticized the Shiv Sena–BJP government in Bombay for their dishonest bargains with foreign capital. The right wing in Bombay had ridden to power in the state of Maharashtra on a platform that opposed the U.S. multinational Enron; then, the following year, after they were successfully elected to power, the right-wing coalition performed a turnaround and signed a highly suspicious deal with the same company. This agreement, Roy points out, is "the largest contract ever signed in the history of India." The contract with Enron has borne bitter fruit. Roy writes, "The power that the Enron plant produces is *twice* as expensive as its nearest competitor and *seven times* as expensive as the cheapest electricity available in Maharashtra."

Since 1999, the contract has been in abeyance because the government refused to pay the exorbitant rates demanded by the company. In raising her voice against such exploitation, Roy also makes a case for a counterglobalization. "In the present circumstances," she told her audience in Massachusetts, "I'd say that the only thing worth globalizing is dissent. It's India's best export." The recent collapse of Enron, the largest bankruptcy in U.S. history, one that is also surrounded by scandal, has given new credibility to Roy's writing. For instance, in January 2002, when the Texas company's collapse was making the headlines, a Scottish newspaper presented Roy as one of the authors of Enron's downfall. The news report now gleefully detailed Enron's wrongdoings in India:

Even though the World Bank said that the project was too

expensive and that other forms of power would be cheaper, Enron

bulldozed ahead. There were no competitive tenders, politicians

were bought off with bribes estimated to run to $20 million and

local police and thugs were hired to terrorize the opposition into

silence. By 1997 Enron had been listed by the New York–based

Human Rights Watch organization as guilty of being "complicit

in human rights violations" in the state of Maharashtra.

Roy's voice is nothing if not preeminently pedagogical. My enthusiasm for it is linked to the ways in which this writing offers itself for use in a classroom. I teach world literature to students at an American university. The category of world literature is vague; it is understood that the "world" in the name primarily refers to the non-European world, as distinct from and outside the canons of English and American literatures; the works placed in it can be reduced, without any exertion at all, to multicultural exotica. Arundhati Roy's novel and essays challenge the assumptions of such categorization. Roy's recent essays make visible the relations between the East and the West, relations primarily of power and exploitation; they foreground politics in a way that doesn't allow an empty formalism to be practiced in a classroom; and their urgency, as well as their link to powerful current events like the protests in Seattle and Genoa, forbid their consumption as multicultural fortune cookies. Roy told an interviewer recently: "The writer is the midwife of understanding. It's very important for me to tell politics like a story, to make it real, to draw a link between a man with his child and what fruit he had in the village he lived in before he was kicked out, and how that relates to Mr. Wolfensohn at the

World Bank." Now, instead of world literature, I find myself teaching World Bank literature.

When asked why she had joined the movement against dams, Roy spoke of the Booker Prize and the attendant flood of publicity: "I felt that each feeling and emotion described in my book was being turned into a silver coin and that one day I was going to be turned into a silver statue with a silver heart. I needed to go back to the world and give back to it." Quite removed from the moral aspect of this response, which again has the characteristic pedagogical or didactic cast to it, is the undeniable fact that Roy has also changed powerfully under the force of social demands. Pankaj Mishra, in response to a question about Roy's writings on the nuclear bomb, had said that Roy was "constantly transforming experience into awareness." This is true of the trajectory of Roy's recent writing as a whole. Her novel had sketched—somewhat dreamily—the portrait of the untouchable Velutha. However, her essays and also her participation in national protests document a more difficult, demanding closeness to the people that Roy has always been writing about. In her public stance, there is also a quality of gathering confidence, in many ways undoubtedly a by-product of fame and wealth, which comes out in a courageous opposition to the state and its institutions. There is a precedent for a prize-winning writer in India turning to active dissent. Rabindranath Tagore, the winner of the Nobel Prize in literature in 1913, renounced his knighthood in 1919 to protest British repression against Indians. Tagore was a writer who had turned from his early days of romantic revivalism to a strong vision of a fight against oppression. Roy's decision to march with the real-life Veluthas recalls that earlier conversion.

Last year, Roy received recognition from two governments during the same week: the Chevalier des Arts et des Lettres from the government of France and a "contempt of court" charge from the Supreme Court in Delhi over her antidam protests. Roy called this simultaneous recognition a "rare honor," and added, "Both are an acknowledgement of me as a writer, and I am happy to accept them both." And yet Roy has been opposed to the label "writer-activist" — it reminds her of "sofa-bed" — and there is a good reason why. There is a normative assumption about both art and writing, and about its distinction from politics and activism, that underlies the yoking together of those two words "writer-activist." Nevertheless, the term allows me to distinguish Roy from someone like Bhabha, or, more accurately, to distinguish between different regimes of hybridity. The cosmopolitan appeal of Bhabha, the model of hybridity that he embodied, would be represented by the combination of qualities of science, art, music, and founder of research. These are important traits. But they also express an order of modernity whose pursuits are all sanctioned by the state and the elite. In Roy's case, on the other hand, the mix of means and ends is an oppositional one. It is directed against the elitism of the state and society, and it doesn't come without costs. After the great success of Roy's *The God of Small Things*, her Indian publisher had written that Roy had "activated some rogue literary gene in India's English reading and writing populace" and "everyone now wants to write an earth-shaking novel." Roy's activism, however, has not won the same number of converts. It has also made her a target of attacks in the press. Roy's response is clear-eyed and presented in a language that she has made her own: "But one of the reasons some people get so angry with me is because I have the space now that a lot of others who think like me don't. It was a mistake maybe for so many people to have opened their hearts to *The God of Small Things*. Because a lot of dams and bombs slipped in along with it."

4

In the past, Bombay was paraded as the prime example of metropolitan openness and plurality. Less bound to a past than imperial Delhi or even Calcutta, Bombay represented industrial dynamism, fashion, and, indeed, the future. In today's Bombay, the cosmopolitan hybridity represented by someone like Bhabha has been marginalized by the brazen ascent of a hybrid alliance of capital and the lumpen underclass. An ideology of purity, of religion and region, has taken strong hold. There is still talk of hybridity, but it is limited to art galleries and the speeches on textuality by a few well-known intellectuals at academic conferences. And ranged against it and apparently victorious, the hybridity of the criminal Shiv Sena is pervasive, and composite, and anonymous. Like garbage. Bollywood films confirm this. A new genre of films play out their fantasies against the backdrop of urban violence; one good example is Ramgopal Varma's *Satya* (1998), which has much to say even about the nexus between gangs and Bollywood films. *Satya* also provides its own ground-level reading of hybridity with the opening voice-over about "the city that does not sleep, the city that dreams even when it is awake, the city of glittering heights, the city of silent, dark abyss."

Given this reality, it is surprising to see that "hybridity," as an abstract concept, remains a mantra of postcolonial identity. It is a word that occurs often in the novels of Rushdie when he is talking about Bombay; by an ideological sleight of hand, Indian writers in English have, by extension, also come to symbolize the acme of plurality and openness. But this is where one needs once again to distinguish among different forms of hybridity and mixing.

Bombay

Arundhati Roy is useful here because she draws a sharp equation between both a dubious hybridity and an equally suspect cultural nationalism. Roy takes up the case of the new "Call Center College" near Delhi where young English-speaking Indians are trained to answer telephone queries from the United States and the United Kingdom. The trainees are taught to speak in British and American accents; they stay in touch with foreign news and the weather; they earn a fraction of the salaries that would be paid to their counterparts abroad. The business is predicted to become a trillion-dollar industry. Roy writes: "On duty they have to change their given names. Sushma becomes Susie, Govind becomes Jerry. Advani becomes Andy. (*Hi, I'm Andy, gee, hot day innit? Shoot, how can I help ya?*)." On the other hand, in India, there are also sites for breeding an indigenous, narrow cultural nationalism, and Roy's example is the right-wing RSS *shaka*, or training camp. This is the place where, Roy writes, "ordinary people march around in khaki shorts and learn that amassing nuclear weapons, religious bigotry, misogyny, homophobia, book burning and outright hatred are the ways in which to retrieve a nation's lost dignity." The two sites — the call center and the *shaka* — are complicitous: "while one arm is busy selling the nation off in chunks, the other, to divert attention, is orchestrating a baying, howling, deranged chorus of cultural nationalism." According to Roy, "They're Siamese twins — Advani and Andy."

It is against the hybridity of Advani-and-Andy that Roy positions the alliances that make up the protesters against the dams on the Narmada. Describing one such protest, she writes: "All of India was represented. Urban, rural, touchable, untouchable. This alliance is what gives the movement its raw power, its intellectual rigor and its phenomenal tenacity." In the context of the

Narmada movement, and the people's movements worldwide, "hybridity" acquires another, narrowly specific meaning. The Indian scientist and environmentalist Vandana Shiva, for example, has spoken against the Rockefeller Foundation's genetically engineered "Golden Rice":

> *Each year of the Green Revolution, they would introduce one rice variety that would last for one or two years, until it collapsed because of a disease outbreak. And then they would introduce a new monoculture. Collapsing monocultures are not diversity! But they are a wonderful treadmill that the big corporations would like us to get on. First they sold us chemicals. Then they wanted to sell us seeds that would require the chemicals. That is why they introduced genetic engineering. . . . The golden rice is part of that same package.*

The specificity of this critique makes it necessary to abandon the mantra of an abstract notion of hybridity. The lesson is that there is no golden hybridity. The only standard to work by has to be, to use Roy's phrase, "the greater common good." It is clear that despite its celebration in Indian English fiction and criticism, hybridity is open to contradictory uses. It is open to history's interrogations. Even the phenomenon of Arundhati Roy's rise to prominence in Indian letters as well as wider circles is a part of that contested terrain. No more but also no less. What is more significant, however, is that we learn that the contested terrain extends not only to Bombay, but also to the rest of India, to its small towns and villages.

IN THE LIGHT   OF SMALL   TOWNS

Arundhati Roy's debut novel, *The God of Small Things*, has sold more than six million copies worldwide. In addition to winning the Booker Prize, the book spent forty-nine weeks on the *New York Times* best-seller list, and was published in forty languages. This kind of worldwide success has obscured the fact that Roy's novel is set in a village "whose population had swelled to the size of a small town."

And yet this location is crucial. And not only because Roy's story is about the claustrophobia of the linked oppressions of caste and class and gender in a closed setting—in this case, rural Ayemenem, in the state of Kerala in southern India. Rather, the location is important because Roy reveals that the larger world, even the Western world, is not wholly removed from that village. In fact, a huge change has overcome Ayemenem. One name for the new upheaval is satellite television: "Blondes, wars, famines, football, sex, music, coups d'état—they all arrived on the same train. They unpacked together. They stayed at the same hotel. And in Ayemenem, where once the loudest sound had been a musical bus, now whole wars, famines, picturesque massacres and Bill Clinton could be summoned up like servants."

The eternal flicker of the television in the dark—"American policemen were stuffing a handcuffed teenaged boy into a police car. There was blood spattered on the pavement. The police-car lights flashed and a siren wailed a warning . . ."—is only a part of broader changes. In Ayemenem, the house of the communist leader has been turned into a luxury tourist hotel (" 'Heritage,' the hotel was called."). The son of a minor local party functionary Comrade K. N. M. Pillai, a young man named Lenin, ends up working as a technician in the Dutch and German embassies in Delhi ("Levin he called himself now. P. Levin"). Communism has given way to a victorious market capitalism and its dubious virtues. There is increased tourism and commodified culture. And there is decay and degradation. The outside world has penetrated the very ecology of the old order. One of Roy's main characters often breathes the changed air on the days that he walks "along the banks of the river that smelled of shit and pesticides bought with World Bank loans."

Is one to be surprised by this depiction? Almost a decade before Roy's novel appeared, Upamanyu Chatterjee's *English, August* had mocked the ready assumption that the *mofussil* towns and villages were places that held no surprises or that their incongruities would be considered absurd by outsiders. A British visitor is amazed that there is a video parlor, possibly showing blue films, in a very small Indian town. And irritated by this, the protagonist of Chatterjee's hilarious novel says to him:

> *"About sixty-five per cent of the population of the block of Jompanna—a block is roughly one-sixth or one-seventh of a*

district—is illiterate. But one doesn't need to be brainy or literate to watch a blue film on video. Your real surprise is just the . . ." he looked for the word, "juxtaposition, isn't it?" and then he was galled by Avery's solemnity (and so began, in Madan's phrase, to "finger" him), "but that's because India is a land of sublime and fascinating contradictions, where the Himalayas of the soul arise out of dung, and dance hand in hand with the phallus of Shiv."

There are also examples in Indian fiction of other, older forms of globalization appearing in the Indian countryside. In Mukul Kesavan's novel *Looking Through Glass*, to take up just one example, we encounter an unusual historical narrative of the world coming to the small town. In Kesavan's story, we are in the thick of the nationalist uprising in British-India. The period is August, 1942. Kesavan's narrator meets Tojo in Azamgarh. The reader learns that Tojo had been a tailor in Malaya but the Japanese occupation had forced him to return to his village in what would be the province of Uttar Pradesh in present-day India. What is the secret of his unusual name? The narrator tells us about Tojo's past: "Ramlakhan was his real name but after the Japanese overran Malaya he had taken on Tojo as a good name to fight the British with. Ramlakhan Tojo." A range of other examples, spanning different ages and types, can be found in other Indian writers in English, who are as different from each other as Amitav Ghosh, I. Allan Sealy, and, preceding them by several decades, Qurratulain Hyder.

In the same year that Kesavan's novel was published, a young Indian writer published a book of travel writing called *Butter Chicken in Ludhiana*. The writer's name was Pankaj Mishra, and his book was the first sustained portrait of travels through the new, tawdry world of Indian small towns. That book was a sardonic look at the attitudes that went with what Mishra called India's "shabby borrowed modernity." *Butter Chicken* signaled a growing interest among writers and readers in understanding the ways in which a new economy was beginning to find root in the whole of India. In fact, in a manner that recalled the pioneering work of R. K. Narayan from several decades ago, the book marked a shift in Indian writing in English, a turn away from the big cities to life in the less glamorous small towns.

Mishra's acerbic, often wry, account succeeded in making one very important point about the changing equation in Indian politics: metropolitan India had been toppled from its position of power by the rest of the country. While discussing the 1992 demolition of the Babri Masjid by Hindu zealots, Mishra wrote that a majority of those who had brought down the ancient mosque came from provincial backgrounds. The English-speaking elite had been reduced to passive bystanders. Small towns were shedding what Mishra called "their earlier, sleepy, half-apologetic air" and were now "pervaded, instead, at least in the wealthier quarters, by a new aggressiveness." This emergence found expression not only in religious bigotry; it was present also in a new sensibility that now sought to create "a whole new pan-Indian culture." Mishra found signs of this triumph in the "taste for strident politics, violent films, ostentatious architecture, lewd music, rumor-mongering newspapers and overcooked food." He found it also in the mixed-up squalor and prosperity in the small towns, and in the ragged confidence of the nouveau riche.

More than any of the above aspects, more than even the small vulnerabilities and the touching little signs of yearning that Mishra came across in the people he met in the Indian small towns, what stuck out for me the most was the philistinism that the writer repeatedly ran up against. For example, we find Mishra in a guest house in Rajasthan, reading Iris Murdoch's *The Word Child,* and a policeman walks up to him and demands to take a look at what Mishra is reading. The older man speaks little English, but that doesn't in any way deter him from carrying out an extended, somewhat absurd, interrogation about the novelist and the description on the dust jacket. At the end, he asks, "Why are you reading this book?" To which, Mishra replies, "For pleasure . . . *Apni khushi, apne maze ke liye."* The policeman looks at Mishra, and then at the book. He says, *"Yeh to badi moti aur difficult kitab lag rahi hai, isme kya maza aayega?* This looks like such a thick and difficult book. What sort of pleasure can you get out of it?"

This question is amusing and also irritating. It can also be put in another way. As a character in *English, August* asks: "What is Jane Austen doing in Meerut?" The answer can come from elsewhere, and indeed, learned sociologists and linguists try to do this all the time. But the response can come also from provincial India itself. And in his more recent debut novel, *The Romantics*, Mishra does exactly that, investing the space of vernacular culture with an aspiration as well as a kind of knowledge that earns for it the seemingly paradoxical title of provincial cosmopolitanism. We are introduced to the violence of change in the new economy, and accompanying that, the frustrations of a small-town existence. The old order is gone, the new one not yet born, and the human lives are caught in the distortions of the interregnum. And yet, it is in that troubled space that literature and reading plays a role—not by staging a rescue but, more simply and movingly, by holding to the reader a strange and surprising mirror of recognition.

The novel's point of entry, as in the earlier travel book, was the transformation of a small town under a predatory new economy. These are the opening words of *The Romantics*:

When I first came to Benares in the severe winter of 1989 I stayed in a crumbling riverside house. It is not the kind of place you can easily find anymore. Cut-price 'Guest House' for Japanese tourists and German pastry shops now line the riverfront; touts at the railway station and airport are likely to lead you to the modern concrete-and-glass hotels in the newer parts of the city. The new middle-class prosperity of India has at last come to Benares. The holiest of pilgrimage sites that Hindus for millennia have visited in order to attain liberation from the cycle of rebirths has grown into a noisy little commercial town.

Tourists, traders, seekers, refugees flit in and out of the pages of the rest of the novel. There is also cable television and talk of David Letterman. In all of this, the opposition is not so much between a placid, small-town complacency and the sudden incursion of both transnational and indigenous capital. Instead, the drama is of a discovery—and loss—by a young, provincial man of the world outside.

The narrator, Samar, picks up a second-hand copy of Flaubert's *Sentimental Education* from a pavement seller in Allahabad. In his rundown college library, Samar has read Edmund Wilson's commentary on the novel. He is amazed to find the "account of an ambitious provincial's tryst with metropolitan glamour and disillusion full of subtle satisfactions." Samar has a friend at college named Rajesh, a student with roots in indigent rural life. Rajesh borrows Samar's copy of Flaubert. And once, while returning in a train from the village where Rajesh's widowed mother lives alone, Samar listens to his friend, as he tells him: *"Yeh meri duniya ki kahani hai. Main in logo ko janta hoon. . .* It is the story of my world. I know these people well." In such plain declarations—about a world that is rendered distant and also made strangely intimate—we confront the vivid energies of an imagination that is often shut-off from the world but never closed to it.

If much of cosmopolitan Indian writing, as typified by Rushdie, has valorized the immigrant and the foreign land, then *The Romantics* is a celebration of the home and its forgotten world. What is remarkable is that this is unlike the nostalgic home of much of expatriate Indian writing. Instead of the bustling, bursting metropolis, we have the carefully drawn pictures of a few, linked lives in the Indian small towns. Provincial India emerges as a place where you can find oddly unexpected details of a complex dialogue with the West and also, of course, a place for the exchange of "gossip, corruption, and sleaze scandals: the size of a politician's wealth, the imaginative ways in which the World Bank or some other rich development agency had been conned, the bridges that existed only on paper, the dual-carriage highways that had never been built."

2

The sociologist Ashis Nandy has written that "Malgudi is English literature's first Indian small town." R. K. Narayan's Malgudi is an imaginary town that is neither city nor country: it suffers an invasion intermittently from the distant, urban world, and its unaffected, amiable pace reflects in many ways the dominant sense of Indian village life. Malgudi resembles the old Mysore of Narayan's youth. It is a town that appeared to him on a certain day in September, a day that had been chosen by Narayan's grandmother for its auspiciousness. Narayan had bought a new exercise book for his novel. He wrote in his memoirs: "As I sat in a room nibbling my pen and wondering what to write, Malgudi with its little railway station swam into view, all ready-made, with a character called Swaminathan running down the platform peering into the faces of passengers, and grimacing at a bearded face."

When Narayan began to write—this was in the India of the 1920s, with no other well-known writer in English in his town or, for that matter, anywhere else in the country—he read out his pieces to his brother and some coffee-drinking friends at the Hundred Feet Road Restaurant. Then, Narayan had his prose typed on demi-sized bond paper because this is what he had learned he needed to do. He had consulted a book named *How to Sell Your Manuscripts*. Narayan later recalled: "The typist, who was really a violinist, owned the Venus Typewriting Institute. He was obliging and efficient and charged me (deferred-payment system) two annas a page. When I had typing work, I visited him at his home beside the Jagan Mohan Palace and waited at his door while he ate his morning chapatti, spreading the ghee on it with his finger."

There are traces of expectant urbanity in the details of the restaurant and the typing institute; there are also the marks of a slow, rural life in the arrangement of payment but also in the picture of the young writer waiting patiently while the violinist-cum-typist spreads ghee with his fingers.

The process that Narayan describes, which one would have expected to take place in any one of his own novels, could not have occurred in a village or a large city. This is the small town of Narayan's imagination and ours. More important, as in his novels, Narayan quietly establishes a small-town world of ordinary, petty commerce. Thus, there is movement but also a sense of space that is for the most part self-enclosed. One can detect among his characters a feeling of satisfaction with the world as it is, and, not far from the surface, also a sense of missed opportunity and half-perceived failure. And as we read Narayan we can see very clearly the shift that has come about in a novel like Mishra's *The Romantics*, which, as we saw above, also opens with a treatment of the economy and real estate, except that the landscape is now more public, and larger, and louder. These are the opening lines from *The Man-Eater of Malgudi*, written about four decades earlier:

I could have profitably rented out the little room in front of my press on Market Road, with a view of the fountain; it was coveted

by every would-be shopkeeper in our town. I was considered a fool
for not getting my money's worth out of it, since all the space I need
for my press and its personnel was at the back, beyond the blue cur-
tain. But I could not explain myself to sordid and calculating peo-
ple. I hung up a picture of Goddess Laxmi poised on her lotus,
holding aloft the bounties of earth in her four hands, and through
her grace I did not do too badly.

The piece of Narayan's writing that for me has most dramatically presented his sense of the village is a short story called
"A Horse and Two Goats." The delightful story begins with a
memorable introduction, one that makes a nearly literal effort
to map rural India: "Of the seven hundred thousand villages
dotting the map of India, in which the majority of India's five
hundred million live, flourish, and die, Kritam was probably
the tiniest." At the tale's center is an old man, Muni, who lives
in Kritam with his wife and two goats. They are a very poor couple. Most of the story takes place beside the statue of a horse at
the edge of the village beside the highway. While his two goats
graze on cactus and lantana bushes, Muni, the narrator tells us,
sits on that pedestal beside the highway because "it gave him a
sense of belonging to the larger world."

On this particular day, a van runs out of gas and stops by
Muni. From it emerges a "red-faced foreigner," an American.
Muni does not speak English, the American does not have any
Tamil. The American begins to ask about a gas station before
he breaks off in the middle to exclaim at the statue of the horse.
"Marvelous," he says. He wants to buy the statue, which, he has
mistakenly assumed, belongs to Muni. Muni, not understanding a word of what the man is saying, first thinks the visitor is
there to find out about a murder that had taken place in the vil-

lage a few weeks ago. Then, he concludes that he is being quizzed about the story of the horse and tells the American, in chaste Tamil, about Kalki, the Redeemer, coming at the end of Kali Yuga, when the world is destroyed at the end of time. The drama and the jest of the story lie in the twists and turns of the mistaken transaction that takes place. Muni comes to believe that the red-faced foreigner is interested in buying his goats. He accepts the hundred rupees the foreigner offers him and walks home quickly so that the goats don't follow him. The foreigner puts the horse in his van and drives away. Muni tells his wife that a foreigner just bought the goats. It is not till the goats bleat outside their hut that his wife accuses Muni of thievery. That is where the story ends.

We return once again to Nandy, who has called Malgudi "a tribute to a remembered village." One gets a sense that Nandy wants us to understand that the small town or even the city is to be understood as space that is surrounded in the imagination of the writer by the memory of the village. As I think of a story like "A Horse and Two Goats," I am struck by a different kind of realization. After finishing *Swami and Friends*, his first novel, Narayan began to seek a publisher abroad. His manuscript would return to him, "with unfailing regularity," every six weeks. It seemed he was not going to strike a deal. The last pub-lisher to reject it was Dent. Narayan had asked them to forward the manuscript, if they were not going to accept it, to an Indian friend at Oxford. This friend, in turn, was advised by Narayan to "weight the manuscript with a stone and drown it in the Thames." The man at Oxford ignored this advice and sent the book to Graham Greene, who recommended it to Hamish Hamilton for publication. The books that followed found read-ers in the West. This happy ending had come out of a lonely effort across a wide geographical and cultural gap. It is a picture that scarcely bears any comparison to what exists on the literary scene today. Narayan could not have easily escaped the sense that any successful transaction involved an act of creative mistranslation, and it is part of the strength of his art that he could inject humor into it. Commentators often link Narayan's fatalism to his Hinduism. I think there is greater reason to see his sense of fate, but also caprice, as emerging from his own private recognition that he had so easily and arbitrarily been plucked out of surrounding obscurity and perhaps sterile struggle. Narayan's art appears all the more original and strong when one thinks that it would have been against that kind of knowledge that he shaped, from an enormous distance and disadvantage, a picture of his intimate world. And if Narayan's stories express a retreat from change or from history, or if they appear whimsical, then it is because his writing is also a protest against the tyranny of real history and, often, the arbitrariness of change.

In contemporary Indian writing in English, the small town, and certainly the city, is already a part of a global planet. In his appropriately named book *A New World*, the novelist Amit Chaudhuri responds to the seismic shifts in the social life of people over the past decade: in particular, we witness the private struggles of individual lives against the backdrop of a new globalization and the circulation of goods and also bodies. The story revolves around Jayojit Chatterji, a professor of economics, who is an expatriate Indian living in the United States. He is also a single father recovering from a divorce. Amala, his former wife, is still in America. She is now involved with her gynecologist, a married man. Jayojit has come back to India with his son. They are visiting Jayojit's elderly parents in Calcutta. As we turn the novel's pages we find a life arranged around new objects in India. There are references to Aquafresh toothpaste and Head and Shoulders shampoo, to MTV, to ads for ATM machines and ANZ Readymoney, and even to the debates on economic liberalization. Jayojit reads an editorial in the *Statesman* and formulates in his mind the beginning of a letter to the editor: "Sir, with reference to your article in the leader, one must begin by sounding a note of caution about assuming that economic deregulation will be a panacea to all our problems; but it will, no doubt, be one to some of them."

When Jayojit goes out on the streets of Calcutta for a walk, he comes across a vendor of roadside snacks. "Bhelpuri, babu? Jhaalmudi?" the man asks Jayojit. This is what we read about the bhelpuri seller: "His eyes were brown-grey, as if they held a little of the twilight of another town in them." On the streets of each Indian metropolis flickers that same vanishing light that has its origins elsewhere in humbler houses and huts. The vendors on the city streets are human milestones that mark the nation's passage down a road that has witnessed famines, natural disasters, civil war, and displacement of populations through projects like the building of big dams. We can see that the street seller is hawking the fragments of another world, the world of the forgotten village and small town.

The "Bihar-Bengal cargo truck" that rumbles by, in Calcutta in the night, in Raj Kamal Jha's *The Blue Bedspread*; the *bhaiya* from UP who knows "all the secret ways to make the chutney and cut the kanda and all" in Ardashir Vakil's *Beach Boy*; in Rohinton Mistry's *A Fine Balance*, the slum dwellers who have migrated to the city from a village, who complain about the government official: "Telling us we are afraid to change. What does he know? Would we have left our native place and come all the way here if we were afraid of change?" All of these characters are migrants into the city. They are the bearers of an alternative cosmopolitanism. Another Indian writer, Vikram Chandra—

himself a cosmopolitan shuttling between Bombay and Washington, D.C. — understands this perfectly when he writes that in addition to his neighbors who travel to Belgium to trade in diamonds, the flight attendants who fly to Beijing, the workers who keep Saudi Arabia running, the merchant navy sailors who carry cargo to Brazil, or nurses who give care and nurture in Sharjah, and the gangsters who shuttle between different ports in Asia as part of their everyday trade, there are also the others in Bombay who are cosmopolitans:

I mean the men who have left their homes in Muzaffarnagar and Patna to drive cabs in Bombay; the chauffeurs who send money home to Trivandrum; the road-laborers from Madhya Pradesh; the maids from the Konkan coast; the cooks from Sylhet in Bangladesh; the Tamil bakers; the struggling actresses from

Ludhiana; the security guards from Bihar; the painters from Nashik who stand on roped lengths of bamboo three hundred feet in the air to color Bombay's lofty skylines.

3

In *A Suitable Boy* by Vikram Seth, the middle-class character named Haresh Khanna finds out that it is the migrants from the hinterland who provide invaluable labor in the shoe factory outside Calcutta. In his factory, Haresh has noticed that "All the toughest jobs on the conveyor, as well as elsewhere, were performed by Biharis." This recognition, in Seth's narrative, is very different from the nods to provincial citizens by the likes of Rushdie or Mistry. This is because Seth's novel, even though it is written in English, is filled with a deep feeling for vernacular culture. Unlike the metropolitan novels, *A Suitable Boy* does not wheel in the "rest of India" in the form of a cardboard cutout for the purposes of showing to the people lining the streets what "real India" is actually about.

Set in the India of the 1950s, *A Suitable Boy* builds much of its narrative around a provincial town, Brahmpur, and it doesn't take the reader too long to discover the presence in that space of sensibilities that find articulation in English and also, more vitally, in Urdu and Hindi. If this were not in itself a delight, because it is an uncommon occurrence in Indian fiction in English, what also comes across clearly is the conviction that this novel could as easily have been written in those other, vernacular languages. Indeed, as Harish Trivedi has noted, *A Suitable Boy* was "one of the first new wave

Indian novels in English to be translated into Hindi." Trivedi had gone on to add: "The nineteen, twenty-six or thirty-seven languages world-wide into which some successful recent Indian novels in English have been translated have included remarkably few Indian languages, curiously." And Seth himself, in his new preface to the Hindi edition, wrote that *A Suitable Boy* (as *Koi Achcha-sa Ladka*, 1998) had returned the novel, as Trivedi reports it, "to its source milieu and medium, so that now even some of the characters in it would finally be able to read it."

In contrast to *A Suitable Boy*, in metropolitan novels by writers like Rushdie, for example, it can be a huge mistake to be a provincial and not speak English. Witness the politician Piloo Doodhwala in Rushdie's *The Ground Beneath Her Feet*: "OK? To my phace you are saying it? Arre, how to surwiwe when I am beset by traitors? When I must phight not only these sacred mooing gods but also my own wife as vell." It is not so much that the speech here is caricatured to resemble the diction of the Hindi speaker who has had very little benefit of primary education in English; rather, my complaint is that provincial origins are here signified in no way other than a failure to speak proper English. It is as if the writer was unable to imagine such people as sentient beings with extraordinarily varied life.

The character of Piloo Doodhwala, his wife Golmatol, and the two daughters named Halva and Rasgulla form a cartoon family probably based on what Rushdie has learned from newspapers of Laloo Yadav, the former chief minister of Bihar. As Laloo belongs to the caste traditionally associated with cowherds in the Gangetic basin, Rushdie calls his character Doodhwala, or the Milkman. Laloo Yadav came to prominence as a leader of the lower castes, and then achieved great notoriety for his corrupt rule. It is the story of his crime— siphoning off money from the state exchequer to provide fodder to nonexistent cows—that provides Rushdie the story of a ghost goat farm in his novel. Rushdie's Piloo Doodhwala, speaking his Laloo English, is a rich and dishonest businessman in the posh and unlikely neighborhood of Bandra in Bombay. There is no history behind him anymore, no perception of a place of origin or belonging. The imposed accent betrays no knowledge of small towns or villages. The sense of a man from a low caste, one who had himself spent a part of his childhood working in a cowshed, now leading a movement against the dominance of the upper castes, is entirely lost on Rushdie. The report of the corruption just becomes a magical realist tale, and cannot come close to an indictment of either the individual or the system that made possible such rot and such betrayal. The satire doesn't stick. One is reminded of Pankaj Mishra's remark about Rushdie's grotesque representation of the rustic politician: "Such crude and witless buffoonery is how the Indian chi-chi class—which serves as 'India' in Rushdie's fiction—responds to the unwashed millions staking a claim to political power. What startles us is that it comes from someone who once complained about orientalist representations of India; the embarrassment we feel while reading it is mostly on the writer's behalf."

I grew up in Patna, where Laloo Yadav lives. My parents still live there, although many of my parents' friends have left Patna for places like Delhi. The last time I went to visit my parents, I got an appointment to see Laloo. My brief account of my meeting is a public service announcement for aspiring cosmopolitan writers who have never set foot in a small town. It seems to me that such writers might sometimes wonder how a small-town politician that they are writing about spends an hour of his time on a slow, summer afternoon.

When I arrived at his house, Laloo was feeding milk cake to his pet dog, Johnny. I wouldn't have known what it was that Johnny was eating with such relish except that he happened to lick me on my arm. I looked at the line of white liquid running down my elbow. Laloo noticed me doing this and said in Hindi, "It's only milk cake."

Laloo was sitting on a rattan chair that had been placed at the end of the driveway leading to his house. It was an evening in May, a little after five o'clock, and the air was already beginning to cool. I got the feeling that feeding Johnny was the evening's entertainment in a town that, thanks to Laloo himself, offered very little else by way of what one could call a cultural life. A member of the security detail had led me inside the barred gates and I had just passed Laloo's sons playing cricket with a tennis ball on the paved driveway of their home. On the part of the road that divided the kids from their parents, hundreds of small, red onions had been spread to dry. The sharp smell hit you many yards before you got close to this patchy evidence of Bihar's agricultural health.

A servant rushed up and gave Laloo a wad of rolled-up chapatis. Laloo looked at me and then began tossing the scraps of bread into the air. Johnny leaped a few inches and caught them expertly in his mouth. He clearly didn't discriminate between milk cake and the chapatis. I asked Laloo if I could take a picture of Johnny. Yes, yes, he said. Then, he threw another chapati in the air when I pointed the camera. Impressed by my interest, Laloo began behaving like a proud and indulgent father. He beckoned another servant and instructed him to hide his blue rubber slippers. *"Chapalwa ko lukaa do,"* he said. We were to witness a demonstration of canine savvy. A distant mango tree was enlisted for this pedagogical purpose. Then, Johnny was released on his mission and he began his zigzag walk toward the hidden footwear of his master, the most famous fraud in Patna.

I had received all the news of Laloo's scams from a huge distance, in the form of small news items tucked away in newspapers. In 1996, for instance, in the "fodder scam," Laloo Yadav was involved in a massive theft from the exchequer amounting to millions of dollars. A year later, Indian intelligence indicted Laloo under the Prevention of Corruption Act and on several other counts, including criminal conspiracy, criminal breach of trust, forgery for cheating, falsification of accounts, and forgery of valuable securities. In 1997, Laloo was arrested, but in a remarkable coup, he retained power through the backdoor by ensuring that his wife took his place in the office from which he was resigning.

In a few minutes, the dog had retrieved Laloo's slipper. The master said, "Shake hand *karo*," and the dog, saliva dripping from its jaws, raised its paw. Johnny had recently won an award in a dog show. The show had been held in a park in front of my parents' home in Patna. My nephews told me that Johnny, a black labrador, had won the award also because there were no other dogs in his category. I asked them if the other competitors had withdrawn voluntarily, but my nephews felt that it might have been more because there are no other labradors in Patna. Both possibilities are equally plausible—and this too reveals a great deal about my hometown.

During my visit, Laloo was now out of jail, although there was talk of his return to custody. I was visiting him in the official residence of the chief minister of Bihar. There were policemen—and one policewoman—scattered around us. Away in the distance, to my right, stood a Black Cat Commando silhouetted against the yellow walls of the bungalow. The house is only a few minutes' drive from Patna's nondescript airport, and every few minutes a small-engine plane flew over us. Laloo, wearing a shabby white cotton undershirt, would look up momentarily and then cover his ears. A silver amulet hung from thick red strings around his neck.

As long as I was there, Laloo's wife, Rabri Devi, the chief minister of Bihar, sat a few feet away on a plastic chair. One of Laloo's lieutenants, Shyam Rajak, bearded and in a black *kurta*, or shirt, sat in another plastic chair at a respectable distance. I looked at Rabri now and then while Laloo talked to me. Rabri seemed fairer in person than in her photographs. Her neck bulged above the line of her blouse, as if she had swallowed a small bird. She was wearing a pale blue sari. I began to wonder whether it was the smell of Rabri's shampoo that was carried over to me when the breeze stirred.

The smell had a faint sweetness to it that I found agreeable. It returned me to my childhood, and to the memories of my aunts in Bihar's small towns and villages. They were simple women, only mildly literate, and they stuck to the routines of housework and worship. None of them would have dreamed of becoming the chief minister of Bihar. I am sure Rabri hadn't either. As she sat there, behind her husband, smiling occasionally and saying nothing, Rabri was only a middle-aged housewife who had just finished taking a bath to get rid of the heat.

Laloo spoke to me in Hindi. Much of our conversation was about our hometown. Laloo spoke briefly about his arrival in Patna from his village, Phulwaria. He said his village "was in a remote area." He had taken the ferry across the Ganges. In Patna, he said, "everything looked new and mysterious." Then, he added, "When I came here I got an opportunity to learn about the wider world." That remark gave me pause. The town that I had sought to escape in order to get a sense of the world outside was the one that had been for Laloo the introduction to the world outside the village. I remembered the story I had heard my father tell us about his coming to Patna from the ancestral village to the north. Like Laloo, my father had taken the ferry. He had slept on the banks of the Ganges after spreading a towel on the sand. I thought also about my mother, taking a train from Ara to come to Patna for her college. It was in Patna that one was afforded a chance to meet writers, artists, and musicians. During Dussehra festival each year, there would be all-night performances by the best Indian artistes. A cousin remembered one year having had the privilege of listening to the legendary Ustad Bismillah Khan playing the *shehnai*. The next day, the cousin was taking a train out of Patna, and he saw the Ustad strolling on the station platform and then squatting on the concrete edge to piss on the tracks.

At some point, Laloo decided to deliver a brief lecture to me on history. He recited the ancient name for our town, Pataliputra, and then mentioned the Chinese traveler, Hieun Tsang. He looked at me and said, "Itihaas padhne ki zaroorat hai" (It is necessary to read history). Then, Laloo mentioned other names, Ashok, Chanakya, Guru Gobind Singh. Rather pointedly, he said, "It was here that we had Chandragupta II. His reign is called the Golden Period in Indian history. Chandragupta II was a shudra. Ask the historians." Actually, the ruler that Laloo had in mind was not Chandragupta II—a ruler in the fourth century A.D., in what is described in school textbooks as India's Golden Age—but Chandragupta Maurya, a ruler in the third century B.C., who, it is speculated, was the illegitimate son of a ruler and a palace maid. Clearly, what was more significant in Laloo's mind, and what he wanted to convey to me in passing, was that Bihar had been ruled by a person who had been born low.

The recognition of this plain but radical truth imparts a moral legitimacy to Laloo's immense, albeit waning, popularity in Bihar. Laloo understands the appeal of this idea. Born in a rural, milkman's family, he has made his own rise to the top the powerful narrative for others to identify with. But it is only through an ideological sleight of hand that the difference between him and today's Bihari poor can be erased: Laloo is only in a very narrow sense like those who vote for him. He is powerful and rich. Further, his irresponsible and corrupt rule takes him away from any comparison that could possibly be made with any of the Chandraguptas in Indian history. For Laloo to invoke that comparison, in however veiled a manner, is the more egregious misreading of history.

When the history lesson was over, it was time for me to leave. I finished the lemon tea that had been delivered in a tiny cup. The conversation had begun to peter out. Suddenly, Laloo shouted that he wanted water. A servant in a dirty white uniform, with a faded gold comb in his turban, came bearing a plastic tub. It was brimming with water.

The tub was placed in front of Laloo, and he proceeded to put his feet in the water. Another servant rushed forward with a bar of Lifebuoy and a brush. The servant sat on his haunches and started soaping Laloo's feet. But the servant's motions weren't vigorous enough. Laloo spurred him on. He said, "Khakhoro! Khakhoro! Aur nahin ho to chhuri se khakhoro!" (Scrape. Scrape. And if it doesn't work, scrape it with a knife).

I wanted to take a photograph but thought it would be impolite to ask. When I got up to leave, I asked Laloo what was wrong with the soles of his feet. He explained the matter to me patiently. Each morning he rubbed oil on his feet. But when he walked out to a place under the tree to pray and perform *puja*, pebbles got stuck to his soles. He preferred walking barefoot when he offered his prayers. This explanation was given to me so directly that it appeared that I could, indeed, have gone ahead and taken the photograph. It probably would not have struck Laloo that in trying to take a picture of the servant washing his feet, I would have been portraying him in an unfavorable light. For Laloo, nothing that he did was wrong. He was now a member of the elite in our town. He behaved in the way that he had always, from a distance, seen the elite behave.

1

I disliked Patna when I lived there as a boy, but what I remember most clearly is how much I disliked myself. The loathing diminished when I grew up and found words and started to write. I began to see myself and the place Patna as two different, distinct entities. But I also learned how both of them had always been very close if not also the same.

I grew into puberty in Patna. Around the same time that adolescence began changing my voice and the way in which I looked at the world, a boy who was a year or two senior to me stunned me by making a sexual remark in the schoolyard about my elder sister. Rage caught me by the throat. Everyone thought my elder sister was very pretty. I adored her. But I stayed silent. I might have been afraid of the older boy, but I was also confused by the anger and desire I felt in myself. The greater part of this confusion was that it seemed to seep into me from my surroundings in Patna: what I despised in the boy who had offended me was not particular to him at all; I saw it as a standard Patna trait. Both the boy and I belonged to this place: how could we have behaved otherwise? To realize this truth was to feel very alone.

I was eleven when I entered a medicine shop on Station Road and asked for a packet of Carefree sanitary napkins for my mother. The man behind the counter said something to the other two men sitting on stools beside him. They laughed. What were they saying? I was upset at my mother for having sent me on this errand. I was learning as I grew into manhood in Patna that I must become distant from the women I had loved the most in my family.

In a sense, Patna forced this on me. My sisters would hire rickshaws to take them to their friends' houses or the cinema. I would be asked to get on my bicycle and accompany them. The men on the streets always made passes at them. In my mind, each street of Patna looked like a permanent leer. Once a young man, chewing *paan* outside a shop on the crowded Boring Canal Road, said "Ehhh, ehhh, dekho, dekho, Red Roj." A film called *Red Rose* had recently been released. Years later, I incorporated that remark in a routine I used to do on Bihari street talk for my friends in college in Delhi. I never mentioned my sisters. I found my trips on the bicycle humiliating. My sisters were much calmer, even indifferent about it. I refused to escort them anymore. But when I quarreled with them at home, I found that I would repeat things that I had heard strange men say about them on the streets. The experience gave me my first divided sense of home and outside.

In a year or two, I became an expert at making remarks about other boys' sisters myself. I remembered my boyhood hurt, so I made sure that the brothers of the girls I was insulting were never around to hear my words. But there were no other restraints. I poured everything I had learned in the classes in physics or geography or biology into my description of bodies and acts that I was, in reality, utterly ignorant about. From the febrile imagination of a characteristically repressed Indian schoolboy poured out a Sadean fantasy of pulleys and hydraulics, elevation and latitudes, skin and glands that sweated sexuality.

All of this did nothing to lessen the confusion or the anger. It was only a part of a process that took me away from home to a life in which I was more and more on the street. This meant that I did no reading or writing; I had nothing that could be called an interior life. My elder sister began to keep a diary. But there was nothing in my life that I felt I could record on a page.

There was a time in the years that immediately preceded my unruly adolescence when I had wanted to write and to draw. When we took the ferry up the Ganges to our ancestral village, I studiously observed the scenes I wanted to paint. I remember a stretch of sand and a small red flag on a bamboo

pole. Some afternoons, I saw men on the riverbank pulling a boat upstream with the help of a rope. I wanted to paint the shape of tall egrets near the water. I wasn't very successful. After a painting competition one Saturday, my art teacher told me that he had tried hard to give me the third prize. With a resigned shake of the head he stopped in midsentence, and I remembered the slim trees and the mountain peaks I had painted for him on far too many occasions. Seen from the window of my classroom—the school was built close to the water—the Ganges did not appear beautiful to me. Crows rode on the carcasses that floated on the water, pecking. I also wanted to write for the school magazine. At a relative's house, I read old copies of *Reader's Digest* and tried to write jokes like the ones I saw printed there. Those jokes had been sent in by ordinary readers. But nothing remotely funny seemed to be happening around me. I had tried to write a story, but I had to abandon that too. And then, within a year or two, none of this mattered anymore.

For, what seemed like the rest of Patna, we discovered girls. Neither I nor any of my friends knew a single girl, but in the abstract, girls dominated our lives. We rode our bicycles obsessively past the girls' school, but I could not bear to look at the red-skirted figures milling around. My sisters were among them and I kept hoping they would call out to me. We also began to haunt the 11:00 A.M. Sunday shows at Veena Cinema. We told our parents we were watching the old Hollywood films to improve our English. Very few in the audience understood or spoke the language. We were all there for the same thing: any hint of female flesh. Whenever there was any suggestion of sex on the screen, the theater resounded with loud whistling. The whistles would only grow louder a moment later because the censors' scissors would already have cut out the rest of the scene. Life seemed caught in an endless cycle that promised cheap excitement but inevitably led to frustration.

2

The older youth in Patna also lived through a cycle of frustration that had in it an element of sexual denial. But their experiences of frustration were also more complex because of their meager prospects in life. Colleges were often shut down. Unemployment was high and corruption was rampant. On the day after my eleventh birthday, this frustration found its release in a huge protest against the faltering government of the Congress chief minister Abdul Ghafoor.

The date was March 18, 1974. The students took out a procession in Patna and the police fired on them, killing several of the protesters. A curfew order was "clamped" immediately. Some of my relatives—cousins and their spouses from a nearby town who had come for the party at our house the previous night—were unable to return to their homes.

The party got extended. We stood on the roof of the house and played *antakshri*. There was one young woman in the group, a distant relative, who was a wonderful singer. She was also beautiful with light eyes and hair that strayed from her forehead in the manner made popular by Bombay film actresses. While this woman sang songs from old Hindi films, in the distance we could see smoke rising from the buildings that had been set on fire.

The students' agitation that had begun that day would bring down the government in Bihar and face the brunt of Indira

Gandhi's emergency rule the following year. The leaders who emerged during that movement, the old and ailing J. P. Narayan and a new student leader by the name of Laloo Prasad Yadav, were to change the political landscape of India in the years to come. In the large sprawling family on my mother's side, my male cousins had so far been inactive and unengaged in campus life. One of them, only a few months earlier, had consumed a pesticide and had laid down on a sack of potatoes prepared to die. That same cousin had now joined the fray as a follower of JP. Other cousins courted arrest.

There were huge gatherings in Patna's Gandhi Maidan. The students were on the rise in the rest of Bihar too. The movement was met with very little repression at first. Then, as a result of other disturbances, Indira Gandhi's rule at the center was suddenly threatened. She imposed the emergency rule; the fundamental rights were suspended; many of the leaders who had gained popularity were thrown in jail.

The superintendent of the Patna jail was my maternal uncle. His house, located right outside the jail's walls, faced the Sujata restaurant, which had been torched during the students' riots the previous year. When I went to eat at my uncle's house, I would hear of the arrests and my uncle would tell me about the leaders in jail. I would get chicken for dinner at my uncle's house. The Emergency didn't mean much to me. People spoke of trains running on time. The landscape in Patna showed a change. Suddenly, new billboards sprouted on the streets; they carried slogans that proclaimed our march toward a golden tomorrow. One of Indira Gandhi's slogans was borrowed for our new urinal in school. On the wall that we faced when we stood in a line to pee, someone had written in pencil: "Aaapka bhavishya aapke haath mein hai" (You hold your future in your hand). This was the way in which politics entered our adolescent universe—as a private part of the human anatomy. This might have been because of our youth, but Patna made it very easy for this to be so.

The 1970s had come to town, for most of us in Patna, after half of that decade was over. The Emergency, as far as I can remember, didn't change our entry into the borrowed culture of the age. We wore bell-bottoms and grew our hair long. We tried to acquire other affects. There was a bookstore in Patna called Tricel—there were excellent bookstores for Hindi books near the Patna College, but only one as far as I could tell for books in English—which sold stickers suitable for the new zeitgeist. I bought one that said "Love" in funky, psychedelic colors. I did not buy any books.

As I look back on those years, I am struck by the absence from my life of all matters literary. I remember reading the report of the local, well-known Hindi writer Phanishwar Nath Renu raising his arm to protect JP from the stick-wielding policemen in Patna. Renu was imprisoned soon thereafter. I discovered Renu's fiction two decades later. Ten years would pass before I'd watch *Teesri Kasam,* starring Raj Kapoor and Waheeda Rehman, a film based on one of Renu's stories. By then, I had already left Patna. And Renu was dead. But back in the 1970s, when I first came across him in the news in Patna, I had not read any of Renu's writings. The report in a Hindi weekly about the writer's protest meant little to me. What stayed in my mind was only a small detail about how Renu's long, curly hair was dry and unkempt in prison. In his cell, the writer lacked hair oil.

The paltry evidence in my life of the aesthetic—if we can call it that—was only the annual elocution at school. At this event, during the final years of my school life, I must have heard Lord Tennyson's "The Charge of the Light Brigade" recited more times than I had even read the poem on paper. For the Hindi version of the event, a popular choice was Ramdhari Singh Dinkar's jingoistic poem "Samar Sesh Hai" (The War Is Not Over). I had declaimed it with appropriate passion myself and won a prize. The poem was actually a critique of Nehru's pacifism, but once again, I did not know any of this. The poet, who had died some years before I had read out his poem in our school auditorium, had also lived in the same city as I. Dinkar was one of the giants of post-independence Hindi writing. But this didn't mean much to me either. His home was simply the house that served as a marker on the road from where I had to turn right in order to go to my dentist.

3

The dentist who put braces on my teeth had hands that always smelled of soap. Every time we were at his clinic, the dentist would tell my mother that he wanted a cut of the dowry that my improved looks would now bring. The dentist was sloppy but we liked him because he was from our own caste. Caste was important in Patna. Later, my sister was married into a family that was linked to the dentist and he became our relative.

The memory of my years in Patna is filled with talk about marriages. Each summer, a female cousin would get married. I would observe the drama of the negotiations about dowry. Then, the portion of the dowry that was to be paid in cash would be brought to my parents' house before being taken to the house of the prospective bridegroom. I remember afternoons when the money would be brought in cheap briefcases or wrapped in handkerchiefs hidden in suitcases. Once I touched the notes: they felt slightly moist.

For some reason, even though I spent so much time thinking about girls, the familiar obsession with marriage in Patna incited no thought about sex. Sex had little to do with the home: it belonged to the street. And it was public, like a pass or an insult. One morning, I was leaving home for school and I saw a crowd collected near our gate. My mother, watching me from the balcony, shouted that I should not look. The crowd was gathered around a pair of dogs. The dogs were mating. Rather, the animals had mated and were now unable to separate. A crowd had gathered to watch. In time, I learned to recognize such crowds from a distance. These crowds were restive and sullen. Our warm faces must have looked like those who sit in the theater, except that there was more fidgeting among us. Boys and men stood around the mating dogs till one man would dart in and prod the animals with a stick. Someone would throw a stone. Or spit. I was always seized by revulsion and excitement.

Marriage didn't have much to do with sex. It dealt with money. There was never enough money for dowries. This left us open to humiliation, but even this was not especially aggravating because the girl's side was expected to abase themselves. Female cousins in our family far outnumbered male ones. A few of the cousins were not very pretty; none of them had much education. Among the males, there was very little talent, too. But when it came to them, the talk was less about marriage and more about jobs. There were very few jobs in Patna other than clerical ones. My cousins took the civil services exams each year. No one got anywhere. As far as my female cousins went, there were other problems too. There was one cousin, older than I, who wet her bed each night. My mother would take her to doctors. Would she still wet her bed after marriage was a question I often asked myself. This cousin slept on a rubber mattress. I imagined the green rubber on her marriage bed. There was another distant cousin who had a deformed foot. Every time the young woman had left our house after a visit, my mother would invariably sigh, "Who will marry her?" Many years later, in a theater in a city in America, I watched the play *The Glass Menagerie* by Tennessee Williams and thought of this relative of mine in faraway Patna. In the figure of this sad but expectant woman — a woman who limped and who was waiting for a suitor who would perhaps never come, or who would come but only to leave after a brief while, when his interest or pity had run its course — in the figure of this woman on the stage I saw the outlines of my own relative with whom I had now lost touch. I do not know whom I identified with more, the woman or the man.

I have an image for this time in my life. I could be traveling on a train in India and I would pass a house in the dark in which through an open window I could see burning a dim bulb. It would be a momentary glimpse, but it would be enough to evoke in my mind a memory of Patna and the lives of many of my relatives. As I reflect on that image, I think that this awareness of the pain of others around me was both deep and genuine. But it was already accompanied by a sense of detachment. This guaranteed a certain pathos: I was inclined toward a romantic cultivation of sadness. I wanted to be the one in the train passing by that dark house barely illuminated by a single bulb. The reality, however, was that I was still living in Patna. I felt trapped in that city and in what I was convinced were only the shallow struggles of the large family. This led to a feeling of dull helplessness. I was not a writer; I was not in love. Nothing seemed to happen. I felt wretched about myself and felt, I think rightly, that this wretchedness also belonged to the place in which I lived.

My elder sister's wedding was the last marriage that I attended in Patna. I was in college in Delhi by then. During my stay in Delhi I had begun thinking of myself in some vague way as a writer. An important intellectual change had overcome me. I had begun to read. I am unable to recall why this should have happened, but it might have been because I had decided that I needed better English in Delhi. I still read only fitfully, but the foray into the world of books made me see the world in a new way. I could be in a Delhi Transport bus in Daryaganj and a voice running in my head would name the objects I saw being sold on the street, their colors, the look in the eyes of the sellers. I was observing the world around me and stringing my observations into sentences. Words gave my world its crucial form. I had not stepped out yet of the confusion that I had felt in Patna, but language was giving me a chance to name my hitherto undescribable feelings.

I wrote a few poems, a couple of short stories, and some journalism. When I was bored in my classes, as when the economics teacher droned on about the relative merits of buying butter or guns, I wrote poems. These poems were filled with metaphysical longing—they were testimony to my sublimated sexual yearnings. My stories and the journalism, however, betrayed other knowledges. I had left Patna; I had been elsewhere. When I wrote of Patna it was with new eyes. I had encountered through films, books, and newspapers the centrifugal energies of the world that took me away from the worries of my family and my own isolated concerns. The world was rich with experience. This knowledge had freed me. It had also made me remember the unremarked intimacies of my childhood, its joys and sorrows. In what I wrote and read, I began to return to Patna. This habit has grown in my self-imposed exile from Patna: I still write about it as if I knew very little else.

4

The stories that Patna offers me—there are only stories, and very few explanations—seem to belong to my past. But for so many in my family, they also make up their present. I, too, am not done with the task of understanding my past. The reports and stories I record or write are ambiguous gestures; it is as if I am waving at Patna, and it is difficult to tell whether I am saying hello or good-bye.

I tell stories about Patna because they are a part of my shame at having come from nowhere. And also my nostalgia because Patna is all I ever had. Both my shame and nostalgia are a part of the experience of having left Patna, where I didn't want to belong, and then coming to America, where I'm not sure I can ever belong.

Patna today provides me a way of orienting myself to the world, even when that world is fictional. I notice that the name Patna occurs once in Arundhati Roy's *The God of Small Things* (p. 259). In Anita Desai's latest novel, *Fasting, Feasting*, the name comes up very early (p. 5). In Vikram Seth's *A Suitable Boy*, Patna is the place where "momentous events" are taking place, events that were likely, in at least one character's view, "to alter entirely the shape and configuration of the political forces of the country" (p. 816). Patna is where a number of political parties, including the Congress Party, "were holding sessions in the mad heat of June" (p. 817). In Salman Rushdie's *Midnight's Children*, we find mention of "Patna rice." Patna does not appear, alas, in Rushdie's *The Ground Beneath Her Feet*. But Piloo Doodhwala, the tycoon who masterminds a fraudulent dairy scheme and is the owner of a ghost goat farm, and whose wife is named Golmatol, is surely based on the rather *real* fictional chief minister and the fodder-scam magical realist from Patna, Laloo Yadav.

Patna is not only my hometown. It is also a place in time. It made me who I am. My own writings bear that address. I had wanted to leave Patna; I am not sure that I ever did, but it is almost a relief to me that Patna goes on being what it is without me.

My elder sister, no longer needing my escort, goes out to work each day in Patna and, when I am visiting, she comes back home and tells me stories. We often laugh. And yet, listening to my sister, I am reminded of what had seemed to me so threatening and confusing about Patna when I was an adolescent. Even the stories about Laloo Yadav and other local politicians, which most amuse us, return me to another time. The lumpen display of power in the Bihar legislature and elsewhere is not wholly removed from the schoolyard in which the boy had made an obscene remark about my sister. I often wonder whether Patna hasn't remained tied to its own adolescence. You can see this in the city's abiding marks of a feudal life: violence, male pride, caste, misogyny. I haven't dared ask my sister how she lives with it every day.

A few years ago when I was in Patna, my sister began telling me about our village, which I had not visited since my grandmother's death the previous year. My sister was talking of our relatives, and the conversation turned to the sons and daughters of our father's first cousin. There were three of them, much younger than we, these second cousins of ours. The eldest was a boy who, in his early teens, began getting into trouble. He stole some grain from my grandmother. It was said that he climbed the *khajur* trees and drank the palm wine from the earthen pots the tappers had hung there. When I was in the village, this boy would bring fruit for me. Like his siblings, he had brown hair and brown eyes and I was very fond of him. His name was Deepak. His younger sister's name was Suneeta. I remember Suneeta being fair and bashful. My grandmother complained that Suneeta took the spinach from the little garden patch behind her house. By the time she was six or seven, Suneeta had begun to lead the animals out to graze. She took care of the goats and a buffalo. Suneeta must have been ten when I last saw her, sometime in the mid-1980s when I left Patna for the United States.

While I was gone, Suneeta had reached puberty, the age that I associate with my time in Patna. My sister told me that Suneeta had an affair with one, possibly two, men who were related to us in the village. One of these men was already married; I knew him well and had seen him in Patna just a few days before my sister told me this story. Suneeta would go out to meet them in the mango grove at night.

People in the village found out about this. Deepak, Suneeta's brother, heard the story from his mother. The tragedy of being a brother in Bihar is second only to the tragedy of being a sister. Deepak beheaded Suneeta with a sickle. He disappeared after that. The police came once to the village and then went back.

Like me, Deepak left the place of his birth. For a while, he worked as a laborer on a railway project in Assam. Then, I heard that he had come back and now worked as a rickshaw puller in Patna.

6

I am unsure of the role of such gestures, but I want to present a poem by a Patna poet, Alokdhanwa, in Suneeta's memory. Alok writes in Hindi. It was a decade ago that I first started reading Alok's poems. His first collection of poems, *Duniya Roz Banti Hai* (This World Is Built Every Day), was published in 1998. Suneeta must have been killed a little before that time.

In the summer of 1989, the well-known leftist poet Gorakh Pande had taken his own life at Delhi's Jawaharlal Nehru University. Pande was a Hindi poet from Patna. Various left-wing publications, gasping between insolvency and the general repression meted out to those who resist, came out with issues dedicated to the memory of the dead poet. One such publication, *Prasang*, in its special issue carried this dedication: "In the memory of Jaimal Singh Padda, Pash, Gorakh Pande, Safdar Hashmi, Shankar Tambi, Somdutt, Kamesh Deepak, Amritlal Nagar, Mohanlal Mahto 'Viyogi,' and all those who were the prey of killings."

In that remarkable issue, *Prasang* presented the poems of many of those poets who had struggled alongside those mentioned in its dedicatory note. One of these poets was Alok. The introductory note read: "From where contemporary Hindi poetry finds a new direction and the consciousness of popular struggles get their poetic voice." I went on to read more of Alok's poetry; for the past few years, I have been translating these forceful poems that with great tenderness recall moments of innocence and violence that seem so familiar to me: "Growing all around my sister's feet/like yellow plants/was my childhood —/ that was eaten by the police *daroga*'s water-buffalo."

But before I offer Alok's poem "Girls in Flight," I want to cite a piece of criticism that was published in a small Hindi magazine that also used to be published from Patna, *Samkaleen Janmat*. Alok's own poetry had also often been published in that magazine. This piece of criticism was written by Maheshwar, a partisan of important left-wing struggles in Patna and elsewhere. Here is what Maheshwar had to say about Alok's poem—and I am presenting these words because they articulate a feminist protest, even though the choice that the critic offers at the end wasn't, I think, Suneeta's at all:

Your women are running away only in their diaries, it is only in the pages of their diaries that they are fleeing. But where are they fleeing in real life, these women? In real life women are being confrontational and the assertiveness of women is increasing these days. Women have begun realizing that they are struggling under the collected weight of patriarchy, feudal oppression and capitalist-consumerist power. The exploitation that exists in India today, in that milieu, each of these things are complicit in making the life of women miserable. And women are moving ahead to confront these things. Where are these confrontational women? You say that they are fleeing in their diaries and we are witnessing that they are not running away anywhere. At this time, compared to fleeing, they would consider getting beheaded a better option.

Alokdhanwa, "Girl in Flight"

One

Chains of the home
become so much more visible
when a girl runs away from home.

Are you faced with memories of that night
which one sees again and again in old films
whenever a girl runs away from home?
Rain surrounding the stone lamppost
the light enough only to show the restlessness of
   the eyes?

And all those songs on the silver screen about
   love's madness
today they came true in one's own home!

Were you used to thinking
that those songs were fashioned
only for the actors and actresses?
And that dangerous play
of Laila's end
that arose complete from the stage
and spread in the private lives of the viewers?

Writer in the Hinterland

Two

You will not, of course, ever share
that letter
which before she ran away
she left on her desk
you will, of course, hide from the whole world
her message
you will steal her mirror, her *para,*
her aabnus tree
her boat with seven sails
but how will you take away
the days of a girl in flight
which might still be left in good number
in the infinite folds of her *dupatta?*

You will burn down
all her leftover things?
Will you burn down also her absence?
That is echoing from her presence
like a *santoor*
so strongly
in your head

Three

You will erase her
you will erase a girl in flight
from the air of her own home
you will also erase her from there
which is her childhood inside you
from there too
I know well
the violence of the superiors!

But the fact of her running away
will not leave your memory
like the old windmills turning in the wind

She is not the first girl
who has run away
and nor is she going to be the last one
now there must also be other boys
and other girls too
who will run away in the month of March

A girl runs away
as if getting lost among flowers
getting lost among the stars
sprinting, clad like a swimmer,
in a crowded, dazzling stadium

Four

If a girl runs away
then it is not necessary
that some boy too should have run away

There are so many other conditions in life
with whom she can go away
she can do anything
only giving birth does not mean being a woman.
Outside the large, locked tank
that is your house
girls have changed quite a lot
I will not give you permission
that now you
swindle them even of their possibility.

She can be anywhere
she can fall
she can scatter in disarray
but it is she herself who will be a part of all
mistakes too of her own doing
she will look at everything
from the beginning to the end
she will also go looking at her own end
she will not die anyone else's death

Five

A girl runs away
as if astride a white horse
on both sides of greed and gambling
so much dust rises
from wretched bridegrooms!

You!
who
keep your wives separate
from whores
and keep your lovers separate
from your wives
how you are struck with terror
when a woman wanders fearlessly
searching for her own self
together in whores and wives
and lovers!

Now she can be anywhere
even in those nations to come
where loving will be a whole full-time job!

Six

So many, many girls
run away in their hearts
in their daydreams, in their diaries
their number is much bigger
than those who really are in flight!

Has any girl run away for you?

Isn't there in your nights
even one road with red pebbles?

Were you handed out your marriage?
Did you bring her here
with your own abilities, and your strength?

You brought here at one go
one woman's entire nights
even the nights that lie on the other side of her death!

Did you not cry on this earth even once
with your head against a woman's chest
Don't go away just this one night
no woman said this to you

Don't go away at least tonight
how many women said this
how many, many
times the world over
at all the sea's doors they came running
don't go away at least tonight
and as long as this world will be
at least tonight will also last.

Writer in the Hinterland

PART II

1

In the early 1970s, I recall reading one or two abridged children's editions of books by Charles Dickens. The memory holds because I also remember a drawing in the book, of a boy asking a man for some more soup. The books were full of suffering, and the suffering involved children. The stories made me fearful. They discouraged me from reading. But it was in Dickens that I would have first come across the city named London.

My first sense of a literary London came much later. By then, I was already twenty-two. At that time, I was living in a tiny room in a hostel on the Delhi University campus; the room belonged to a friend who was preparing for the civil service examinations. He didn't mind my staying with him. Each morning, my friend would read the *Times of India* diligently and ask me the meaning of unfamiliar words ("What is a 'truism'?" "Is 'asperity' related to 'disparity'?"). This exercise brought me little comfort. But then I read a book that my friend kept in his room. On the wide windowsill of the room, my roommate had placed all his books: mostly they were textbooks on Indian history and government. Among the flimsy books on "general knowledge" that were staple reading for the examinations stood, rather incongruously, a hardbound copy of a book published by Andre Deutsch. The book was V. S. Naipaul's *Finding the Center.* It was a book whose first seventy-odd pages, a section entitled "Prologue to an Autobiography," I would read several times during the year and a half I spent in that room in the hostel.

The very first sentence of Naipaul's book established in my mind the idea of London as a city of beginnings. That sentence conveyed to me, with its movement and rhythm, a history of repeated striving, and of things coming together, at last, in the achievement of the printed word: "It is now nearly thirty years since, in a BBC room in London, on an old BBC typewriter, and on smooth, 'non-rustle' BBC script paper, I wrote the first sentence of my first publishable book." This first sentence — about a first sentence — created an echo in my head. I read the line that followed. Naipaul revealed that he had been a few months short of his twenty-third birthday when he wrote that sentence. As I read those words, I realized that I was the same age. This discovery was like a charm. I was filled with a new desire. I did not know what I could write there, but suddenly I longed to leave for London.

The book that Naipaul had begun late that afternoon in the BBC room was *Miguel Street.* The sentence Naipaul had written, without knowing anything about where it would lead, was the following one: "Every morning when he got up Hat would sit on the banister of his back verandah and shout across, 'What happening there, Bogart?' " Naipaul added to those words and discovered that he had a story. In a few weeks, he had finished writing the book. But he could not think of himself as a writer. He was uncertain and he lacked conviction. Nonetheless, he persisted, continuing to use the nonrustle BBC paper because "it seemed more casual, less likely to attract failure." More books followed.

I too wanted that life of hopes and fears about putting words on a page, the life that Naipaul had described in a single phrase in the book that I was reading: "such anxiety; such ambition." The account of the struggle that Naipaul had offered in his autobiography stayed with me as a story also about the city in which its drama had taken place. And even after I had moved to the United States, I continued to think of London as a city where if you were writing in English you could get a start. London was not for me the city of eminences buried in Westminster Abbey. It was not even the city where nationalist Indian leaders like Gandhi and Nehru had acquired their higher education and training. Instead, London was the place where, arriving from the colonies, Naipaul had begun to write.

There was an immediate difficulty for me, however. Naipaul had ended in London via Oxford, where he had gone on a scholarship. I did not see this happening to me. Two or three of my friends who were students with me in Delhi and who had done well in their studies had been awarded scholarships to attend Oxford and Cambridge. But my examination results had been dismal; I had considered dropping out of college altogether. I had told myself each year, just before the examinations arrived and caught me unprepared, that I had wanted an education that was vastly more interesting. It was only partly an excuse. I saw myself as a writer. And yet, I wrote little and I read without plan or direction.

One morning, an old friend came back from Oxford. He was a Rhodes scholar at Balliol, and he had returned to the hostel where he had spent three years. When my friend got out of the taxi, he appeared changed. As the morning passed, I realized what had changed in him: he seemed to have rid himself entirely of that air of customary indolence that had been our protective armor for the past few years. The Oxford man told me that his days were now filled with movement. He made frequent visits to London, which was an hour or so away from his home. I imagined trips to libraries, museums, lectures, theaters, parks. I got a gift from him: a pack of postcards showing scenes of life at Oxford. Sunlight slanted across the narrow brick street; bicycles were propped against walls covered with ivy; cricket was being played on the immaculate greens. My friend fed me stories of tutorials and discussions in bakeries and pubs, stories that I would later rediscover, with a sense of nostalgia that would seem to be almost my own, in the novel *Afternoon Raga* by Amit Chaudhuri.

Our visitor from London had come bearing other gifts too: shaving cream and disposable razors and duty-free cigarettes. Tepid tea with toast and omelette in the Hindu College canteen on winter mornings had never tasted so good before because awaiting me at the end of the meal were the imported Silk Cuts that I had just received. The London that the Oxford man described seeped into the winter mornings and became a part of my dream. London became a bright place—there was warm sunshine on the canteen lawns where we were sitting, on metal chairs with seats of blue and white plastic weaving—and I wanted to be there instead. Home was the room in the hostel that did not even belong to me. Each night I would unroll a thin bedding on the floor in the space between the desk and the bed used by the friend who was preparing for a career in the civil services. I wasn't unhappy in this small room. A little later, I was provoked to try and find a room only to take away the uncertainty of the future. This seems unusual to admit, but it is possible that I had not even dwelled on the pleasures of privacy.

London

Perhaps I could not afford to. I had not had any luck getting a place in the university hostels with my low grades. One day there was news that some rooms would be falling vacant in the hostel attached to the Delhi School of Social Work. I wrote about this to my parents in Patna. My mother sent a quick reply. She wanted me to do something to help myself. An uncle who dabbled in astrology had advised my mother that I should put a small shred of saffron in the hollow of my navel after my bath each day.

I acquired the saffron from the nearby Kamla Nagar market. On the morning I was to be interviewed at the hostel, I bathed and, with the help of a fingernail, pushed a thin thread of saffron in my belly button. I wore a clean blue shirt to the meeting. But the warden, a tall, bearded man with the mark of white sandal paste on his forehead, seemed suspicious of me. He stood at the door and refused to take my application. For many months after that, before I placed it somewhere else and lost it forever, the small, plastic box of saffron lay unopened in one of the pockets of the suitcase that I kept under my friend's bed.

I suffered from the warden's paltry act of rejection, however. And somewhere in my response to this feeling of worthlessness, my destination shifted from England to America. In the weeks that followed, I began making inquiries about taking tests like the GRE and TOEFL. All the test takers were headed for places like Chicago, New York, and California. I cautiously added my name to their ranks. Another student who lived on the first floor of the same hostel was willing to help. He gave me a list of universities in the United States where he was going to apply. This man was a little younger than I. He never seemed to be reading but he exuded a quiet air of learning. His main work for the day was to use smack. With a flame lit beneath a tinfoil, he chased the brown powder, a coin placed at the tip of his tongue to catch the residue. As soon as he had finished doing this, my friend would lean over and vomit delicately in a large, clay pot in his room. Actually, the pot sported an oversize rubber-plant that pushed out thick, dark-green leaves every couple of days; the plant had been stolen during a collective raid in the corridors of the college across the street from us, and it now gave the darkened room an elegant, relaxed air. A few months later, when we took the tests together, this quiet drug user performed brilliantly.

Like my roommate upstairs, this young man also kept his books on the windowsill. He, too, had a book by Naipaul. Next to Robert Pirsig's *The Zen of Motorcycle Maintenance*, he had kept Naipaul's *The Mystic Masseur*. The title confused me. I did not pick the book up. But I wanted to read more of Naipaul; I needed to feel stronger in my desire to leave for the West. As it happened, I came upon another book by him very soon.

On my roommate's windowsill, where I had earlier found Naipaul's *Finding the Center*, also stood the "general knowledge" books that were compiled in regularly updated editions by one Mr. Khanna. In those volumes, there was invariably a section called "Books and Authors." Without my having read the books named on the list, I learned that *Future Shock* had been written by Alvin Toffler, *The Prophet* by Kahlil Gibran, *The Guide* by R. K. Narayan, and *A House for Mr Biswas* by V. S. Naipaul. Naipaul had already made me want to leave for London. Now, the Indian name in the title of his book mentioned on the list pleased me. I went to the Hindu College library and borrowed the novel. It was thick and its yellowing pages were bound between cheap red cardboard covers. I began reading *A House for Mr Biswas* while lying on the floor of the future civil servant's hostel room in Delhi.

London

2

Mr. Biswas never makes it to London.

V. S. Naipaul's father, Seepersad, whose story is the subject of A *House for Mr Biswas*, kept an unused passport in his desk. The fresh, unused passport lay there in the drawers—and this detail from *Biswas* was to be narrated again, in the nonfictional account in *Finding the Center*—along with the letters from a London writing school and the pink young of the mice that nested among the papers.

As I read Naipaul's novel in the borrowed room in Delhi, I came across the part where Mr. Biswas learns that his brother-in-law is being sent abroad to study medicine. I flinched at the recognition of an emotion that I had experienced so often in recent days: "Mr. Biswas was overwhelmed. More and more students were going abroad; but they were items of news, remote. He had never thought that anyone so close to him could escape so easily. Concealing his sadness and envy, he made a show of enthusiasm and offered advice about shipping lines." Mr. Biswas had reason to feel bitter. He had bought a secondhand portable typewriter on credit and decided to pay for it by writing for English and American periodicals. He had not had any success with his plans. Mr. Biswas had even responded to an advertisement for the Ideal School of Journalism, Edgware Road, London. He had sent them several articles about the seasons; these had been needed as a part of the first exercise. Mr. Biswas received a printed letter in reply: "We regret to inform you that your articles have been submitted without success to: *Evening Standard, Evening News, The Times, The Tatler, London Opinion, Geographical Magazine, The Field, Country Life.* At least two editors spoke highly of the work but were forced to reject it through lack of space. We ourselves feel that work of such quality should not be consigned to oblivion. Why not try your local newspaper?"

Seepersad Naipaul wanted to get his stories published in England. He had sent his stories to his son at Oxford. A few months before his death, Seepersad was writing letters to his son, urging him to send the stories to publishers: "Try more than one publisher; or try to get the thing through an agent, if necessary. Some of those recommended by Kilham Roberts in an old copy (1940) of *The Authors' Handbook* include. . . ." Fewer than four months later he was dead. The drama of this anxiety and love is vividly expressed in the collection of family letters recently published under the title *Between Father and Son*. Naipaul's sister, writing to her brother at Oxford after their father's death, summed up the disappointments of Seepersad's life: "There are so many things I want to say but I don't know how to say them. That Pa is dead—well, I guess I have to reconcile myself to that, but I can't. There are few things which haunt me—he didn't see you, who he so much wanted to see; to see England, and most of all to have his book published." The letters exchanged within the Naipaul family touch upon an extraordinary pathos, but they also link colonial life with the promise of writing: that is why Pankaj Mishra has identified their themes as "poverty, the fear of extinction, the hope for justice, and writing as redemption."

These themes find their full elaboration in Naipaul's novel. Critics go on at length about the symbol of the house in *Biswas*. It is undeniably the book's central motif; Mr. Biswas's flawed pursuit of the house is a grand narrative of anxious striving and failure. But what makes the search meaningful is not the house in itself but the reason why Mr. Biswas longs for it. He wants to write. Even the mismatched pieces of furniture that Mr. Biswas carries with him are the props for the stage on which he wants to define his selfhood. This self is a writing self, and it comes into full being with the son, who leaves for England. The book he writes, now held in the reader's hands, is recognized as the son's record of the father's failure and triumph. This recognition is what unites, in our experience of reading *Biswas*, the story of the ambitions of the father and the son, the writer and his subject.

The single line that comes to Mr. Biswas every time he wishes to test a new ribbon in the typewriter is the following one: "*At the age of thirty-three, when he was already the father of four children. . . .*" The half-finished sentence lights up momentarily a whole dark universe of desire and futility. And yet, despite the terrible isolation of his ambition, it is also true that Mr. Biswas's haphazard, incomplete actions carry him from the plantation to a life of writing. It is a supreme achievement. Whenever I think of that, the symbolism of the house pales in comparison with those other symbols that represent the writer's journey: in the beginning, the brushes and the paint for the signs that Mr. Biswas painted with such care; then, the fresh newsprint on the pages of *The Sentinel*, where he was employed; his books and the writer's desk that was made from packing crates; his typewriter with its song of escape and despair: *At the age of thirty-three, when he was already the father of four children. . .* ; the short stories attempted by Mr. Biswas in bed, putting pencil to paper while making sucking noises with his teeth.

These accumulated symbols tell their own story in *Biswas*. A part of this story is that London comes to the colony. And this is not simply the background of the empire and its history, but the meeting of Mr. Biswas with Mr. Burnett, a London man who is the newspaper editor at the *Sentinel*. It is the latter who provides

Mr. Biswas with copies of London newspapers to help him develop a feeling for the journalistic story (one Burnett headline for a story by Mr. Biswas was "WHITE BABY FOUND ON RUBBISH DUMP *In Brown Paper Parcel* Did Not Win Bonny Baby Competition"). Soon, Mr. Biswas is able to turn out presentable prose. Mr. Burnett gives Mr. Biswas a sense that the city was populated with stories that were waiting to be told. He encourages Mr. Biswas to write stories with a jaunty edge. Most important, or at least this is how it felt to me when I first read the account in the Delhi hostel, after the void and the blankness of the nervous breakdown that Mr. Biswas had suffered on the plantation, what Mr. Burnett offers are elementary lessons in precision and clarity (" 'Several' has seven letters. 'Many' has only four and oddly enough has exactly the same meaning."). As a part of his reporter's job, Mr. Biswas goes aboard the ships that came from America and Europe; he feels that "within the walls of the office every part of the world was near." Thus, even without having left Trinidad, Mr. Biswas becomes a part of the culture of the desirable, outside world. The desire to write for publications in England and America, and the purchase of the typewriter on credit, are the results of this change and cause Mr. Biswas a great deal of frustration and grief. And yet, this chapter in his life is the most glorious episode of transformation and literary awakening.

I stopped reading the novel soon after I had read a few more pages of the book. I had been enjoying the book, but it seemed to me that the story had already been told. Or perhaps I had sensed, in my own nervous way, that I did not want what Mr. Biswas had gained to be threatened by what he had experienced as darkness at the plantation. He had found both stability and a sense of achievement, simply by stringing together sentences, but was now confronted by the terror of the abyss.

London

The threat of failure had begun to appear in the pages I was reading. Mr. Burnett was sacked, and Mr. Biswas had become fearful of losing his job. By turns angry and helpless, Mr. Biswas now used more of Maclean's Brand Stomach Powder. He struggled ineffectually against his smallness, and became unpopular not only with his divided family but also in his neighborhood. He "discovered the solace of Dickens" and shared it with his son. But at work, his writing suffered. The cruelties of life continued, and so did Mr. Biswas's cruelties to those around him. Then, a letter came to Mr. Biswas from Chicago. It was from Mr. Burnett. It was a brief letter. It ended with the words: "Now and then I see a copy of the *Sentinel*. Why don't you give America a try?" The closing question did not register with Mr. Biswas. Instead, he sat down to write a long letter with "detailed denigrations of the new members of the staff." Mr. Biswas had begun his reply immediately because he had been moved by the fact that Mr. Burnett had written to him. In talking of his colleagues he had intended frivolity, but the letter, when he reread it, appeared bitter and revealed too much of himself. "He tore the letter up. From time to time, until he died, he thought of writing. But he never wrote. And Mr. Burnett never wrote again."

I would have stopped reading *Biswas* somewhere there. I was all in favor of giving America a try. It was not till many years later that I finished reading Naipaul's novel. By then, I had already published my first book. The threat of extinction was not so immediate anymore. During this belated reading of the complete novel, I was living in the United States and, as a part of the broad diasporic Indian community, found more to marvel at in this grand saga of displacement and invention. This time, oddly enough, I also lingered on the descriptions of the drowning of a calf and other scenes from rural life that, when I was in India, I had found familiar and without interest. At that time, I had only been looking for London. London as a point of entry; writing as a record of arrival. I think I understood why I had stopped reading *Biswas* where I had, and chosen to remember, at that time, other words by Naipaul. When I completed reading *Biswas* in America, something stirred in my memory. I thought back to the moment of my departure from India and how I had tried to imagine my own story at the airport by recalling the line from *Miguel Street* that Naipaul had quoted in *Finding the Center*: *I left them all and walked briskly towards the aeroplane, not looking back, looking only at my shadow before me, a dancing dwarf on the tarmac.*

3

In an interview given only a few months prior to his being awarded the Nobel Prize in literature, Naipaul talked in a high conservative tone about delinquent youth in England. His actual words were, "I see that several generations of free milk and orange juice led to an army of thugs." (This after a long summer of rioting in Lancashire and Yorkshire, in which British youth of Pakistani and Bangladeshi origin battled racist attacks as well as police heavy-handedness.) Such pronouncements are not wholly surprising from Naipaul. In his thinking, it is liberalism and not the destruction of the welfare state that needs to be blamed for many of the ills of the society in which he finds himself a reluctant citizen. This is wrong thinking, but it also involves, on Naipaul's part, a kind of amnesia.

It is a forgetting about the lessons of mentorship and social nurturing that we have received from Naipaul himself. Let us return to *Biswas*. Mr. Burnett had been drawn from someone

Naipaul had known as a child—Gault MacGowan, a man from Fleet Street, who had been brought to Trinidad to revive the *Trinidad Guardian*. It was MacGowan who had trained Seepersad Naipaul to look at the world as a journalist and a writer. No one else in colonial Trinidad at that time, the younger Naipaul later wrote, could have given his father such a sense of vocation. It was an inestimable gift. And it was this inheritance of a calling that the father passed on to the son. From Seepersad, a young Naipaul learned about the writer's craft; the less confined world of the writer's imagination; and, most important of all, the redeeming power of the word.

While Naipaul was still away in England, where he had gone after earning a government scholarship, Seepersad suffered two heart attacks. He did not survive the second one. At his death, Seepersad Naipaul was only forty-seven years old. The death came as a great shock to the son. But it also liberated Naipaul from the close relationship that would have prevented him from writing about his father. Over several years that followed his father's death, Naipaul wrote *Biswas*, which he has described as "very much my father's book." The book redeemed the failure that had haunted the elder Naipaul, who had dreamed of success as a writer. But first and foremost, *Biswas* was a tribute to what Naipaul had been taught by his father: "It was written out of his journalism and stories, out of his knowledge, knowledge he had got from the way of looking MacGowan had trained him in. It was written out of his writing."

It is impossible for any serious reader of literature not to be affected by this acknowledgment. Naipaul's *Finding the Center* was one of the first literary autobiographies I had read. The book had appealed to me as a story about a literary beginning, but there was a greater claim attached to it. To believe seriously in what Naipaul had written about his influences was also to be, in turn, influenced by him and find oneself linked to a wider literary circle. When I read it in that hostel room in Delhi, I did not know any writers and was uncertain about my own, vague yearnings. *Finding the Center*, with its story about a start in village life in India, suggested a narrative for my past. The book was my personal example of London coming to me: it planted in my mind the idea of leaving home. But in retrospect, what was more important was that Naipaul had allowed me to imagine, through his example of mentoring, an idea of a wonderful community of writers and readers.

In the years that followed I read more of Naipaul. His well-known distaste for Third World radicals exercised my patience, but I read anything new by him with interest and often pleasure. He said many provocative things to people (when asked by Elizabeth Hardwick what the dots on the foreheads of Indian women symbolized, Naipaul had replied, "The dot means: my head is empty"), and such comments invited laughter and also dismissal. What he said about writers and writing, however, always held my attention. More than a decade after having read *Finding the Center* for the first time, I read an interview with Naipaul in the pages of *The New Yorker*. While reading the interview, Naipaul showed me how I needed to expand my notion of what I had thought of as mentoring. The act of teaching or communicating a deep purpose could not be limited to the literary members of one's society. This circle of inclusion needed to be a wider one. This came through to me in the interviewer's account of his being shown by Naipaul a portrait of Emperor Shah Jahan from the writer's private collection in his London apartment. Let me quote from the story:

> *"I think the most important thing about that picture is its condition," Naipaul said. "The eyes, the lips, the ears—very fine. But*

then it's so damaged around the head. And it's awful to say that within a hundred years of that picture being done and being locked away in the prince's library, it was plundered. And it was because that prince hadn't created a state. He hadn't created institutions to protect the painting, and, in a similar way, he hadn't protected his people. All that art, all that training, all that talent, and it's for the prince alone. It doesn't educate the country—it's part of nothing else, because the prince has provided nothing that will remain when he has been wiped away. When I make this point to scholars of Indian art, they think I'm making some antique point about Indians being barbarous and uncivilized. They're incapable of understanding what I'm saying—that all the energy should have gone into creating a self-aware, analytical society with its own intellectual possibilities.

Art cannot last in a vacuum. For books to be written, and for them to be read, we need schools. We need an enlightened state. We need institutions of learning, and we also need roads, and parks, and hospitals. What we have above is not Tory talk, contemptuous of ordinary people and their needs, but actually a discourse of thoughtfulness and concern. With this understanding, the notion of the mentor giving another person a powerful sense of literary vocation gets amplified. It touches on broader aspects of life, it spreads out, and it becomes all-encompassing. The concept is in its essence democratic and social. It sees in the provision of free milk and orange juice the promise of a protected people.

It cannot be doubted that Naipaul is among the most accomplished practitioners of the art of writing today. He also takes a prized place at the very beginning of the phenomenon that we now call the literature of the Indian diaspora.

An acknowledgment of my debt can come only in the form of a piece of writing: a record of what I have received from Naipaul as a lesson about the literary life. I want to present him in return with a very brief narrative about mentoring. The mentor in my story is not a father but a mother; my story takes us not to London but to the place from which I had sought escape. My mother, decades after her children left her household in search of their own separate futures, has begun to hold free classes in a room next to her kitchen. Her students are the poor children of her neighborhood in Patna. Some of the children are homeless; others live in the "servant's quarters" of nearby homes. My mother's class begins soon after most of the children finish their first round of chores as domestics, washing dishes and sweeping floors.

My mother tells me that the students have now learned to write short words on their slates. The children want notebooks and pens. This is their biggest wish. When I first heard this, I thought of *Biswas*. I thought of small beginnings and a hard life. And how the attainment of desire in that novel is built around the small signs of a writer's life: alphabets on a page, a few books, a desk. I wish for a lot of notebooks in the lives of the children in my mother's little school. I wish for books in their future, books that they themselves will write. I wish that the children will be literate citizens of the world who will demand their share from society and the state.

1

Now that you
have come, I will dream
in two languages.

Now that you
have come, I will live
each hour
twice over.
Greenwich Mean Time
will only mean so much.
Darkness at noon
in New York will only mean darkness
before dawn in New Delhi.

Now that you have come
we will think of the others
who came on the Fatel Razak,
the Komagata Maru,
and the Bostan.

Now that you
have come to London
(it could also be Durban or Port-of-Spain)

I will not take the train
by myself to a restaurant
called the Taj Mahal again.

Now that you have come
to this street in Chicago or Toronto,
Bollywood will come to Hollywood
and curry will be eaten in a hurry.
Only the impure
will endure.
In the bad new days
we will find our bold new ways.

Now that you have come
Malgudi will be in Manhattan.
The seth will be on Wall Street
and his servant not far away.
Now that you
have come, we will join the fray—
arm in arm, waving red flags,
with the other workers on Broadway.

Now that you have come
there will be bhaji on the beach.
There will be the satanic verses and the
imam's curses.
Bhangra will rock
rock
and ragas will join reggae.
There will be a brimful of asha
to lighten our day.

Now that you have come
there will be more ethnic chic
in the downtown boutique
and hazaar megabytes
of expertise near L.A.

In Panipat or Sasaram, however,
things will remain the same.
Now that you have come

there will be two types of Indians:
those who have the green card,
and those still waiting
for a ration card to come their way.
But, hey, things need to change
even if we're here to stay.

Now that you have come
I'm here, there,
everywhere.
This is pure chutney.
Would you have it any other way?

2

To be an Indian from Trinidad, V. S. Naipaul had written in an article in 1965, was to be an "unlikely" being and "the embodiment of an old verbal ambiguity." The word *Indian* was for Naipaul a much abused term. And the examples the writer had chosen to make his point were apposite. Indian ink is really Chinese ink, and what we call India paper is paper that first came from China. Naipaul wrote of the case of Columbus landing on the island of Guanahani in 1492 and misnaming its people: "He called them Indians, and Indian they remained, walking Indian file through Indian corn. And so, too, that American bird which to English-speaking people is the turkey is to the French *le dindon*, the bird of India." One of history's ironies, of course, was that the "real" Indians were later brought to the islands that Colum-bus had mistakenly assumed to be India. The new arrivals, back in 1845, were indentured laborers from British India.

They were transported to Trinidad and Guyana to work on the plantations after the abolition of slavery. Naipaul's ancestors belonged to that stock.

In the essay that I have been quoting from above, Naipaul had gone on to write that to be an Indian from Trinidad was not only to be "unlikely and exotic," it was also to be "a little fraudulent." Naipaul was here making a statement about all immigrants. "Immigrants are people on their own," he wrote. "They cannot be judged by the standards of their older culture. Culture is like language, ever developing. There is no right and wrong, no purity from which there is decline. Usage sanctions everything." This was not in any way a complaint. For Naipaul, it was important that the Trinidadian Indians were creatures of the New World. India persisted in their midst in the form of temples and some customs; its truer associations were perhaps the buried memories of famines and past sorrow. The immigrants had escaped all that. Although they were able to "recreate eastern Uttar Pradesh and Bihar wherever they went," Naipaul also saw that new currents of history had liberated the Trinidadians from India. World War II and the coming of the Americans meant that "a new people seemed all at once to have been created."

I was born in Bihar. In the mid-1990s, I visited Trinidad to work on a documentary film on the descendants of the Indian indentureds. The film that resulted from my visits was called *Pure Chutney*. In the preceding decades, Naipaul, and his younger brother Shiva, had journeyed to India and to Bihar. Shiva Naipaul had called Bihar "the subcontinent's heart of darkness." When I went to Trinidad, I was traveling in the opposite direction from the Naipauls. I did not know what I would discover at the end of my journey. The newness that the elder Naipaul had written about—the people that were left when

India had fallen away from them—interested me. I had been living outside India a decade; the accidents of history in the diaspora had suddenly acquired meaning for me. When I was a boy, growing up in India, a dark-skinned cousin was called "West Indian" by some of the members of my family. In a racist joke, this cousin was often confused with Clive Lloyd, the legendary cricketer who had led the Caribbean team. But there had also been a cricketer of Indian origin on that same team. His name was Alvin Kallicharan. I now wonder how it came to be that in my family Clive Lloyd's very dark skin had meaning, but Kallicharan's difference was neither noticed nor explained. I thought of questions like these in the plane that took me to Port-of-Spain, and it seemed to me, at times, that I was returning to an enigma of my childhood. I was rediscovering my past.

In Trinidad, I was a stranger in a familiar place. On my first day there I found the name of my hometown in India, Patna, which was now the name of a street in Port-of-Spain. I drank beer at Kumar Bar. The food in the Indian restaurants was very little like the food served in restaurants in India; it tasted a lot like the food you will get in the homes in rural parts of Bihar. This was peasant food. Away from Port-of-Spain, I was startled by the sight of small, colorful flags fluttering on bamboo poles, a scene that I associated only with my own ancestral home in the village. I was finding that in some ways Trinidad had remained Indian in a way that much of India itself no longer was. And yet, everything was different. Everyone spoke English. The religious festivals, the weddings, even the funerals were conducted in a form that mixed the rituals of village India with customs that belonged to the communities with whom the Indian migrants had come into contact. Caste had undergone a massive change, even if it had not disappeared outright. The rigidity of the social conventions that I had grown up with as an Indian, and the cultural divisions that I had inherited, suddenly seemed happily obsolete here in the Caribbean. I was invited to lunch one day at a Trinidadian-Indian home where I learned that one half of the family was Hindu and the other half Muslim.

At the same time, however, where invention and change should have fostered a greater openness to social mixing, there were also some Trinidadian Indians who eagerly, even zealously, sought the marks of religious and cultural purity. One Hindu activist, with links to the right-wing Vishwa Hindu Parishad in India, railed at length against secularism. In his view, secularism was an ideology that had been imposed from the outside, from the West, a history from which he considered himself protected. In faraway Trinidad, at the end of the twentieth century, he was full of rage against the injustices of the

medieval Moghul emperors. "It is a part of my history," he said, "I must not forget it." It was as if other histories had not happened since, and that several centuries of further complexity hadn't woven their strands into our perceptions. Other Indian-Trinidadians were as eager to practice this form of self-denial. One man, a member of a Hindu reformist group, made disparaging remarks about African Trinidadians: most of their children are born out of wedlock, he said calmly. He was anxious that I see Indian Trinidadians as a separate, superior group from their fellow citizens. It seemed to me that, in many cases, Indian Trinidadians had become more insular. Or perhaps, it would be more accurate to say, they wanted to assert their distinctive cultural identity, much of which had been disparaged for long, and they fell back on a tactic that was shortsighted if not also bigoted. And yet, while ideologues were busy drawing lines of

distinction, it was also true that in realms like popular culture, "Indian" and "African" cultures mixed with dynamic force. In a form of music called "chutney soca," for instance, Indian-Trinidadian musicians combine Bhojpuri songs with calypso tempos and even hip-hop rhythms. In the creolized language that is shared by all, in the food that is eaten, in the mix of the people who walk on the streets of Port-of-Spain, a genuinely multiethnic society has come into being.

All of these changes are a part of the promise of diasporic cultures. Naipaul, writing his essay about the "unlikely" Indian, was describing what had happened in Trinidad. But what he was saying in the abstract was also true of what was by then beginning to take place in London itself, where Naipaul was probably putting those words to paper. For the truth is that the newness Naipaul had seen coming to the periphery was also a part of the story of the center. The new arrivals themselves were the agents of that change.

3

Dean Mahomed (1759–1851) was born in Patna and, at the age of twenty-five, emigrated to Ireland. Later, around 1807, when he was in his late forties, Mahomed moved to London. In India, he had been a member of the English East India Company's Bengal Army; in London, Dean Mahomed chose to become a medical practitioner, and then a restaurateur. When he was in his mid-fifties, Dean Mahomed moved to the coastal town of Brighton, where he set up a business in "Indian Medicated Vapor and Shampooing Baths." It is very likely that Mahomed introduced the word *shampoo* into the English language.

An advertisement from 1826 has the name "Sake Deen Mahomed, Shampooing Surgeon" emblazoned on the top. It mentions that this art of applying steam to the human body has long been familiar in "the eastern parts of the world" and that "the art of Shampooing was first introduced into England, by S. D. Mahomed, in 1784." King George IV was one of his patrons. And so was his successor, King William IV. However, the business in baths, which reportedly attracted public attention, did not garner a significant fortune. Mahomed was not well off when he died. Yet in 1794, Dean Mahomed had written of his life and Indian society under the East India Company. The book was published with the title *The Travels of Dean Mahomet.* This was the first book written by an Indian author in English.

In the years that followed, especially in the nineteenth century, in its closing decades, there would be a spate of books written in English by Indians. When one reads the writings of someone like Mohandas Gandhi, who had arrived in England as a student in 1888, what emerges is the picture, once again, of the Indian as "unlikely" and "exotic." Gandhi's writings were written in the form of reminiscences, in the 1920s, when he was already an established leader of the Indian freedom struggle. He published his essays in his newspaper, *Navajivan,* and then, in English translation, in *Young India.* The Indian leader was in his mid-fifties then. However, his writings convey no sense of a political interrogation of identity. Instead, there is a touching experimentation with a sense of newness, even as the young man carries the whole burden of his puritan past. Of course, the experimentation is all within the norms of the late Victorian society, but, nevertheless, what is also very much in evidence is a remaking of the self, much of it carried out with a nervous glance at the bill. Thus, in Gandhi's account of his life in London, we read of him buying a violin for three pounds and a "chimney-pot hat" for nineteen shillings, taking lessons in elocution and dancing, reading the Sermon on the Mount, and even being a "dissembler," passing himself off as a bachelor with the girls he met although he was already married and a father. Here, even in the tale of the origins of our principal nationalist icon, there are the details of diasporic travel and a great mixing of cultural influences. This is the condition that I have been calling pure chutney.

Recalling his life in London, Gandhi began one chapter with the words "There were comparatively few Indian students in England forty years ago." By the time he was writing those words, there were many more students already coming to England from India. The children of the Indian bourgeoisie, sent to London to acquire degrees, also picked up liberal ideas of participatory democracy and a desire to live with the British as equals. In one of India's major post-independence novels, *Aag Ka Dariya* (River of Fire), originally written in Urdu then translated into English by its author, Qurratulain Hyder, we get a glimpse of this nationalist ferment. Hyder mentions Sajjad Zaheer, who "in 1931 came from Oxford to India for six months and published *Angarey*, rebellious short stories in Urdu," a book that, incidentally, was banned by the government in Uttar Pradesh. Hyder also provides the names of the women who went to England to get an education, and adds that this was rare at that time. Then, she writes: "In 1935 Sajjad Zaheer and his comrades in London launched the Indian Progressive Writers Association, and its Manifesto was written by Dr Jyoti Ghosh, Dr Mulk Raj Anand, Promod Sen Gupta, Dr Muhammad Deen Taseer and Sajjad Zaheer."

Mulk Raj Anand, one of those progressive writers that Hyder mentions, had been influenced by Gandhi. Anand had also been a student in England, first at Cambridge then at University College, London. Many of his novels, beginning with *Untouchable* and *Coolie*, were inspired by Gandhian ideals—Anand was later to spend time with the Mahatma at his ashram—and also Gandhi's own unadorned writing in *Young India*. But here, too, there was no chance of any sacredness or purity of influences. When he was beginning to write his books, Anand had entered the charmed Bloomsbury circle of literary figures like Virginia Woolf, T. S. Eliot, E. M. Forster, and Aldous Huxley. In a memoir written almost six decades later, Anand recalled what London, after India, had meant to him: "I arrived in London after a brief jail-going in the Gandhi movement in the early twenties and found myself removed, suddenly, from the realities of the freedom struggle into the world of Bloomsbury where the pleasures of literature and art were considered ends in themselves."

The conversations with the aesthetes left Anand feeling both overwhelmed and frustrated. As a provincial graduate of Khalsa College in Amritsar, Anand had read very little so far: two Shakespeare plays, Thackeray's *Henry Esmond*, and some books of poetry provided by his professor. He wanted to be on equal terms with the learned writers he admired, but it seemed to him that they did not know much about India except what they had picked up from Kipling. Leonard Woolf and Huxley were exceptions, people who "had doubts about our benign white sahibs." The others "seemed to believe, more or less, in the 'Empire on which the sun never sets.'" This angered Anand. He wrote, "I had left home because my pro-white-sahib father had beaten my mother for my going to jail." After one of the Bloomsbury parties, while helping with the cleaning of the dishes, the young Anand reached a resolve: "I would fight for the freedom of my country forever, though I may admire these English writers for their literary skills."

Anand's resolve is touching and might to some appear simpleminded. But this was in the early 1920s. To me, it speaks of nationalist zeal but also of a literary and cultural vacuum in which the Indian writer in English had to look elsewhere for a model. In an essay in the *New York Review of Books* a few years ago, Pankaj Mishra commented on this particular history, remarking that Anand had "no tradition or model to support his attempts to write a novel in English about India." Mishra wrote that, at that time, even the European idea of the novel as "a means of social and political inquiry" was new in India, not only to someone like Anand but also to those writing in Indian languages. "More discouragingly," added Mishra, "few Indian writers before the 1930s had ever attempted prose fiction in English."

When we read these words, we can begin to understand why Anand, leaning over the sink in a bookshop, would have felt torn about liking writers who appeared ignorant of his past. There were no others that he could follow. He had his authenticity, but in the absence of a record of cultural production in the language in which he wanted to write, this authenticity didn't count for much. Or it counted only as a piece of exotica.

The London of the expatriates, of our earliest nationalists and our earliest writers in English, offered not only a mix of influences. It also presented a rather precise problem: the Indian, in that setting, could not find retreat in some myth of purity. Here is Anand once again: "The thing that disturbed me was that I might get a scholarship from the Silver Wedding Fund of King George and Queen Mary, which my Professor in University College had recommended me for. And then I would be a hypocrite, hating British rule in India and living on its dole."

Three decades later, Qurratulain Hyder was wryly commenting on an inescapable impurity of another sort when, in

River of Fire, she wrote of the revolutionary Indian students, of impeccable bourgeois background, spouting slogans in the London of the 1950s. She called these left-leaning students "Red Indians" as in "Inside, some Red Indians were making fierce anti-American speeches." One of these students had been overheard in an earlier chapter, saying to a friend in India, "Honestly, I don't feel like running away to England at a time like this, when the country is plunged in total disaster. But higher education is necessary, too, for rebuilding India. Although right now it would be a kind of bourgeois opportunism, don't you think?" Her friend replies, "Quite right. . . . But it is so difficult to get admission into Cambridge. I've managed only because my father studied there."

4

Hyder was writing in the shadow of the Partition. In her novel, Indian and Pakistani students met in the BBC canteen in London of the 1950s, their words carrying with them memories of cultural mixing, memories now made all the more dramatic, and also tragic, because of what had happened only a few years ago. One of the students, Kamal, mentions a wedding song and asks: "Can any western sociologist understand the beauty of this scene, this fusion of Muslim and Hindu imagery in a song sung at Muslim marriages?" In London, then, what is recalled, rather mourned, is a half-mythical, half-real time when the massacre of impurity had still not taken place. Hyder's writing about London was a protest against the cut-throat sectarianism of both the Hindu and the Muslim Right at home.

Hyder's London was a far cry from the London where Gandhi had arrived in 1888 and noted that there were not many Indian students around. In Hyder's London, Indians and Pakistanis congregated in places as varied as the BBC Canteen and a boarding house in Camden; yet their numbers were hardly overwhelming. At one point, Hyder wrote: "A few leading movie stars like Raj Kapoor and Nargis began arriving in London, but they failed to make a splash because the Indian population in the city was quite small." By the time we come closer to the present moment, this picture has altered almost beyond recognition. In Indian fiction, this change is perhaps most dramatically represented in Salman Rushdie's novel *The Satanic Verses*, in Gibreel Farishta's decision to turn London into a tropical city. Farishta lists the civic improvements in the city: "increased moral definition, institution of a national siesta, development of vivid and expansive patterns of behavior among the populace." Then Farishta settles his eye on the advantages of heat in the cold city: "A new mass market for domestic air-conditioning units, ceiling fans, anti-mosquito coils and sprays. A coir and copra industry. Increased appeal of London as a centre for conferences, etc.; better cricketers; higher emphasis on ball-control among professional footballers, the traditional and soulless English commitment to 'high workrate' having been rendered obsolete by the heat. Religious fervor, political ferment, renewal of interest in the intelligentsia. No more British reserve; hot-water bottles to be banished forever, replaced in the fetid nights by the making of slow and odorous love."

The list is enough to make an Indian immigrant bathe in nostalgia—"Spicier food; the use of water as well as paper in

English toilets; the joy of running fully dressed through the first rains of the monsoon" — but the greater truth lies in what it says of the confidence of the novelist. An Indian writer could not have imagined such a literary legislation twenty or thirty years ago. Although the weather in England has not changed, alas, the ecology of literature certainly has. The map of London has been altered by the arrival of the Indian writer. A couple of years ago, in a special issue on London, *Granta* magazine published four maps of "Literary London" by Martin Rowson. The map of "Modern London" showed an entire section that was marked "India." The landmarks in that space included icons labeled Rushdie and Hanif Kureishi. The literary topographer had peppered the landscape with bags of money that, according to the key, meant "Booker Prize" and "Agents/Advances."

The literary phenomenon is very much a part of a larger change, a product of the sizable migration to Britain from its former colonies. In the 1960s, the northern mill towns were importing labor from the Indian subcontinent and the Caribbean. Workers who would work long, cheap shifts were needed also for the railways and the hospitals. Immigrant labor fulfilled that need. In addition, professionals migrated; doctors, academics, and artists from the Indian subcontinent took advantage of the lax immigration laws in the 1960s. Following the ouster of the Asians from Uganda under the dictator Idi Amin, people of Indian origin also came to England from Africa. The changes that resulted were not simply at the level of the population; the former empire's basic cultural character was forever transformed.

In the mid-1980s, Hanif Kureishi wrote a travelogue about a visit to the northern town of Bradford. Kureishi recalled that, for T. S. Eliot, culture had referred to a whole way of life. Thus, for Eliot, British culture had meant "Derby Day, Henley regatta,

Cowes, the Twelfth of August, a cup final, the dog races, the pin-table, Wensleydale cheese, boiled cabbage cut into sections, beetroot in vinegar, nineteenth century gothic churches and the music of Elgar." A contemporary list of the characteristic activities of the British people, Kureishi went on, would include "yoga exercises, going to the Indian restaurant, the music of Bob Marley, the novels of Salman Rushdie, Zen Buddhism, the Hare Krishna Temple, as well as the films of Sylvester Stallone, therapy, hamburgers, visits to gay bars, the dole office and the taking of drugs."

Kureishi's essay was a penetrating portrait of a working-class city in England, a city with districts where there wasn't a single white face around. The writer's visits to pubs and a school led him to wonder aloud about why the immigrant community needed to pursue separate education for the sexes. There was a fear of impurity there, a turning away from all the principles of a liberal education. Kureishi asked whether the Asian community leaders were "a few earnest and repressed believers, all men, frightened of England and their daughters' sexuality?" The writer himself belonged to another generation, one that had been born in England, and whose lives, he wrote, "seemed to synthesize disparate elements: the pub, the mosque, two or three languages, rock 'n' roll, Indian films."

Early in his visit, Kureishi drove through the rundown city and passed Priestley Road. Kureishi wrote, "J. B. Priestley was born in Bradford, and in the early sixties both John Braine and Alan Sillitoe set novels here. I wondered what the writing of the next fifteen years would be like." One cannot read those words too without thinking of Meera Syal writing her first novel, *Anita and Me*, about an Indian girl growing up in a white working-class mining town in Wolverhampton. It was this emergence that Kureishi was anticipating in his remark. In Syal's prose what comes alive is a portrait of a people, at once tentative and also terribly courageous; we see them taking over, as if they were a cheerful army of occupation, the far land from where their former rulers came. The young Meena in Syal's novel witnesses the following scene: "I stood uncertainly on the front porch and watched helplessly as the Aunties and Uncles began reclaiming the Tollington night in big Indian portions, guffawing Punjabi over fences and hedges, wafting curried vegetable smells through tight-mouthed letterboxes, sprinkling notes from old Hindi movie songs over jagged rooftops, challenging the single street light on the crossroads with their twinkling jewels and brazen silks."

The 1960s that Meena recalls are filled with memories of quieter revolutions, of finding jobs or homes when they were only for whites. Of being able to see a brown face on the telly. The news of Rita Farrier, the reigning Miss India, winning the Miss World Contest meant that the news in Meena's home remained on full blast, the phone never stopped ringing, and the Aunties and Uncles arrived with food for an impromptu party. Syal's novel tells the story of a girl growing up in the Black Country, but it is also a tender tribute to the early Indian immigrants, the immigrants who belonged to the generation of Syal's parents, the ones who wrapped themselves in nostalgia and silence when Meena's father brought out the harmonium and, in a rich vibrato, his face taking on an expression of a Hindi film star, began to sing *"Mera Saaya Sath Hoga, Tu Jahan Jahan Chalega."*

In Syal's second novel, *Life Isn't All Ha Ha Hee Hee,* published in 1999, the scene has shifted to the Indians, who are, in a more practiced sense, British. The children of the first generation of Indian immigrants have grown up. Nostalgia has given way to new pleasures and problems. Syal builds the novel around the stories of three young women, three friends, as they manage their lives, their relationships, and their careers. In *Anita and Me*, the reader was shocked to hear that Meena's best friend, Anita, who was white, had been involved in a violent attack on a stranger named Rajesh Bhatra. Anita had said, "And we went Paki bashing, it was bosting! This Paki was standing at a bus stop, he was in a suit, it was dead funny! Nah, I only watched, the lads like did it, you know, and us wenches, we just shouted and held their lager. . . . They really did him over and you know what, the stupid bastard didn't do nothing back!" But over and over, in the pages of *Life Isn't All Ha Ha Hee Hee*, what we discover is a complex mapping of the violence that we are capable of inflicting on each other. In this novel, Syal brings the critical energy she had brought to her script for the feature film *Bhaji on the Beach*. The film had brilliantly followed a group of Asian women, of different generations, as they go on a visit to Brighton. The film had focused on gender and patriarchy, but never strayed too far from related concerns about race and class and sexual orientation. The women in *Life Isn't All Ha Ha Hee Hee* pick their way through the same social minefield. There's nostalgia here too, but it is not for a distant place. Or if it is, the distant place is only the past, the past that took place no further away than London's East End. One of Syal's main characters, Tania, driving along the Broadway of Little India, past places like Pradeep's Sweet Mart and Lahori's Kebab Hut, is suddenly surrounded by her memories. Her nostalgia is fueled not by Hindi film songs but by the music of the British *bhangra* bands that had come to her on bootleg tapes during her teen years. Tania and her friends Chila and Sunita had been knocked back by "the wall of sound and fury" that had come out of the speakers at Riz's Music Mart:

The drums they knew, their parents' heartbeat, folk songs sung in sitting rooms, the pulse of hundreds of family weddings; but then the guitars, cold steel and concrete, the smell of the Bull-ring, the frustration bouncing off walls in terraced houses in Handsworth, hurried cigarettes out of bathroom windows, secret assignations in libraries, hurrying home with a mouthful of fear and desire. The lyrics parodied I Love You Love Me Hindi film crooning, but with subtle, bitter twists, voices coming from the area between what was expected of kids like them and what they were really up to.

Tania slides down the windows in her jeep and listens to the music pulsing in the air. The youth are lounging at the side of the street, and the music climbs in over the sounds of the evening. Tania recognizes "a line from one of her favorite old Hindi songs, but repeated scratchily, laid over jerky violins and a soporific single sitar note, with a pounding acid beat below it."

Pure chutney!

But I—who was born in India and who sees in this new music the realities of the *desi* youth who pass through my classes and with whom I want to talk, even though their realities are very different at times from mine—I seem to be hearing all this from a greater distance. I have listened to this music and I like it, I want to say to the *desi* teenagers. At the same time, I also feel the need to quickly recognize that the Indian youth in the West, the children that are being born to my friends, are going to produce a new, mixed culture where I can be only an outsider. It is very exciting to imagine that future.

5

For Rohit Dev Goswami,
Six Days Old Today

Fertility rates in many places are dropping rapidly, especially
in the richest countries, where, to put it simply, any two people
are not producing two more people.

The New York Times

I cheer for you,
one so little,
for taking on the *New York Times*
so early on in your

career. This should make
the news in your own
grandfather's paper in Assam,
Janambhumi, The Birthplace.

In Texas, you arrived around sunset
while in India
it was already dawn
the Brahmaputra red like your name.

Later that night
in India, everyone lit lamps
for Diwali,
the festival of light.

According to *The Hindu,*
which I read on the world wide web,
Indian schoolchildren
on the day of your birth

took an oath to not use fire-
crackers during Diwali
as a protest
against child labor.

Also that day, if you're interested
in matters of the weather,
a full 28 mm
of rain fell

in Thiruvananthapuram,
but Calcutta for some reason
remained completely dry.
Oh, was I boring you—don't cry. . . .

*

Your arrival was announced
in the homes
of your family in Assam
by the ringing

of the telephone.
From Corpus Christi,
the good news was e-mailed
. to me post-post-haste.

I don't want to mess
with Texas, but even India,
sometimes, is only a bit of electronic data
on my computer.

The photograph of your face
will forever be
for your grandparents
their only passport.

The land of your parents' birth
you will receive

in the bright shapes
of postage stamps.

When I see you at play
I hope the faraway
fairyland in the stories they tell you
will always have mangoes in it.

Later I'll tell you
that even in this TV global-nation
that joins Boston
with Bombay, only twenty miles

from your home, more
and more people try to cross
the border, doing what only the bull
from Merrill Lynch is allowed to do.

*

Today your mother
placed outside the door
an oil-lamp, a coin,
grains of rice, a bowl of water

and a pen.
For that's how Destiny
comes and writes
one's future in Assam.

I can only add
to those invitations:
a toy car, an Olajuwon jersey,
a Tickle-me-Elmo,

a can of Coke,
a computer disk.
When you can
rent a video

from a *desi*
grocery store.
Promise me, you'll find
Nargis beautiful

and Dev Anand
dashing. In doing this
humor your parents'
past
and remember
they actually like
Batman
and Demi Moore too.

Make of your parts
what you will.
Visit us often
in ours.

1

In the folder of papers that I collected during my first year as a new immigrant in the West, I have a newspaper clipping from the Indian newspaper *The Statesman*. The report is about the visit to Delhi of a literary critic who had emigrated from India in the early 1960s. The critic told the reporter that she liked to eavesdrop on conversations in Delhi's buses. She had noticed how people would switch to English whenever they wanted to express "a noble thought or a higher emotion." The critic went on: "It would be interesting to study how many people, who otherwise conducted their courtship in one Indian language or the other, have said that vital sentence 'I love you' in English." While sitting in the basement of a library that offered the privilege of reading two Indian newspapers about a fortnight late, I read the report about the critic's visit, and that line about the use of the English language arrested me. The phenomenon that the critic had described was for her proof that we Indians had imbibed the colonizer's language, and, equally important, that there was no way of wishing away this fact. To deny the place that English had in our lives, the critic said, would be to deny our past. All this seemed quite indubitable to me. But the critic's remarks were actually of interest to me for an entirely different reason.

I had left India behind. In my new life, I wanted romance. It was not only my untried sexuality that bothered me; rather, the feeling of sexual inexperience seemed to gather into itself the more visible sense of social and financial insecurity in a new, foreign society. Love and sex, I had told myself, would make me an insider. However, there were obstacles in my path. I was worried that I would not know what to say when I was going to ask someone for a kiss. Or how exactly I would tell a woman I had fallen in love with, which I did with alarming frequency, that I wanted to be in love with her forever. As a result, I was extremely attentive to any insight into the language of love. The news item in *The Statesman* had posed a problem for me. In a place where everyone spoke English, how would I switch languages? This question didn't emerge in a vacuum. Although I wanted to fall in love with white women, women with golden hair and glittering smiles that I had seen in magazine ads, I was nostalgic for home. I would have given much to be able to say to someone *in Hindi* that I loved her very much.

During that first year away from India, *Masterpiece Theater* was screening the adaptation of Paul Scott's *Jewel in the Crown* on television. Salman Rushdie had pilloried this film as a part of the Orientalizing "Raj revival." He was right. But for me, the weekly screenings were a way to reenter a space of romance and Indianness. Within the frame of the film, I could still speak English and be at home. Perhaps it even gave me pleasure that the people around me were watching a television show that portrayed India, and therefore Indians, as erotic and dangerous. I wanted to look in the mirror and see Art Malik, the actor who played Hari Kumar. I longed for a tie, a jacket, and a British accent. In the weeks that followed, I acquired two of the three. In those days, while I awaited the weekly screenings of *Jewel in the Crown*, I also read other Raj fiction. I came across E. M. Forster's "Kanaya," a short, fictional journal of the writer's days as the secretary to a minor maharaja in Dewas, in central India, in the early 1920s. I had not known that Forster was gay. As I learned later, the writer was putting some distance between himself and the England of the Oscar Wilde trial and the Sodomy Laws; his love affair with Mohommed el Edl in Egypt, and his later furtive relationships in India, were attempts to find a flawed fulfillment in the colonies. In Dewas, Forster was having trouble finding a suitable person to have sex with. The Englishman received advice from his Hindu employer—"you must not masturbate, that's awful"—and also assurances that he could procure someone from among the hereditary servants. Kanaya was the name of the barber boy that His Highness thought Forster would like.

Kanaya was pretty, wrote Forster, "with a clear complexion, thick black eyebrows that met, and a thin black moustache." He was "somewhat overdressed, in too yellow a coat and too blue a turban," and, to Forster, "he rather suggested the part." But the barber boy was amiable as he shaved Forster, and the writer was pleasant in return. At his next meeting, Forster "caressed the buttons of his coat." And when he drew the boy to him, Kanaya shook his head. Forster wrote, "To shake the head means 'yes' in that country." (Ah . . . the treacherous ambivalence of the sign in that alien country called sexuality. And also the ambivalence, of course, of colonial power, and the desire that meets domination.) "Are you willing?" Forster asked the boy. But even as the question was posed, there was the sudden noise of water being splashed against the tattie that covered the door. A servant had returned. Kanaya went away.

At the third meeting, wrote Forster, "Kanaya was punctual and gratified my desires." But the satisfaction, it seemed, didn't last. Forster had expected more by way of a friendship with Kanaya. But this seemed unlikely. Forster wrote, "I couldn't get from Kanaya the emotional response of an Egyptian, because he had the body and the soul of a slave, but he was always merry and he improved my health." There were other hindrances to the companionship that Forster seemed to be seeking. It was difficult for the two to meet, and then, after he had been away for ten days, Forster returned to Dewas to find that Kanaya had been talking to others. He had told someone that "Sahib's fond of boys." When the rumor spread, people responded with a change in their behavior; they acted with what Forster called "a good deal of impertinence and ill-breeding."

The scandal spread. In another two months, Forster was to leave Dewas. And the tensions in the court persisted till he left. In Forster's account, there was little joy. The illusion of imperial romance, across races and classes, could not possibly have lasted, not in the form that Forster, a Cambridge intellectual, wanted it to take when he chose to have sex, almost exclusively, with illiterate, working-class men. This, too, is perhaps a part of the famous "not now, not yet" declaration in the novel that Forster was to write the following year, *A Passage to India*. The book ends with this lament about the impossibility of friendship between Aziz and Fielding, one man an Indian and the other British. Forster himself saw the division between the colonizer and the colonized clearly enough even when he was writing "Kanaya." But more clearly, he saw his own place in the state of things: "I see myself disintegrated and inert, like the dead cow among vultures at the edge of the road." This was less about judging one of the two parties; Forster had decided that neither was any good. In a letter to his friend Syed Ross Masood, Forster confided why he had turned away from fashioning his novel as a bridge between the East and the West: "I think that most Indians, like most English people, are shits, and I am not interested whether they sympathize with one another or not."

This unsentimental education was not proving a very great help to me in my search for romance. I had begun reading "Kanaya" with excitement because the writer's negotiation of the taboo against homosexuality could be instructive. It spoke to me about accepting desire and then speaking, or at least writing, about it. Forster's agonized presentation of his needs to His Highness, his sense of frustration, even the small, touching details about the Englishman fondling the buttons on Kanaya's coat, spoke to me of candor and even maturity. But my reading of "Kanaya" didn't lessen either my ignorance or my confusion, and there was a reason for it.

In India, when I was an adolescent, there was an incident in a nearby small town. I read about it in the papers. It was my first, shocking introduction to homosexuality. An upper-caste hoodlum had got into a quarrel with a teacher; he had picked up the teacher's son, taken him to a small house that served as the office of a political party, and sodomized the boy. Years later, in the mid-1990s, I was back in India, traveling with a group of Naxalites, the leftist activists organizing peasants in the Bihar countryside. A young man asked me I had come across any handbooks on guerrilla strategy, especially any that had come out of El Salvador or Nicaragua. I said I hadn't. He then asked me about the Persian Gulf War. He wanted to know whether I had made contacts with groups in the United States that had opposed the war. I said that I had. On the campus where I had been a student at that time, the leftist as well as the gay and lesbian organizations had been at the forefront of the protests against the war. I had many friends in those groups. After a pause, the young man asked me the meaning of the term "gays and lesbians." When I answered him, my interlocutor fell silent. Then he said, "In this region we are organizing a campaign against homosexuals." When I asked him why, he told me that the local landlords had taken to terrorizing the lower-caste landless peasants by raping their boys. The campaign was a part of the protest against this brutality.

I suddenly remembered that autumn some years ago when I had read Forster. I told the young man that, till I came to the United States, I was not aware of having met anyone who was gay. The signs of gayness, I could see with hindsight, were everywhere in India. I just did not read them as such. At the university that I joined in the United States, however, there was an active gay and lesbian organization. It had Indian members and, crucially, the members were progressive and active in a number of organizations. I considered myself a committed leftist when I left India, but the freedom of sexual choice had not before been articulated for me as an important right worth fighting for. I narrated all this to the young man in the village in Bihar and, later, our discussion that afternoon broadened and the whole group discussed the difference between rape and homosexuality. I did not talk on that occasion about Forster, but he had been an important link in the story I was telling that day. Forster's brief, unpublished piece had been an odd revelation to me: at one level, it offered me a new, empathic portrayal of gay sexuality, and even, more generally, of sexual desire; but at another level, it stirred in my mind, which might have been unguarded against prejudice, the memory of what I had read in the newspapers so long ago about the boy and the hoodlum in the town not far from my own.

When I look back at it now—my reading the news item in the library basement about English as the language of love in Delhi, or my search for writers who were broaching the subject of sex with Indians, or just the desire deep inside me of wanting to be in love—I am struck by a different thought. My desire to be welcomed into love by white women, the idealized sexuality of glossy magazines mixing somewhere with my tormented silence, did not exist alone. Its obverse was the limited—and limiting—view that Forster took of the Other. After Kanaya had come back to beg forgiveness for having said too much, Forster shunned him with the thought: "What relation beyond carnality could one establish with such people? He hadn't even the initiative to cut my throat?"

2

Hanif Kureishi swam into my universe like a new planet. Here was an entirely other world, I thought. Kureishi was the right antidote to Forster. And to me. The first work of Kureishi's that I encountered was *My Beautiful Laundrette.* I watched the film in the university auditorium only months after I had begun dutifully sitting in front of the television whenever *The Jewel in the Crown* was being screened. The pathetic relics of the Raj, to which I had attached myself, were quickly washed away during the screening. There was India in Kureishi's film too, but this India was in the living rooms and laundrettes of England.

The people from the older generation were Indians I recognized: the hero's father was a down-the-hill socialist, alcoholic, and now dependent on the dole ("Oh dear," he says mournfully, mockingly, at one point in the film, "the working class are such a disappointment to me"). The youth in the film didn't say "sahib" every time they opened their mouths: they spoke in British accents and had skinheads for friends. Omar, the protagonist, was in love with a skinhead named Johnny. The gay theme was an important and very open part of the film. But it was also very much taken for granted; it wasn't a part of a big announcement or a program. And the film bound this story with other stories about large Indian and Pakistani families, and immigration, and the corroding power of Thatcherism. (When asked why he evicts people from his property, proving those people right who say that "Pakis just come here to hustle other people's lives and jobs and houses," Nasser, the entrepreneur, gives a response that would warm the cockles of a Thatcherite heart, "But we're professional businessmen. Not professional Pakistanis. There's no race question in the new enterprise culture.")

Some in the Indian and Pakistani community were shocked by the representation of gay sexuality and adultery in *Laundrette*. To them, the film was a betrayal by a renegade Muslim. In New York City, the film was picketed by the Pakistan Action Committee. The *New York Times*, reporting on a later visit by Kureishi to America, quoted the writer as saying: "People think you're supposed to show them exclusively as strong, truthful and beautiful. . . . It's just exactly what Philip Roth went through." Kureishi then added, "Looking back on it, I can see in it the seeds of the Rushdie situation." The writer's own aunt, living in England, castigated him in a letter: "I tried to phone you, but I believe you were in the U.S.A. boring the pants off the Americans with your pornography. . . . We didn't know you were a 'poofter.'. . . Why oh why do you have to promote the widely held view of the British that all evil stems from Pakistani immigrants? Thank goodness for top quality films like *Gandhi*." (The aunt was rewarded for her troubles when, in *Sammie and Rosie Get Laid*, Kureishi gave her name to the Asian lesbian.) I came across more of Kureishi's writing in *Granta* magazine. After *Laundrette* came out, Kureishi published a novella in *Granta* with the not-so-easy-to-forget title *With Your Tongue Down My Throat*. Earlier, he had published in the same magazine travelogues like "Erotic Politicians and Mullahs" about a visit to Pakistan, and another one called "Bradford," about the discovery of the changes that have turned the city into what one later film was to call "Bradistan." I told myself that I was reading each word that Kureishi published—I later found out that this was not quite true—and talked to my friends about him. The first woman I kissed in America looked at Kureishi's photograph in a magazine and said, "What a face, what a face." I might be adding this to my memory of the moment, but I do seem to remember that I felt very close to my friend when she spoke those words.

When *Sammy and Rosie Get Laid* was released, it had the salient virtue of having as one of its stars a well-known actor from Bollywood films, Shashi Kapoor. He was playing the role of a Pakistani politician—he spoke all his lines in English—and reluctantly received lessons in London in deviant sexuality. I lapped it all up. The lesbian who had been named after Kureishi's aunt, and played by Meera Syal, dismisses heterosexual sex with the line: "You know, that stuff when the woman spends the whole time trying to come, but can't. And the man spends the whole time trying to stop himself from coming, but can't."

Rafi Rahman, Kapoor's character, has returned to a London where he had been a student. His youth lay in the memories of a city that had now changed beyond recognition. The city had changed, but so had its people. Now, for example, there were Bangladeshis in London who remembered what Rafi's army had done to their families. History came back to haunt Rafi. Kureishi had staged a dramatic confrontation in a restaurant between Rafi and his daughter-in-law, Rosie. Rosie asked Rafi, "What does it feel like to kill, to torture, to maim, and what did you do in the evenings?" In reply, Rafi rails at Rosie: "You are only concerned with homosexuals and women! A luxury that rich oppressors can afford! We were concerned with poverty, imperialism, feudalism! Real issues that burn people!" Rafi's paltry defense, a familiar left-nationalist argument, sounded so hollow. And yet, this is what, I thought, I too might have said earlier.

The most affecting exchange, however, took place between Rafi and Alice, the woman whom he had loved when he was a student in London. Rafi, it seemed, had found his white woman. She had loved him back. He had made promises of return, but never did. Alice, played with a kind of luminous fragility by Claire Bloom, takes Rafi to her cellar and shows the clothes she had packed, the books, the shoes, the bottles of perfume. She shows him the diaries from 1954, 1955, 1956, inscribed with letters to "My Darling Rafi." But Rafi has no response for Alice when she says to him bitterly, brilliantly uniting politics and passion: "I waited for you, for years! Every day I thought of you! Until I began to heal up. What I wanted was a true marriage. But you wanted power. Now you must be content with having introduced flogging for minor offences, nuclear capability and partridge-shooting into your country."

In 1990, Kureishi published his debut novel, *The Buddha of Suburbia.* "My name is Karim Amir, and I am an Englishman born and bred, almost." That was the book's opening line; I loved the stumble at the end, which I read more as a feint, our own declaration of "not now, not yet." The book presented an England strung high on what one character in *Buddha* called "race, class, fucking, and farce." Kureishi was less Forster, and more Ackerley. J. R. Ackerley's *Hindoo Holiday*, which was a memoir written of his employment at an estate that his friend Forster had recommended to him, offered a hilarious portrait of colonial India. In Ackerley's writing, a kiss rarely carried the burden of gross cultural generalization. Once, Ackerley was kissed on the cheek by his young friend Narayan. Ackerley returned the kiss, but Narayan drew back immediately, saying "Not the mouth! You eat meat! You eat meat!" Ackerley had written, "Yes, and I will eat you in a minute." Then followed the writer's observation that this time when he kissed, Narayan did not draw away. There was kissing in Kureishi too, and it had a light, subversive quality to it. When Karim joins the theater he meets another actor, Terry, an active Trotskyite, who asks him to join the party. Karim narrates the exchange: "He said I should join to prove that my commitment to the ending of injustice wasn't all hot air. I said I would sign up with pleasure on one condition. He had to kiss me. This, I said, would prove his commitment to overcoming his inbred bourgeois morality. He said that maybe I wasn't ready to join the Party just yet." Forster would not—could not—have accused Karim Amir of lacking the initiative to cut—or kiss—his throat.

When I read Kureishi, a whole generation of earlier writers who had written about race suddenly seemed dated—and old. In the presence of Kureishi's characters like Karim, the older writers could finally be seen for what they were in the England to which they had traveled from their old countries: aliens. In this new world, the white Englishmen that Karim met were, funnily enough, sometimes more Indian than he was. And those who weren't were right-wing reactionaries who wanted

Karim to keep away from their daughters. One of them told Karim: "We're with Enoch. If you put one of your black 'ands near my daughter I'll smash it with a 'ammer! With a 'ammer!" (Then, he let loose his Great Dane on Karim. The dog, less racially prejudiced, put its paws on Karim's back and planted dog jissom on his jacket.)

Kureishi's candor appeared novel to me because it was both contemporary and sexual. I read later that while he was studying philosophy at the University of London, Kureishi had supported himself by writing pornography under the name Antonia French. That piece of information led me back to India and made me speculate on the place of the pornographic imagination in Indian fiction in English. Steamy, soft-porn writing has flourished in the books by very minor writers, Shobha De being one example, but no major writer, over a long span of time, has applied his or her talent to the elaboration of an erotic aesthetic. The only writer who comes close is Upamanyu Chatterjee, who had emerged as a voice in *desi* writing around the same time that Kureishi was gathering fans in the West. Chatterjee is a member of the Indian civil service and, in my opinion, it is the juxtaposition of sex and bureaucracy in his writing (especially in his debut novel, *English, August* and his latest, less impressive *The Mammaries of the Welfare State*) that gives his prose its particular touch of perversity. In Chatterjee's writing, there is no trace of the reticence that many think is characteristic of Indian English writing about sex. It is not only that the dull acts of reading files and attending meetings are transformed by the fantasies of the eternally bored and stoned Agastya Sen, who serves in the above two novels as Chatterjee's doppelgänger. Rather, Chatterjee's strength is that in his novels the more ordinary, everyday acts of Indians get imbued with sexuality. As a result, the whole world appears in a wonderfully sordid light.

Agastya Sen, and his colleagues with their families, go on a picnic to a forest area where there is a Shiv temple. The temple that the group is visiting had been built in the second half of the tenth century. The temple's walls are covered with intricate erotic sculptures. As can be expected, the sculptures invite bawdy jokes. But it is the more banal, perhaps repressed, practices of the people in front of Agastya, rather than those given form in the tenth century, that catch Chatterjee's eye, and as a consequence he produces writing that is more shocking and also revealing. Agastya is asked by someone, "Have you ever seen how women behave in front of a shivaling?" The narrative goes on: "There was a tube-light in the innermost sanctum directly above the black stone phallus of Shiv. There the wives came into their own. They took turns to gently smear the shivaling with sandalwood paste, sprinkle water and flowers over it, prostrate and pray before it, suffocate it with incense, kiss their fingers after touching it."

There was a lesson here also about language. I had been carrying with me the knowledge imparted by the literary critic traveling in the Delhi bus, the knowledge that Indians switched to English whenever they wanted to express "a noble thought or a higher emotion." But in Chatterjee's writing, English was being made Indian precisely by expressing a less than noble thought and by giving voice to what would be called a lower emotion. An early chapter in *English, August* offered the lines: "District administration in India is largely a British creation, like the railways and the English language, another complex and unwieldy bequest of the Raj. But Indianization (of a method of administration, or of a language) is integral to the Indian story."

An oft-quoted line from the novel, in fact from the opening page itself, is: " 'Amazing mix, the English we speak. Hazaar fucked. Urdu and American,' Agastya laughed, 'a thousand fucked, really fucked. I'm sure nowhere else could languages be mixed *and* spoken with such ease.' " But it isn't so much the mix of Urdu and American, I'd argue, that represents the abstract and somewhat elusive quality of Indianness. Instead, it is the quality of the burlesque: the staidness of colonial English tickled, harassed, abused, and caressed by proper as well as improper Indians: this is the world where memories, with a shift in the accent, get easily transmuted into mammaries. If anything separates me from that moment years ago in the library basement, where I sat contemplating a news item about the use of English in India, it is the realization that Indians, with all the ambiguity that accompanies the following term, get fucked in English.

3

"Your life is so pristine, mine's like the Hanif Kureishi scene," is a line from a song by the British Asian band Cornershop.

When I reminded Kureishi of this line in my interview with him, Kureishi laughed and said, "Yeah, I remember that. What were they talking about?" I said, "I think it has to do with sexuality, the idea that your life was rife with excitement." "It was!" Kureishi said. "At that time, it was. Until I had kids." He laughed again, and then looked at me. "You'll find that after you have kids, it just changes."

I asked Kureishi how he might be different from a writer like Naipaul, and he began by talking of the similarities between his father and Naipaul's father. Both men had an interest in education and in writing. Kureishi said, "They were fastidious men who wanted to be journalists, but they were bitter men, failed men." Then he outlined the differences between himself and Naipaul. The two of us, he said, are "completely different." He didn't have Naipaul's interest in India, for example. Kureishi said of Naipaul, "He has a basically conservative sensibility, and I don't only mean politically. . . . Also, I like women. I like women and I've always been interested in sex and relationships between men and women." Naipaul's books fail, Kureishi said, because Naipaul "can't write about relationships between men and women, and he can't write about marriage, which seems to be the central institution of the West. Most of the great novels of the West are about sexual desire—*Anna Karenina, Madame Bovary*—they are all books about marriage and adultery."

In 1998, Kureishi published *Intimacy*. It was a novella about a single night, when the protagonist, Jay, has decided to leave his unsuspecting wife and two kids for someone else. Kureishi's prose in the book was lucid and elegant. Jay was a mixture of doubt and desire. As a result, the clarity of the writing produced a strange effect, a tense sense of disquiet. In the novel, Jay is a screenwriter. And on that night, he wanted to record what he was feeling as he went through his separation, because he desired "an absolute honesty that doesn't merely involve saying how awful one is." In other words, he wanted to achieve an intimacy with himself at the very moment he had become certain that he had lost every shred of it with his wife. Perhaps the tension that the reader experienced while reading the novella was that it mirrored the disturbing closeness that lies between the intimacy of the act of love and, on the other hand, the intimacy of the act of infidelity.

I asked Kureishi about *Intimacy* and he described the book as an attempt to write a book "about how painful it is when a marriage falls apart. . . . I wrote a story about what happens on the night you leave. The violence of it. The viciousness, the hatred, the fury, the strength of feeling that you have when you fall out of love with somebody." The book had very close auto-biographical parallels to Kureishi's own life, and it was widely attacked for it. In the interview, Kureishi did not sound guilty, though one can imagine his critics wanted him to be precisely that, at least to start with.

Kureishi's own attitude has been to regard desire as libera-tion. When he was a kid, he read D. H. Lawrence, Henry Miller, Erica Jong, Philip Roth, the Beats, and others. Kureishi said to me, "You need other people to liberate you." But liberation from what? What interests me, finally, about Kureishi's elabo-ration of the idea of sexuality and desire is that it comes into play in his work not as a nostalgic, return-to-sixties rebellion against bourgeois norms but as a way of coming to grips with the con-temporary landscape that is mined with politics. In a 1988 arti-cle that I have saved from an era when I copied and kept everything about Kureishi, the writer told another interviewer: "I like to write about sex as a focus of social, psychological, emo-tional, political energy—it's so central to people's lives, who you fuck, how much you love them, the dance that goes around it, all the seduction, betrayal, loyalty, failure, loneliness."

The following year, Khomeini's *fatwah* against Rushdie had a decisive impact on Kureishi. He was outraged by the threats to a writer's freedom. Many others were too, but, for Kureishi, sex now became a way of opposing fundamentalism. In *The Black Album* and later, in the short-story "My Son, the Fanatic," which was more recently made into a film, the absolutism of faith and its austerity is arrayed in battle against the human heart and its waywardness. Love, sex, alcohol, rock music, literature, fashion, and even food are defenses against the crushing cer-tainties of strict religious doctrines. Not too long ago, I read a reviewer's comment on a film about Asians in England, *East Is East*, and I was struck by how much both the script and the review owed to Kureishi's pioneering work: "Sex in *East Is East* means a genital urge; but it also means the desire to eat pork sausage, or the aspiration to design hats, or the need to be admitted without hassle to the local disco, as if you were as good as white. For Dad, it's a drive toward rectitude, as much as power; for Mom, it's a longing for recognition and company, including that of her family."

All this is a part of a liberal belief in openness and freedom. It is also a part of a strong belief in plurality. In many ways, the brilliance of the film *My Son the Fanatic* lies not simply in the moment in which the fundamentalist son, after being hit by the father, asks him, "You call me fanatic, dirty man, but who is the fanatic now?" Rather, beyond even this gesture of irony and reversal, is the father's desperate, loving statement to the son, as he watches the boy march away with his militant friends, "There are many ways of being a good man." This belief is combined in Kureishi with a commitment to the benefits of education. And the possibility that education offers an individual choices and the chance to grow. One can surmise that a faith in those liberal ideals, and in the promise of art to give shape to experience and lead to understanding, is the bedrock on which Kureishi bases his own practice as a writer. Yet, as always, things are more complicated than that. Kureishi told me during our interview that the book burnings and the *fatwah* against Rushdie were only part of the reason why he wrote *The Black Album*. His own life, at that time, "was falling apart." Kureishi said that he was "very involved in drugs and all kinds of dissident sexuality," and scared that he would, if he continued in the same way, stop writing altogether. His father had died recently, and he was getting addicted to cocaine. He said, "And that's when I started getting interested in fundamentalist religion. I could see that a puritanical religion could be very helpful." In other words, we begin to see that it is not liberalism pitched against fundamentalism, or even the other way around, but each of them acting as a check on the complete autonomy of the other. That essentially is the truth of the Hanif Kureishi scene, where life is not so much confusing as unstable and open-ended. It is also remarkable that in his fiction, Islam and the West have not clashed as opposing civilizations where one is modern and the other primitive, but, instead, they emerge as two contrary modernities. In the interview, Kureishi explained this point to me: "Islamic fundamentalism was a completely new phenomenon in the eighties. Of course, the fundamentalists would say, 'We're just following tradition,' but actually it was the invention of a brand new tradition. There hadn't been such a thing before."

The talk of paradise and eternity is as much a part of the contemporary moment as fusion and Ecstasy. An aggressive, unequal form of globalization has produced as its equally dangerous underside a culture of fundamentalism. This is not a matter of the past and the future; instead, it has everything to do with our inseparable present. Kureishi's lucid lesson is that our desires, even when they are opposed to our more austere orders, are inextricably bound in conflict. The writer does not stand apart from this confusion. When we grasp this, we attain clarity.

In this way, we also learn that saying "I love you" is not so much a matter of choosing between English and Hindi, as I had believed when I first left India. Nor, for that matter, is it a case of choosing between promiscuity and commitment. Rather, we learn how our choices are threatened by, and even drawn toward, their opposites — and, forever famished, they crave language and, inevitably, also silence.

My Hanif Kureishi Life

PART III

1

During a recent winter, only a few days before Christmas, I sat in a theater in New York City watching a play called *The Indian Wants the Bronx*. This award-winning work written by Israel Horowitz was first performed in 1968. In the play, an Indian man named Gupta, who is a newcomer to the United States, waits at a Manhattan bus stop hoping to find his way back to his son living in the Bronx. While watching the play, I could not but ask how much has changed in this country.

Gupta has his son's name and address written on a card. He is accosted by two delinquent youth who cannot decide whether Gupta is a Turk or an Indian. At one point in the play, one of the boys snatches the card with the son's name from Gupta and calls the telephone operator. He finds out the son's number easily enough—there is only one Gupta in the whole of the Bronx. Today, the telephone book will yield an unimaginably higher number. It is estimated that there are now nearly 1.7 million Indian Americans. An Indian father might not be able to find his son in the United States, but he will find many others who have the same name.

My earliest memory, a dim, inexact picture in my mind, is that of an uncle, whom I called Mausaji, leaving for New York City. We are at the train station in Patna. There is an old man sitting with a flower garland around his neck. My uncle sits on the opposite side. I only remember the old man with the garland. He was a leader. He did not enter my life again till I was eleven. On the day after my birthday, within miles of my home, he led a huge protest that finally brought down the government of Indira Gandhi. The old man had weak kidneys and died a few years later. My mother is there inside the train too. And her mother, who is crying. Mausaji was one of those who came to the older United States, the one that had only one Gupta in each borough of New York. I was a little older than two at that time; I did not see Mausaji for another twenty-one years.

When my uncle left our town in Bihar—this was in 1965— the war between India and Pakistan was being fought. There was some anxiety in the family about my uncle's safe passage. But he arrived safely and enrolled in graduate school in Florida, where he studied physics. A year or so later, his wife, Saraswati, whom I called Saras Aunty, followed with their little daughter. Saras Aunty is my mother's younger sister. I used to call Saras Aunty "Mausiji" before she left India; when she started living in the United States, I decided to switch to the English word *Aunty*. That must have been my earliest act of translation.

When she wrote letters to Saras Aunty, my mother would save some space on the pale blue aerograms where my elder sister and I would write a few words. In all those years of my boyhood, these must have been the only letters that I wrote in English. Did my aunt also know that in these letters a boy was discovering language and using it, for the first time, to say half-understood words like love and loss?

For our efforts, my sister and I were rewarded each year with birthday cards with postmarks from—as the years passed—Buffalo, New York, a place in Delaware, and then, Virginia. I loved the cards from my aunt. Saras Aunty's words never varied over the years. But my appreciation was more basic. I was responding to the quality of the paper from which the cards had been made, their firmness and solid color. As pleasing as these cards were, however, what had a more powerful effect on me were the color photographs that we received from America.

They were a novelty. Another ten or fifteen years would pass before color photography became familiar in India. By the time I was six or seven, I was as much taken by the images of my two cousins—my aunt and uncle had a second child in America—as I was by the sight in these pictures of huge American cars and the clean spaces of the middle-class home. A part of my boyhood is made up of these memories, as if I were experiencing my own life as an elsewhere, as a place called America.

For the *desi* immigrants of that generation, the 1960s meant—more than the Beatles and Vietnam and Martin Luther King—the reality of greater isolation and pain that is quite unimaginable in the altered landscape of America today. Part of the reason for this lay in numbers. It was really the Immigration Act of 1965 that opened the gates to professional Indians, doctors, engineers, and academics. Earlier, the Barred Zone Act of 1917 and the Asian Exclusion Act of 1924 did not permit immigration of Asians; in 1946, after the passing of Public Law 1983, one hundred Indians were allowed into the United States each year. The laws changed in 1965 to permit what was called "occupational immigration," because the

American economy was in dire need of an educated and skilled labor force. According to INS figures, more than 27,000 Indians immigrated to America in the 1960s and another 164,000 in the 1970s, up from under 2,000 in each of the previous two decades. By 1980, there were almost 400,000. Since then, that number has more than tripled. But part of the reality for people like Mausaji and Saras Aunty also lay in other details. As Mira Kamdar has written: "India was far, far away. Airline tickets were expensive. There was no direct dial international calling, no fax machines-cum-answering machines attached to people's phones, no e-mail. We were a little island of India in a vast land of *Leave It to Beaver.*"

Late in the 1960s, like many other Indian scientists, Mausaji was recruited in the American effort to put a man on the moon. In my home in Patna, and often at the homes of my relatives, there would often be talk of my uncle's brilliance. Till late in high school, when asked what I wanted to do in life, I would unhesitatingly say "scientist." But what was the interior life like for my Mausaji and Saras Aunty? This question often bothers me — more since my arrival here in the United States — when there are festivals or when I get news of a death in the family. Consider Diwali, the festival of lights. It is celebrated on a night during late fall in India, sometime between Halloween and Thanksgiving on the American calendar. For most of the years that I have been away from India, the only sign of Diwali has been a yellow sheet of paper in my mailbox from the *desi* grocery store announcing holiday discounts.

On a recent night, I went to one of the Indian restaurants, in the small town where I live in Pennsylvania, to pick up some food that I had ordered. When I got there, I looked through the glass walls of the restaurant and saw that there was a party going on inside. The woman standing at the door was a student I recognized. She was wearing a sari. She said, "Happy Diwali." I was invited to join the celebrations. The people inside were all students at the university where I teach. Even the waiter offered me sweets. But I did not stay. I took the food and left. In the car, I was filled with a creeping sadness. The sight of the student in the sari—she had joked that this was the only occasion she had for dressing in this way—made me think that I often miss home. It's just that I am not even conscious of this fact anymore.

I try to go back to India as often as I can, but given the way in which the schedules at school are arranged, the fact remains that I have not celebrated Diwali for the last fifteen years. And yet, what is also undeniable is that, if I wanted, I could join Diwali celebrations in small towns and big cities in this country. There are fair-sized Indian communities in much of the United States. This would have been very difficult for those others who migrated to the United States in the first few decades after Indian independence.

When I was growing up, it is possible that we wondered whether Mausaji and his family celebrated Diwali. I have another memory. When several years had passed since Mausaji's departure, I came to know that there had been a lot of financial anxieties for Mausaji and Aunty during their first years in this country. Mausaji regularly sent money home to his widowed mother. He paid for the education of his younger brother and his sisters. Then he took responsibility for paying for his sisters' marriages and their dowries. When my cousins had grown up and gone to school, Saras Aunty had begun working in a library. By then, I think, the demands from home had lessened. It was around this time that I first spoke on the phone to my aunt, in 1986. I had been accepted for admission at an American university and wrote to my aunt with the news. My aunt called at my parents' home. I picked up the phone. No one else was home. I felt very close to my aunt when she said "hello." But I found that I had nothing to say. She told me to call her when I arrived in the United States.

But I did not call her. This had to do with the fact that I did not exactly know how to make a collect call. In addition, each day would come and pass and there were so many new things to learn and to do that I did not feel the need to call anyone. I had wanted to come to America, and I was happy to be here, but I missed my home in Patna very badly. Then, one evening, after I had drunk a couple of beers, I came out of the bar and went straight to the public phone at the street corner. I attempted to make a collect call. The operator was having difficulty understanding me — I might have been slurring — but I got through and spoke to my aunt. My aunt said that she would come and visit me with Mausaji soon. They were several hours away but they would drive. Where would they stay, was my first thought. The apartment in which I lived was not suitable even to receive anyone for fifteen minutes. It smelled of cat piss and gas. My roommates — an international cast of poor fellow international students — assured me that my uncle and aunt would find a place in a hotel.

When Mausaji and Saras Aunty showed up at my door, I was delighted. Both of them looked very elegant, and also young. My uncle looked like, well, what we'd call in India, a foreigner. They had brought a new blanket for me and delicious *rasgullas*. They also took me to Sears and bought a coat for me that I would end up using through graduate school. Finally, we went out for dinner.

My uncle now worked as a senior scientist in the government. Someone had said Mausaji had a post in the Pentagon. I began to think that there perhaps lay one clue to why they had never gone back for a visit. Mausaji would not have wanted his employers to think that he remained an alien. He had tried to tell them that he had no other home. Perhaps he had even come to believe it himself. Small beginnings in a village in Bihar amid acute poverty had now led to a secure life still hedged by a strange insecurity. I didn't ask Mausaji and Saras Aunty that evening, or any time later, why during the past decades they had never returned to India. I remember very well that Mausaji and I got into a small argument over politics and I had shown impatience when he spoke about India. My aunt touched my elbow. When Mausaji went to the restroom, my aunt said, "He feels very lonely."

We met a few more times. I took a Greyhound to their home the first year during Thanksgiving. I recall with shame that I pronounced the turkey "tasteless," thinking that I would please them by saying that Indian cooking was better than American concoctions. My aunt had made *samosas* for me. She took me to the Indian grocery store so that I could pick out Bollywood films. I learned that both she and Mausaji watched only Hindi movies of the 1950s and 1960s. One night my parents called us while I was there. They had brought Mausaji's old mother from her village. She was on the phone. She had not heard her son's voice for more than two decades.

Mausaji was choked with emotions that I could not presume to name. He said "Ma" once, and then again very loudly. Then he heaved away from the phone and began to weep on his daughter's shoulder.

A year or so later, I saw Mausaji and Saras Aunty again. I was visiting them because my parents wanted me to look up an Indian man in Washington, D.C. They had decided that he would be a good match for my sister in India. The young man was from our caste. He was a software engineer. Mausaji and Saras Aunty had had an arranged marriage like everyone else around them at that time. Such a marriage taking place in the United States might have seemed odd to them. Their own daughter had gotten married recently. I had not known about it, but I met her husband, who was a pleasant American man she'd met at college in Charlottesville.

I haven't seen my uncle and aunt again. They were very helpful at our last meeting. Following my father's instructions from India, they presented a suit and some cash to the young man that my parents had chosen for my younger sister. This was a way of effecting an engagement. I remember Saras Aunty asking me whether my sister had been asked for her views on the matter; I said yes, I had called her at her college in Delhi, and she had told me that I should do what our parents had asked me to do. I added that my elder sister's marriage hadn't been brokered by relatives. She had married of her own will. I had been uncomfortable when my parents pushed me into this role, but now, when confronted by Saras Aunty's questions, I felt that I was suddenly being turned into a representative of another civilization, or more accurately, a degraded culture.

We did not have any further conversation. This was about eight or nine years ago. I called a couple of times but felt that Saras Aunty was finding it difficult to talk to me. I concluded that she felt that there were problems with India and with Indians—or at least, with Indian relatives—that were insurmountable or took her to a past that she'd rather avoid. I didn't call again, and I too was left alone. The silence that has now surrounded my relatives, these relatives who played such a large part in my imagination when I was growing up, is a mystery I cannot solve.

Now and then, as on Diwali, I begin thinking of Mausaji and Aunty. Sometimes I am suddenly back in their past, as if

New York

I were inhabiting a photograph. During my first visit, Saras Aunty said to me that when she shut her eyes, she could always see India. Later on, unkindly, I thought of saying to her, "You need to open your eyes." I wanted to tell her that the India she had known was no longer there. It had changed. Perhaps I was afraid that Saras Aunty would see me as a person who was not modern. She would not perceive the changes either in the home she had left or those who came from '.iere. There is some truth in this. But the issue also lies outside the circle of my own fears.

The experience of my uncle and aunt hides, beneath its middle-class solidity, a terrible sorrow. First, there had been all the years of hard struggle to keep families running both in India and America. Saras Aunty's mother — my grandmother, whom I called Naniji — died a few years after her daughter's departure from India. I remember that a telegram had been sent. With each passing year, the nephews and nieces married and had children. Every marriage season, my mother would be asked by someone or other to supply the current address so that cards could be sent to America. Soon after having spoken to her son on the phone, Mausaji's mother passed away. Someone must have written a letter informing them that she had died calling out her son's name.

When I spoke to him last, Mausaji said that he would visit India after he retired from his job. In these thirty-odd years of absence, the family that Saras Aunty had left is no longer there. Each one of her brothers is now dead. A nephew and a niece died too, within a year of each other, both choking to a painful death from asthma, alone in their rooms. Two large, once closely knit families have been altered beyond recognition and scattered mostly in the small towns and villages of Bihar. For my uncle and aunt there has been nothing through the years but a passage of wedding cards and letters bearing good or bad news. Now, as I think of the telegrams that came, and sometimes only black-lined letters, I ask myself whom did Mausaji and Saras Aunty mourn those deaths with? I can understand why, after the first few years and their losses, Mausaji and Saras Aunty decided that they could not go back. Everything they left behind had been precious. They liked to believe it was still all intact. It was *they* who had not changed. They had lost so much that they wanted to hold on to what was left of the past.

Mausaji was the first person I knew who came to America. It was of him that I thought first when I heard the news on the radio, one April evening, that Jhumpa Lahiri had won the Pulitzer Prize for her volume of short stories, *The Interpreter of Maladies.*

I had read Lahiri's book earlier that year. Her stories of Bengali immigrants in the United States were precise, evocative, and also convincing. Indian immigrants have not seen themselves portrayed in the mainstream U.S. media except as spokespersons for stereotypes with awkward sentences and funny accents. In several of Lahiri's stories, such readers were likely to find themselves, and their voices, registering a record of their transplanted lives. As I listened to the radio—the announcement providing the bare details of Lahiri's past—a few lines from the last page of *The Interpreter of Maladies* came back to me. The story that I remembered was called "The Third and Final Continent." Lahiri had given those lines to an Indian man, her father, who had arrived in Boston on the day that two Americans landed on the moon. Recalling that day, the man in the story says: "While the astronauts, heroes forever, spent mere hours on the moon, I have remained in this new world for nearly thirty years. I know that my achievement is quite ordinary. I am not the only man to seek his fortune far away from home, and certainly I am not the first. Still there are times I am bewildered by each mile I have traveled, each meal I have eaten, each person I have known, each room in which I have slept. As ordinary as it all appears, there are times when it is beyond my imagination."

2

Only a few months before Lahiri's award, I was driving out of New York City and, once again, listening to the radio. It was New Year's eve, the last night of the departing millennium, and I was making my exit from the city. My wife, Mona, had turned the keys over to her landlord. We were headed into a new time and a new place.

In our household, I am not allowed to say anything bad about the city. If I do, Mona reminds me gently that it is the city in which we met. Mona came to New York City from Karachi via Cambridge; I came there from Patna via New Delhi. When I think of what happened between Mona and me, I am reminded of something else. The writer Suketu Mehta, who has his roots in India and now lives in the same neighborhood in Brooklyn where Mona lived, is a friend of mine. In an article called "The Fatal Love," Suketu wrote about the city: "The first time I met the enemy people, Pakistanis, was when I went to New York. We shopped together, we ate together, we dated each other and had each others' babies."

That night, however, as we drove away from New York City, a different kind of drama between India and Pakistan was being played out. The news on the radio repeatedly returned to Kandahar airport in Afghanistan, where the passengers on the hijacked Indian Airlines flight had been released. It was only when I heard the happy news that it struck me that the new year had already arrived in India. Flight IC 814 had taken off from Kathmandu with 155 passengers and was headed for Delhi when it was hijacked. The hijackers had initially demanded the release of thirty-six prisoners who were incarcerated in Indian jails; thirty-three of them were Pakistanis. The Indian government had agreed to free three, including the cleric Maulana Masood Azhar, who was in custody at the Kot Bhalwal prison at Jammu. After his release, Azhar would return to Pakistan and establish the jihadi outfit Jaish-e-Mohammad, which, after the September 11 attacks, would have its assets frozen by the U.S. government because of its links with the Al-Qaeda network.

However, on December 31, 1999, all that Americans were worried about was the Y2K bug. In the aftermath of the attacks on the World Trade Center and the Pentagon, I can look back at that moment and tell myself that Indians have struggled with terror and violence for a long time. There might even be a little bit of pride in that feeling, as if to say we were on the moon first. But this is a flawed pride. It overlooks the fact that what American power has meant for the world, and how America has, rightly or wrongly, been hated for it, is exactly what India and its hegemony has meant among the smaller countries of South Asia. Thus, it is not simply that America now, like India, has tasted terror; it is also that we Indians, like Americans, have long been disliked for being bullies. An Indian can be reminded of this even in New York City. And yet, it also needs to be said that we cannot reduce the individual lives of immigrants to their national identities alone.

New York

On that New Year's Day, I stopped at a gas station on the highway and bought newspapers. There were pictures of confetti and fireworks. The news of the end of the more than week-long hijacking drama found space on the front page of the *New York Times*. I bought other newspapers too, trying to get as much news as I could about the hijacking. There were pictures of the bearded Taliban soldiers around the Indian Airlines plane in Kandahar. One couldn't see the hijackers' faces. The terrorists wore masks as they were escorted to the waiting vehicles that would take them to Pakistan. As I skimmed over other photographs in the *Washington Post*, I stumbled across the photograph of an Indian in another section. The face that had caught my eye was of a woman who was one among a hundred readers of the *Post* who had written a hundred words to describe their identity.

This is what face number 33 had to say about herself: "My name is Sushma Sodhi, of Sterling. I am from India. We came to America with a dream to give our boys the best life. We sacrificed our settled life in our home country for our boys. One son, 19, met a much older woman who has two children from two different fathers. We asked him to complete his education before getting involved. He said, 'Go to hell. Stop calling me.' There is no bigger sorrow than to hear these words from your loved ones."

The words saddened me. My wife and I were sitting in the car, drinking coffee, before we got back on the highway again. I read the words once more, and did not know how to respond. Perhaps I was also suspicious—even without knowing enough myself—that there was some prejudice in Sodhi's words about her son's partner. Or I was annoyed that this was hardly the way to welcome a new year. But I began asking myself whether Sodhi, like Saras Aunty, had decided not to change. I could not easily distance myself from Sodhi's sense of who she was. She had formed an idea of herself around what she needed to do for her children, and also built into this was her sense of what the children owed their parents, and this was all she had in the new country. Perhaps she also told herself that this is what made her Indian.

Several months later, when Lahiri's award was announced, and I was commenting on it for an Indian magazine, I mentioned finding Sodhi's words in the *Post*. It occurred to me that the immigrant reader would find in Lahiri a "seasoned translator." A seasoned translator is described by Pico Iyer as a global soul — Kazuo Ishiguro and Salman Rushdie are the exemplars — who commutes between cultures and writes from a space of "in-betweenness." As hybrid souls, these writers give voice to hyphenated identities. Lahiri, and others like Iyer himself, citizens of the West who have easy access to the East, are able to make sense of either part of the cultural equation in terms of the Other. Seasoned translators are seasoned travelers between cultures. A person like that might present a great contrast to a recent immigrant of a working-class background. The Indian immigrants of the 1960s and 1970s had a median household income that was nearly 50 percent higher than that of the Indians who came in later years. At her best, Lahiri would strike an immigrant as one he or she can never be: one who is able to speak in her own language as well as the language of the immigration officer. For such an immigrant, Lahiri is a symbol of upward mobility: one who speaks Bengali and writes flawlessly in English. And yet, as both Lahiri and Iyer would recognize, this supposedly different immigrant from the working class is also a translator of sorts, fashioning a world out of bits and pieces of different languages.

Lahiri herself recognizes her role as that of performing "simultaneous translations in both directions, of characters who literally dwell in two separate worlds." More than a linguistic act,

New York

translation becomes a cultural act. For Lahiri, it means "the continuous struggle, on my parents' behalf, to preserve what it means to them to be first and forever Indians, to keep afloat certain familial and communal traditions in a foreign and at times indifferent world." Lahiri's parents, originally from Calcutta, speak Bengali at home. I cannot but also think that what Lahiri is doing in her work is giving, to words uttered in one language, both beauty and dignity in another language. At the same time, Lahiri also writes, "My writing, these days, is less a response to my parents' cultural nostalgia, and more an attempt to forge my own amalgamated domain." Any translation is also an act of betrayal, a sharing of intimacy with another tongue. What Lahiri calls her "own amalgamated domain" represents a transgression into a new identity outside the parents' control, and also outside the closeness and isolation of the mother tongue.

Today, as I look at the copy of the *Post* in which I found Sushma Sodhi's words on a New Year's Day long ago, I am reminded of another image I found there. It was the photograph of another person who looked Indian. Face number 86. I turned to the page where her one hundred words appeared. This is what her note said: "My name is Pratiti Kaka. As a child I learned dancing, and my mom thought I'd grow up to be a dancer of renown. I soon joined skating classes. She assumed I'd break Olympic records. When I started swimming, she hoped I'd swim across the English Channel someday. But all her dreams crash-landed when I grew up to be an ordinary, amiable girl with varied interests. After managing an office, I married a wonderful man of my choice and am enjoying life. Just the other day, someone told Mom, 'I want my daughter to be like yours.' " The confidence in the unexceptional, rather, the dream of being part of the ordinary, is also indicative of the process of the immigrant becoming a citizen. You don't stand out, or stick out, anymore. You are like any other American.

I read in Pratiti Kaka's remarks above a declaration of independence. I believe we are beginning to see a change. The second-generation writers of Indian origin in the United States are drawing the maps of their own amalgamated domains. This represents an imaginative departure from what had been accomplished so far in this country by older, first-generation immigrant writers like Bharati Mukherjee and Ved Mehta. The work of the young writers and artists, which we can take as a sign of a certain coming-of-age, has also allowed the Indian community as a whole to grow up. A few years ago, Aasif Mandvi performed his play *Sakina's Restaurant* at the American Place Theatre in New York City. Mandvi, who was born in Bombay, grew up in Yorkshire and Florida. Made up of a set of six monologues, Mandvi's play was built around the question asked by one of his characters, Azgi, who has migrated from India to serve in one of the restaurants on New York's Sixth Street. The young waiter Azgi asks his mother in a letter: "Where did I go, Ma?" In the play, Mandvi skewered not only a racist mind-set unable to distinguish between its ethnic citizens, it also hung out to dry all the dirty linen of patriarchal attitudes in one Indian family and the general hypocrisy surrounding an issue like an arranged marriage. Mandvi later told a journalist writing for *The New Yorker* that he had "expected to be inundated with criticism" from the Indian-American community. Instead, largely because of its support among South Asians, the show's run was extended. It ran for months. The journalist had written: "Mandvi took the play's popularity as evidence of the community's growing confidence in its standing as an integral part of a new American mix."

For me the mark of the second generation's ability to abandon the cultural nostalgia is most visible not in a novel about life in Sacramento, California, or even a bildungsroman written about an Indian kid in Edison, New Jersey. Instead, it is a novel written by a Wall Street banker in the voice of a middle-class fifty-seven-year-old man in Delhi who says: "Misery often makes me want to look away from the present and leads me to nostalgia." The narrator wishes an escape to a rural past: "As I swallowed my heart medicine in the blue dark of the common room, I imagined walking through Beri's sugarcane fields and sitting beneath a mango tree. I wanted to be a child again, with the future a wide, still river in the afternoon." What makes this nostalgia for an unsullied past both poignant and problematic is that it is the desire of a man who cannot escape the memory of the newspapers soaking up the blood beneath his daughter's thighs each night after he had raped her.

Akhil Sharma's *An Obedient Father* has as its narrator Ram Karan, a corrupt official in the Education Department in Delhi. Lucid and perverse, like the solipsistic narrator of Nabokov's *Lolita*, the confessions of Sharma's antihero are sharp, even empathetic, and loathsome. There can be no doubt that Ram Karan is evil, but because he almost always is given a voice, he also remains in some measure human. At one point early in the book, Anita, the daughter that he raped when she was a child, is listening to Ram Karan as he recounts a dream that he had the previous night. He says that he had seen Anita's dead brother, Baby, in his dream. Ram Karan adds, "He didn't recognize me. Baby didn't look at all like me. I was surprised, because I had always expected him to look like me." In Anita's voice we are offered the following response: "There was something polished about the story, which indicated deceit. My hatred increased." The freshness of the imagery in Sharma's novel, its narrative tone as well as its candor, reveals polish but inspires no suspicion of deceit. This is how Sharma describes Anita's presence in Ram Karan's room: "That first night she came into my room and sat down at the edge of her cot. I shut the door. I would have locked it, but it could be bolted only from the outside. I was excited and nervous. When I turned around from the door, Anita was leaning forward with her shoulders curved in, looking like a bird in winter. My eagerness, which had been laced with doubt, turned to self-disgust. I gave Anita my little transistor radio and left the light on through the night." Dark, and certainly difficult to read, *An Obedient Father* is nevertheless a novel that puts an end to the debate about the authenticity of Indian expatriate writers. The question is rendered nearly moot.

Soon after Sharma's book was released, I reviewed it for the *Nation*. I praised it. I found the voice of the writer utterly original, but it was also that I had found the moralism of most Indian reviewers who had dismissed the book quite reprehensible. As a result, I was less critical than I could have been about the book's unevenness. Then an opportunity came for me to meet Sharma. I was asked by an Indian magazine to interview the writer. We met at his office in New York City and then walked to a nearby diner to eat. I found Sharma terribly arrogant, but this only made me think that he was honest. In an interview with the *Financial Observer* several months after I had spoken to him, Sharma said: "I am as good a writer as anyone that I have interacted with, aside from a few people. Most first novels I read are such awful shit." He had said the same thing during the interview with me.

A few days after our meeting, I sent Sharma the transcript of our interview. He soon sent it back to me. He had scratched out the more offensive things he had said about the Indian writers he had not read. I had mentioned in my introductory note that Sharma had eaten an omelette for dinner and drunk water. Sharma had written beside that sentence: "This level of detail makes the author look like he is incapable of picking the meaningful detail." I had also written that after we had eaten, Sharma walked back to his office, where he was going to work till one or two at night. There, Sharma made another insertion, so that the phrase read "After we had eaten, Sharma paid for both our dinners."

Sharma had taken creative writing courses at Princeton with Toni Morrison. This, too, is a fact about most Indian writers in this country: all of them have either been students or teachers of creative writing. But that might be a less meaningful detail in my story. I hurried down to the end of the transcript. Near the end of our interview, Sharma and I had an exchange that showed that the new does not emerge in a vacuum; it relies on a past, and it has a complex relationship to that which we do not see. I looked for those lines and found that Sharma had left them intact. Now, as I read these words again from that interview, I think with tenderness, touched with ambivalence, of Mausaji and Saras Aunty, and the wounds that their silence has always hidden from me.

> AK: . . . But let me have you talk about other Indians. Your parents, for instance. Did they come here a long time ago? Are they traditional?
> AS: Yes, they are traditional. They came a long time ago but they never adapted.

New York

AK: *You also mention a brother on the dedication page of your book. . .*

AS: Yes, I have an older brother who is sick. He drowned when I was a child and he suffered brain damage.

AK: *That must have been an enormous burden to grow up with.*

AS: Hmm. Yes. I think it gave me a sense of guilt and an ability to identify with the victimizer instead of the victim.

1

The same year that Arundhati Roy sold millions of copies of *The God of Small Things*, another Indian, named Sabeer Bhatia, the inventor of Hotmail, made about $400 million from the sale of the e-mail service to Microsoft. More than half of the yearly H1-B visas granted by the U.S. government go to Indian software programmers. It is the software writers from India rather than the fiction writers who are wired to the circuits of global production. Indeed, the needs of a cyber-linked universe has meant that Indians, even without having left their country's borders, can now pretend that they are in the United States.

According to an Associated Press story, "When an American calls a toll-free number in the United States to report a broken appliance or complain about the wrong sweater ordered from a catalogue, the call is often routed through fast fiber-optic cables to a center in India. . . . A polite, friendly voice on the other end is eager to assist—and sounds just like the boy or girl next door, not 8,000 miles away." The business-process outsourcing is a

$200 billion industry. In the past, such work had been farmed out to the American Midwest or English-speaking countries like Ireland. But the lower costs in India, as well as proficiency in English, has meant that Indians take the billing calls from AT&T, frequent-flier miles for SwissAir, and tech support for Compaq. The educated Indians who line up for such jobs—which Chidananda Rajghatta calls "the tech version of burger flipping"—get months of speech training. The training is in American or British accents, depending on the client being represented. The employees also work on using slang and sports terms and, as the AP story puts it, get "a good dose of 'Baywatch' and 'Friends' to bridge the cultural divide between Bombay and Boston."

If the widespread use of English by the middle and upper classes in India has meant that novels by Roy and other prominent writers convey an easy idiomatic familiarity with the language, then it is also true that the pervasive use of English has made India, as Rajghatta puts it, "the frontrunner to be the back office to the world." For a month's labor, the worker at the call center interviewed in the AP story earns just $213—this, incidentally, is the worker's earning on the overnight shift, it being night in India when it is day in the United States. This might be high compared to the average earnings of an Indian, but the pay is low when compared to the profits that the work generates.

Such call centers demonstrate, Arundhati Roy writes in *Power Politics*, "how easily an ancient civilization can be made to abase itself completely." Prakash Gurbaxani, the founder and chief executive of call center in Bangalore, opposes Roy's argument and is quoted in the AP report as saying, "It's easy to preach on a full stomach. . . . If I didn't have to work for a living to support a family, then I can be on my high horse. Most of these kids are just trying to make ends meet." Rajghatta observes that Indian graduates outperform Americans at the call centers because they treat them as "serious careers." He cites a Nasscom survey that "estimates that India could employ more than a million people and earn $17 billion from IT-enabled services by 2008." I cannot share Rajghatta's elation. Would such youth not outperform graduates elsewhere if they were given jobs that were more challenging than trying to sound like someone from California or Illinois? Rajghatta writes that, in Bangalore, "General Electric has opened the Jack Welch Technology Center—its biggest research facility outside Schenectady—employing more than 600 scientists, researchers and programmers, including some 200 PhDs." Are they too being paid only a fraction of what their counterparts get in the United States?

The changes that have been wrought by information technology are not limited to the lives of workers in new jobs in India. The experience of being Indian in America has also altered significantly. In the film *Masala*, made more than a decade ago by an Indian-Canadian filmmaker, we see an old Indian immigrant praying to Lord Krishna: "Help us Bhagwan. We are outsiders here. Make life the way it was before we came to this land of supply-side economics and no-money-down real estate." The joke then was that the old woman happened to be praying to a video image of Lord Krishna. Now, several years later, the irony has been displaced. Indians have done rather well in the world of supply-side economics and no-money-down real estate. Indian Americans rank among the highest-income ethnic groups. One quarter of Indian families earn more than $80,000 a year. And even as late as July 2001, when the information technology boom was already going bust, an article in an Indian-American newspaper still gushed: "In 1998, there were 788 Silicon Valley hi-tech companies led by Indians, according to a Dun and Bradstreet data included in a recent

University of California at Berkeley study. And the numbers are growing—385 of those firms were founded in the period 1995 to 1998."

A year prior to that report, an American journalist, Jeff Goodell, who had grown up in Sunnyvale, California, returned to what had been his family home till 1990. He found a transformed place, "the wreckage of the American dream, circa 1963." Instead of the home of the stable nuclear family, Goodell, who is white, found a renting space for transient, ambitious Asian techies. In his essay "The Venture Capitalist in My Bedroom," Goodell summed up the change in the following words:

> The defining character of Silicon Valley today is not the pasty-faced, plaid-wearing aerospace engineer, but a young geek from Taipei or Bangalore with an H1-B visa and a fondness for American pop culture. These new immigrants are escapees from small villages and moribund economies; they are attracted to the valley by its reputation as a digital meritocracy, where nobody cares what color your skin is as long as you can speak the global language of entrepreneurs.

For Goodell, what unites these new immigrants with the older ones who came through Ellis Island a hundred years ago is that "they believe America is a land of opportunity." This is correct. But the comparison also holds true in another way. The greater truth is that the H1-B workers not only share with the older immigrants a bit of the heaven of the American dream, they also share its disappointments, when the dream turns to dust.

One summer, while I was living in New York City, I walked into the Sara Delano Roosevelt Park on the lower East Side and found sculptures dedicated to America's immigrant history. The artist's name was Janet Goldner. Engraved on one of Goldner's sculptures were the words of a nineteenth-century Italian immigrant: "When I got here I found out three things: first, the streets weren't paved with gold; second, they weren't paved at all; and third, I was expected to pave them." It is undeniable that, as *Fortune* magazine reported in a major story in May 2000, Silicon Valley Indian immigrants have created companies that account for more than $235 billion of market value. However, it has also become increasingly clear that for the more ordinary techie, the reality is that cyberspace "is not simply a medium for free expression and wealth accumulation; it is a labor-intensive workplace." With the economic slowdown, the realities of the workplace, which have always included uncertainty, firings, and exploitation, have only intensified. In September 2001, the *Washington Post* reported that with the decline in the decade-long boom in demand for imported technical labor, a racist backlash is being felt in the workplace. A computer programmer named Singh, living in Silicon Valley, told the reporter about receiving an e-mail from a former colleague: "He told me foreigners should go home. . . . I am a U.S. citizen." This situation is much worse lower down on the food chain. A recent story in the *San Francisco Chronicle* by Raj Jayadev described the woes of the growing number of temp workers in Silicon Valley. Jayadev's report, speaking of immigrants from India and Mexico, focused on a Hewlett Packard "back property" in San Jose two years ago: "There's no better place to work than in Silicon Valley, where vast amounts of wealth are being made; the average wage is more than $75,000. But I quickly learn that the engine

of the new economy is fueled by methods and labor practices more commonly associated with the old industrial era —
assembly plants, conveyer belts, physically demanding work
and low pay."

2

In the pages of the Indian "ethnic press" in the United States,
at the height of the technological boom, there was a lot of discussion of the role of "bodyshops" — contracting firms, mostly
owned by Indians settled in the United States, that hire H-1B
workers from India. To give an example, a report entitled "The
Blood Suckers" began with the words, "Let me relate the
experience of a typical victim — we can't give him a better
name than Mr. Oracle Rao." Oracle Rao in this narrative is a
composite of the varied experiences of Indian H1-B workers.
The story of Oracle Rao, a newly arrived Indian programmer,
depicts both the anticipation and the disappointment that typ-
ify the H-1B experience.

Shortly after arriving at the offices of his contracting firm in
the United States, Rao learns that he is being charged for food,
lodging, and transportation but that he does not yet have a job.
He undergoes interviews for jobs that "could be anywhere from
California to Maine or Texas." Rao may be moved at the whim
of a client. Or he may be subcontracted to another firm, in
which case his earnings will be shared by the two firms that have
now invested in him. He may not get a job at all; in the lingo of
the trade, he could be "benched." During this period, it is
possible that he will not be paid — but at the same time, he will

continue making payments for his expenses to the firm that brought him here.

The boom in Indian writing in English—which arguably has paralleled the rise of the Indian computer industry—has very little to say about the Oracle Raos of our world. But it does touch upon other significant realities of the digital city. In a short story by Vikram Chandra entitled "Artha," we find not one but two rarities of Indian fiction: gay lovers and computer programmers. In fact, to make matters more complex, the gay lovers are Hindu and Muslim, and Sandhya, the main programmer in the story, is female. This is how the story's narrator, even as he moves closer to his male lover, explains his difference from Sandhya:

> *I put my hand on the back of his hip, with a finger looped through a belt hoop, and told him again that I coded high and she coded low, that when I cranked out my bread-and-butter xBase database rubbish I was shielded from the machine by layers and layers of metaphor, while she went down, down toward the hardware in hundreds of lines of C++ that made my head hurt just to look at them, and then there were the nuggets of assembly language strewn through the app, for speed when it was really important, she said, and in these critical sections it was all gone from me, away from any language I could feel, into some cool place of razor-sharp instructions, "MOV BYTE PTR [BX], 16." But she skated in easy, like she had been born speaking a tongue one step away from binary.*

Chandra's story is set in Bombay. The program that Sandhya has written is running into technical difficulties. And the narrator tells us that their business bid for doing inventory and accounting software was poised against "all the old men who owned the company" who would act unkindly "if they found out that this program written by a woman was not only crashing but losing money here and there."

This comment gestures at the ways in which technology, even when it promotes access to a better way of life for many, insinuates into an iniquitous system one more element of oppression. In 1999, I interviewed a Wall Street executive named R. Mutthuswami, who, when I read out the Chandra passage to him, shook his head and said, "There are zero women at that level." He explained that while there are several women, including some Indians, in design as well as management, he hadn't met any who worked with those computer languages that "shield the way the machine actually works." In other words, the inequities are even greater in the United States than the one that Chandra portrays for Bombay.

R. Mutthuswami noted that in addition to these gender divisions, there is also a "clear dichotomy" between two classes of Indian programmers. One class comprises highly educated Indians "who have given up an academic career to start their own companies" in places like Silicon Valley, and the other is mostly made up of graduates from regional colleges and less prestigious programs who perform "low-level coding jobs in the U.S., Europe, or Australia." Those who fall in the former category, according to Mutthuswami, today serve as the CEOs of 25 percent of the companies in Silicon Valley. The members of the second set form "a larger portion" of Indian cyberworkers in this country. They perform only "manual work," Mutthuswami said, and added, "It is a class system, like any other class system."

I asked Mutthuswami whether Oracle Rao, our composite H-1B programmer, would have any say in where he was placed in this hierarchy. Speaking broadly of the class of Indian cybertechies on H-1B visas, Mutthuswami said, "No. They don't get paid very well, they don't have any power or clout. They have skills, but they are mostly for maintenance jobs. I see nothing intellectual coming out of their work here." And yet there has also been a refusal on the part of the Indian press to recognize the ugliness of this picture. One report, for instance, argues that it is inaccurate to suggest that all H-1B workers are low-skilled workers and adds that "many of them provide sophisticated expertise to most of America's Fortune 500 corporations."

A sense of the various, interlinked inequities can allow us to see that the shining digital city is a complex and contradictory space. It is divided between transnational capital and workers, men and women, highly skilled and less skilled. Even when we are talking only of the United States, the picture is no less grim. Long hours and uncertain conditions of work, along with the coercion of immigration laws, produce a vulnerable labor force. A report by William Branigin in the *Washington Post* gave the name "high-tech braceros" to the migrant cyberworkers from countries like India, China, and the Philippines. These conditions are likely to be exacerbated as a result of recent setbacks, including the September 11 attacks, which resulted in a loss of 100,000 jobs in New York City alone. The Immigration and Naturalization Service is yet to come up with guidelines on how long H-1B workers can remain in the country after losing their jobs.

The impact of such injuries is not felt by the workers alone. A report in the *Village Voice* in October 2000 presented what it called "a little-known but growing class of battered spouses: the wives of foreign computer professionals." The wives of the H-1B worker have very limited rights: their right to stay in the

United States depends on the wage earners. A battered spouse, when confronted with divorce, is suddenly threatened not only with poverty but also deportation. Thus, as the *Voice* put it, battered women "are held prisoner by immigration policies that give their husbands complete control over their wives." This also means that if a woman presses charges against her husband, he can start divorce proceedings that throw her immigration status into jeopardy. And, as the H-1B is only job-specific, the man can always change his job—and not petition on her behalf, leaving her with no legal standing for being in this country. Furthermore, if they are deported, women will not be able to take their children with them unless they have gained custody. Domestic abuse is an extreme example, of course, but the ways in which the immigration laws are structured make clear that, as an immigration lawyer put it, "These laws are biased toward those who contribute to the economy. . . . These women are not even a priority for lawmakers. The attitude is that they have not earned any right to protection."

A South Asian women's group in New York City, Sakhi, told the *New York Times* a few years ago that it had helped about two thousand women over ten years, women seeking help against emotional and physical abuse. Another group, Narika, a California-based help line for South Asian women, estimates that it gets about eight new cases each month. Manavi, an organization for South Asian women, is active in New Jersey. During the India Day parade in New York City last year, its volunteers distributed flyers among those watching the parade. The flyers said that over the last sixteen years, Manavi had assisted over 1,700 women who had experienced family violence.

The oppression of women is the other side of the story of technological success. This oppression extends not only to wives but also to women employed as domestic help, and I see in their stories a general, broader story that is ignored when we celebrate the success of immigrants. On October 31, 2000, I conducted a phone interview with a fifty-four-year-old Indian woman who identified herself as Ms. Kaur. She had just won an out-of-court settlement against her former employers, two New York City doctors of Indian origin who had grossly mistreated her as an employee. In the Long Island home of the doctors, Ms. Kaur worked sixteen-hour days for six or seven days a week. There were few breaks and no overtime. According to one of the complaints filed by her, Ms. Kaur was "required to clean the grout between tiles in the large kitchen, dining room and greenhouse with a toothbrush." Her former employers were forced to pay Ms. Kaur $50,000 as part of the settlement.

The pages of the classifieds in the Indian newspapers in the United States are full of ads like the following: "Professional couple seeks live-in housekeeper/babysitter. Please call _____." It was an ad like this that Ms. Kaur had answered that got her the job on Long Island. It was in the same newspaper that she also came to learn about a group called Workers Awaaz, an organization of South Asian women based in New York City, with its volunteers committed to fighting on the behalf of domestic workers. Workers Awaaz coordinated a legal action against Ms. Kaur's employers; several South Asian activist organizations also picketed the Beth Israel Hospital in New York City, where one of her employers worked as a doctor.

The contrast of the Silicon Valley enterprise with the reality of domestic abuse is a more complete portrait of recent Indian immigration to the United States. It tells us of a world ushered in by technological change where hidden behind the stories of success are also the stories of exploitation and sexism.

But what presents a more meaningful juxtaposition, perhaps, is the picture where we set side by side the fact of domestic violence and the struggles of women's organizations like Sakhi, Narika, Manavi, and Workers Awaaz. This picture of change speaks of the emergence of social identities and of possibilities that are as vital as all the other changes brought about by the digital revolution.

3

The digital revolution, and access to technology, has also altered the cultural landscape of the *desi* communities in the West. "In contemporary culture," George Lipsitz has written, "artists from aggrieved communities often subvert or invert the very instruments of domination necessary for the creation of the new global economy—its consumer goods, technologies, and images." The examples of cultural expression that Lipsitz has in mind are the following: the literature of formerly colonized nations, Third Cinema, and hip-hop music. Hip-hop rarely gets mentioned in the same breath as literature, and Lipsitz's argument is especially interesting because he speaks of hip-hop as a diasporic art form. According to Lipsitz, hip-hop is particularly suited to such immigrant communities because it "brings a community into being through performance, and it maps out real and imagined relations between people that speak to the realities of displacement, disillusion, and despair created by the austerity economy of post-industrial capitalism."

If we think of the technological culture and the place of the ordinary immigrant in it, then practices like digital sampling leap out as stunning exemplars of diasporic realities. The remembered songs of the parents, in Hindi or Punjabi or Bengali, are altered through repetition, scratching, and mixing, so that nostalgia is turned into an affect that is wholly different and new. And still, as a memory of the past, we are left with what is repeated because it is recognizable, as if to say that there is no way of being without that history. This particular fact also perhaps explains why remixes—*bhangra* or Bollywood songs, mixed with rap and reggae—are more popular in the diaspora. In a *Newsday* story in January 2001, DJ Pinto Johal, who lives in Jackson Heights, New York, and owns a music store, told the reporter, "Bhangra mixes are really hot. For every one traditional disc, we sell 10 remixes." It is this brand of music that is pumped out at parties across college campuses and certainly dance clubs and restaurants that host *desi* parties in New York City. A news report entitled "To be Young, Indian and Hip" in the *New York Times* captures vividly a *desi* night at Planet 28 in Chelsea: "He scratches for a few bars, throws in the Fugees and then, some Junior Mafia, its 'get muh-ney' chorus punctuated by a mystery voice that cries 'India' on the downbeat, over and over like a mantra. The dancing masses nod in unison. Later, Lil Jay tosses a few surprises—a Hindi song from the popular Bombay movie, 'Disco Dancer' or a perennial 'bhangra' favorite, a folk song from the wheat fields of Punjab, laid over a frenzied house track."

One of the popular DJs on the New York City *desi* scene is DJ Siraiki who says that for him "music, technology, and politics are intertwined." DJ Siraiki is the club name of the filmmaker Vivek Bald. Bald's first film, *Taxi-vala/Auto-biography*, was a documentary on South Asian cabbies in New York City. The film that he is working on now is called *Mutiny: Asians Storm British Music*. We begin to get a sense of a materialist history for Bald's understanding of music, technology, and political or cultural identity when we hear him talk, during an interview, of the electronics market behind Jamma Masjid in Old Delhi, "where you have men who sit in stalls surrounded by wires and transistors and soldering irons and bits and pieces of all kinds of equipment. I swear they can make anything out of anything. And I think you'd find electronics bazaars like these in just about any 'Third World' or any formerly colonized country." This translates into a practice that, arising out of a sense of limited resources, actually stretches and expands the limits of the aesthetic field in which it is deployed.

In *Mutiny*, the viewer gets to see a different kind of innovation. The bands that we see—Fun^Da^Mental, Asian Dub Foundation, the Kaliphz, Voodoo Queens—are skilled at using technology for self-expression. But what you also see is the way in which technology mixed with performance is being used to

build communities that didn't exist before in this form. For example, the group Asian Dub Foundation (ADF), Bald says, "grew out of a music technology workshop that was being run in East London for Bengali youth." Band members had worked as music technology tutors at a place called Community Music, and now they have started their own institution modeled on the CM. The ADF Education is an organization that is training young people to be producers of music. Youth around fourteen years of age are being trained, Bald says, "on a small, portable, and easy-to-use package of equipment that consists of a sampler/sequencer, a MIDI keyboard, a mixing board, and a mic. Because the equipment is so immediately accessible, the youth form a fast and close relationship to the technologies." The philosophy behind such organizations is to empower people through music, with a focus on performance. Bald explains this by quoting one of the ADF members, John Pandit, who says "if you can get up and stand in front of people to perform music, you can get up and speak at a political rally."

The social context for such activism and such innovation is racism and the necessity of protest. This becomes clear from the opening moments of the work-in-progress tape that Bald has sent me. One of the musicians tells the camera that in the Britain in which he grew up, if teachers wanted to punish white students "they'd have you sitting with the Asian kids for the rest of the term." Bald's opening collage of black-and-white images mixes a family portrait from what looks like the 1950s or the 1960s: a bearded Asian man in a restaurant holds a tray of samosas under two portraits of the queen; the children of Indian and Pakistani immigrants play under the spray-painted signs of the National Front; there are shots of Asians at a protest, and a riot; one sees a youth caught in a cop's headlock. The picture is stark. There is an austerity that oppression imposes on the frame and the viewer. And it is in this atmosphere of repression that you hear the explosion of music and dance. These songs carry the rhythm of protest. What makes them particularly strong is that none of this music ever pretends that it is about an elsewhere. In Bald's film about the Asian music in Britain, one of the artists named Nadeem Shafi says: "I am made in Britain. I define Britain."

When I hear the statement above, I also begin to wonder whether Indians in America can make similar claims. Or whether they'd even want to. The violence of the National Front attacks on Asians in Britain forged a different, more resilient culture of resistance. The United States has not offered a similar challenge to Indian immigrants; the riots that had plagued the life of the earlier, working-class migrants to California or Oregon in the nineteenth and early twentieth centuries have never been a part of the collective memory of recent, post-1965 migrants to this country. Indians have not encountered the need to announce their presence defiantly as a part of the American social fabric. We have not, by and large, had any need for a group like the ADF producing a song like "Free Satpal Ram." Satpal Ram is a British Asian jailed in Britain after he fought off a racist attack. His imprisonment has been turned by the ADF into a cause for popular mobilization against a racist system. One of the lines in the ADF song is "An Asian Fights Back Can't Afford to be Meek / With Your Back to the Wall You Can't Turn the Other Cheek." Similarly, a song by The Kaliphz goes "We're not pacifists, we're paki-fists." If the *desi* musicians and artists in the United States were to form schools like the ADF Foundation, what would they want to teach the youth to perform?

And then, a second thought strikes me. Is it possible that the truth is more complex than the simple assertion that America is more tolerant than Britain? Is it not closer to the truth to say that America and its institutions are more powerful? Dissent and real opposition is more difficult to imagine in these parts, and the path of protest, especially for immigrants, cuts through the broad space of culture. This reality can lead us to recognize the importance of performance, not as an overthrow of the state or a grand inauguration of the revolution, but, rather, as Lipsitz puts it, a "desire to work *through* rather than *outside* of existing structures" that surround us. Our words and our rhythms become a way of powerful assertion about our being inside and yet outside this nation, its cities, and its institutions of power. It begins right here, as a performance, in New York City. . . .

4

Trotsky in the Park

I

She screams into the microphone, lips hitting
thin wire mesh of this thing that wants to take in
    every sound she makes,
and her voice rises, she says I'm not violent, I read
poems in public places,
I had promised I'd hold nothing back
    in my poetry,
so this is her name, and she lives on First Avenue near
    St. Marks Place,
I know dykes, she is no dyke,
and when she moved out she also stole the red
    lip-liner
that belonged to my roommate.

This poet calls herself Pubic Enemy and we cheer
    her performance, forever
glad that poetry can offer such sweet revenge.

Poetry gets numbers here. And like Olympic judges
from former East European countries five people in
    the audience
mark poems on a scale of ten: for that somersault
in the air, 7.8, that shaky-start in the cloud of chalk-
    powder,
the score can't be more than a 5.6, for your
    relentless display
of open vulnerability, risking failure with words,
    landing somewhere
between the sixth and seventh stanza on your feet,
you my darling will get a 9.8. Tell me again
    of the time
you heated the olive oil for your pasta
and then rubbed it softly—I think you used the word
    slowly—
you forgot the pasta and rubbed the oil slowly
on your guest's willing body.

A black woman
wearing a Crooklyn baseball shirt proudly like a red
    dashiki
breathes softly her delicate words about moons
    bathed in melancholy
the many moons of unwanted pregnancies and
    deaths
in poor homes. And even those who tonight have
    their cars parked
in the suburbs, and if they don't their parents do,
begin to clap and applaud this performance, we're
    glad,
I guess, that poetry can extract such sweet revenge
    against white suburbia.
When we come out my friend says it was kind of
    predictable. Well,
why doesn't America do something new then to
    black people

so that this woman in the red shirt can start
  sounding like Woody Allen
—or not?

II

Beneath the green statue in the Tompkins Square
  Park, a carpenter writes
a letter to put in a packet for his two nieces in
  Poland, a Madonna tape
and a rubber eraser in the shape of the Statue of
  Liberty for the younger one.
On the next bench, an art-student is learning about
  an outsider in Paris:
"Picasso was a vertical invader. He came up from
  Spain through
the trap-door of a Barcelona on to the stage of Europe."
The Psychic Palm Reader half a block away sits
  behind that red eye
of neon all-seeing and unblinking like fate. Her
  shoulders are square
like those of the women Picasso drew; she has had
  her imagination stretched
across barbed-wire fences that divide rich nations
  from the poor. Two girls
walk out of an MTV video and step past with lots of
  grunge sounds
and an old black guy shouts "I'll give you thirty-five
  dollars. Fuck
you should marry me for that . . . hey, I know women
  better-looking than you."
I am writing a note for the *Voice* personals, a public
  display of affection:
"Hey babe: Let's snuggle in bed and read the poetry
of the future or even the missionary-position
  Marxist writing
you so greatly admire. XOXOXO"
There is someone reading Trotsky in the park. He is
  a Pakistani student,
away from home for five years now, thinking of
  Lahore's streets, the brown, burnt

ancestral land, the men on bicycles as he reads in
   his book the words:
   "Yet every time a peasant's horse shies in terror
   before the
   blinding lights of an automobile on the Russian
   road at night,
      a conflict of two cultures is reflected in the
      episode."
Puerto Rican kids come out of the laundromat with
   a ball
and while the ball thrown from one hand turns and
   turns in the bright air,
the rest of the city that I know so little hurtles
   inside a subway car;
the white men in dark suits reading the New York
   Times, eyes lingering
over the bodies of humans of a certain gender
   who've taken
off their clothes for these men, in a row of ads for
   Bloomingdale's. A man,
class negative, color negative, makes an awkward
entry into the car singing hoarsely about a rainbow, holding in his hand the 2X3 cardboard sign:
      "My mother has multiple sclerosis
      and I can't see out of my left eye.
      Will you help me?"
and there's a middle-aged woman who, having
   carefully rubbed
moisturizing cream on her hands folds them in her
   lap,
and looks away from the man even though she's
   on his sightless side.
Before her station comes, she'll have time enough
to quickly read half of the poem on the orange
poster above the door:
      "Thank you my dear
      You came, and you did
      well to come. I needed
      you. You have made

      love blaze up in my"

III

The man who begins reading
a poem about queer love and clear rage
is clean-shaven and bald, a little
like a Hare Krishna with a Kalashnikov.
This is not poetry for beginners. To his party,
you bring your own anger.
Then someone with Bobby Kennedy's smiling face
printed on her trousers
finishes reading her poem, and an Indian woman in
    the audience
says she wants a 10 for that one. She says, "I love
    poems
which have nipples in them."
The emcee tilts his bearded face
and says, "Let's have a tete-a-tete about that, ha-ha."
He is wearing a tweed jacket one size too small
for him, but his satire is in good form
and he knows the audience well.
He quotes Williams Carlos Williams
and says "He had a Puerto Rican mother.
Now, they didn't tell you that, did they?"

Poetry is about nipples and Puerto Rican mothers.
It is about Trotsky going mad in the park
because they took it back from the homeless.
Poetry is about the hat that Thelonius Monk wore.
It is about poor nations protecting their land and their
    languages.
Poetry is the hiss you make
when you don't like the poem someone else
    is reading.
Poetry is the hiss you make. Period.

I read in a book, baby, that this is the hour
of the immigrant worker—
after the milkman and just before the dustman.
With his immigrant love, the poem that he comes
    seeking

is not the hiss you make, but a stammer
at your doorstep at dawn,
a terrible, trapped-up hope in this hour of becoming.
It has nothing
of the certainties of those who give names
to bottles of wines in the languages of Europe.

A woman just into her twenties, from Shanghai,
    alone
at an underground train station
in the middle of New York at night
after working overtime in a garment factory,
looks at her hands
for a long moment
in the bluish light of the station.
Around her is the silence of Trotsky's tomb.
In that silence is born
the silence this poem makes.

1

Once, when I came out of the subway in New York City, I saw
a sign that said "Gandhi was a great and charitable man."
Beneath, in smaller type, were the words, "However, he could
have used some work on his triceps." The sign was an advertisement for the Equinox Fitness Club. If you joined early, the
sign said, you could save 150 dollars.

I confess I like the use to which Gandhi is put by the Equinox Fitness Club. No doubt the Mahatma would have found
the price of the packet a bit steep. But I think he would have
liked the thriftiness of the early-membership plan. Gandhi
came from a family of traders. The name his family gave him—
Mohandas Karamchand Gandhi—was translated by the writer
G. V. Desani as "Action-Slave-Fascination-Moon Grocer."
What a tantalizing mix of qualities! The qualities of a man of
the world! This kind of man would even have understood
advertising. I am sure the Mahatma would have had a witty
quip for the use to which Microsoft has put his bald visage. In
America, Gandhi's image appears on huge hoardings with the

words "Think Different." There is a tiny logo in the corner showing a rainbow-striped apple. Salman Rushdie has commented on this phenomenon: "Once a half-century ago, this bony man shaped a nation's struggle for freedom. But that, as they say, is history. Now Gandhi is modeling for Apple."

In India, Gandhi had been a face smiling at me from the walls of the decrepit offices in the small towns of Bihar. The use of his image for a New York City gym has returned me to a different use of Gandhi, one that takes the Mahatma out of the museum. This use has not been unknown in India, it has just been ignored by official pieties. This is the irreverent Gandhi of the Indian marketplace. Long live Gandhi Safety-Match. Long live Bapu Mark Jute Bag. Long live Mahatma Brand Mustard Oil.

Do I really want to see Gandhi selling deodorants to a guy in Dadar? "Cleanliness is next to godliness. Free your body of foreign odors!" Perhaps not. But the point that I am moving toward is that a more robust, and perhaps muscular, Gandhi is visible in the pages of Indian writing in English these days. The sanitized Mahatma of early Indian fiction has given way to a maverick Gandhi. Let's take as an early example the memoirs of a writer like Nayantara Sahgal, who was also Prime Minister Nehru's niece. Sahgal described her return from New York to New Delhi in *Prison and Chocolate Cake*. India had only recently won freedom; it had not recovered from the trauma of the bloody Partition. Then, Gandhi was assassinated. In Sahgal's book, we saw Gandhi through a young woman's eyes that are full of adulation: "My own reaction was mingled with reverence. Could it be true that a man could talk of love and truth and goodness, and apply these religious terms to politics and not be laughed at? Could it be true that such sentiments could actually guide a nation's policy? Yet in India all these things were true."

A few decades into the realities of independent India, and the scene appears irredeemably altered. In Upamanyu Chatterjee's *English, August,* what we are left with is the post-apocalyptic image of the Gandhi Hall that looks like "something out of a TV news clip on Beirut." Outside this building with its broken windowpanes and bombed-out appearance is the "statue of a short fat bespectacled man with a rod coming out of his arse." This is the postcolonial Gandhi. And I like him because—I don't know how to say this without irony—nothing seems foreign to his body. Which is to say, my worry about his being used to sell deodorants is really an irrelevant question. Gandhi can take in anything and still keep smiling. A *satyagrahi* always stays on top of the world. This is also nonviolence taken to its real and proper extreme. In a country sodomized by its leaders, here is a leader who has chosen to stand among the people with a rod up his arse.

In the early 1980s, I was in college in Delhi. Each morning, I rode on a bus that took me past the memorials to national leaders, including Gandhi's. During those years in college, I came across *Kanthapura* on my required reading list in an English course. Raja Rao's *Kanthapura*, a novel about the Gandhian revolution, was first published in 1938, almost a decade before independence. The novel was about the inhabitants of a village, innocent of any history, suddenly swept by the powerful tide of Gandhi worship. Rao, along with R. K. Narayan and Mulk Raj Anand, formed the triumvirate of Indian writers in its early stages.

While our teacher discussed the book with us, in the world outside our classroom, another myth of Gandhi was being born. The British film director Richard Attenborough was shooting his movie on Gandhi in Delhi. The newspapers printed updates of the film shoot. There were complaints about Gandhi being played by an actor who wasn't an Indian; then came the giddy news that Ben Kingsley was at least half-Indian. One of my fellow students, a stocky man who studied history and rode a motorcycle, had a small role in the film. One day someone came to class with the news that there were buses waiting outside the college gates. We could all go and join the scene of Gandhi's funeral that was being shot that day. Attenborough needed a huge crowd of well-behaved extras. Hollywood was going to bring our freedom struggle alive for us. In *Kanthapura*, Rao's highly mannered syntax had conveyed to me the removed grandeur of idealism. I was discovering the past in a stylized way. Then, in the world outside the classroom, Hollywood brought peace and popcorn together, and gave Gandhi the honor he deserved. An Oscar.

It would be impossible for someone like me, born some decades after independence, to imagine Sahgal's or Rao's awestruck relationship with the Mahatma. Our freedom as a later generation of Indians has also meant a freedom from Gandhi worship. Newer Indian writers have undoubtedly played a small part in this whole process of demystification. Consider Vikram Chandra's portrait of Gandhi where he appears less a holy man on a pedestal and more a tactical mix of East and West, of high and low, of the sacred and also the secular:

> Be fearless, like that suave cosmopolitan M. K. Gandhi, that most international of khiladis, who told us repeatedly that while his political gurus were Gokhale and Ranade and Tilak, his spiritual gurus were Tolstoy and Thoreau and Ruskin, and that he got his nonviolence not from the Gita but from the Sermon on the Mount. Remember that Gandhi's audience was not just Indian but also everyone else; that all his actions, the spectacle of his revolution and the revolution of his self, were performed simultaneously before a local audience and a global one. He spoke to us, to those he loved, but in speaking to us he was also speaking to all the world, and in speaking to the world he wanted nothing less than to change all of it.

Chandra's Gandhi is a happy borrower. He is not unlike the Bombay criminals whom the writer describes as "those CCTV-using, Glock-firing, Bholenath-worshipping gangsters." Chandra finds them appealing because they "do whatever it takes to get the job done." From Gandhi to the Glock-firing gangsters . . . in less than 60 seconds! This is not only taking Gandhi off the pedestal—it is more like pushing him into the ring, with red boxing gloves and a rakish grin.

The historian Partha Chatterjee has written: "The 'message of the Mahatma' meant different things to different people." According to Chatterjee, what Gandhi's words "meant to peasants or tribals was completely different from the way it was interpreted by the literati." Following Chatterjee, it is quite interesting to me how what newspaper editors call "ordinary Indians" also in their own unremarkable ways have made Gandhi their own. I think that the Gandhi of the Indian marketplace that I was earlier championing is an example of that easy accommodation.

The people, in fact, might be ahead of writers and editorialists. As the research of Shahid Amin reveals, peasants in Gorakhpur, in the eastern India of 1921, were producing a "many-sided response to Gandhi." In the spring of 1921, *The Pioneer* carried an editorial about a report in a Gorakhpur newspaper that had cited reports of miracles popularly attributed to the Mahatma. "Smoke was seen coming from wells and, when water was drunk, it had the fragrance of *keora* (pandanus odaratissimus) an aloe-like plant which is used in the manufacture of perfume; a copy of the Holy Quran was found in a room that had not been opened for a year; an *Ahir* who refused alms to a *Sadhu* begging in Mahatma Gandhi's name, had his *gur* and two buffaloes destroyed by fire, and a skeptical Brahmin, who defied Mr Gandhi's authority, went mad and was only cured three days afterwards by the invocation of the saintly name!"

In this list of magic and change, I see a lesson about our buried, peripheral modernities. The lesson becomes clear to me long after I come out of the subway and see Gandhi's name on a sign advertising a gym. But the lesson, slow in coming, is clear enough. It is about people mixing the rational with the ritual, science with séance, and politics with the poetry of magical transformation. Long before Richard Attenborough, the mythmaker, long before the admen from Madison Avenue, long before our politicians had invented the Gandhi Jayanti Samaroh, long before Indian writers had found magical realism . . . were the peasants of Gorakhpur giving life to Gandhi. Long live the peasants of Gorakhpur.

2

But, what are peasants doing in New York City?

In Rishi Kapoor's popular Bollywood film *Aa Ab Laut Chalein*, the festive Indians in Manhattan sing a song whose refrain is "Kyaa ab bhi wahan khaliyanon mein log neem ke neeche sote hain?" (Do people in the farmyards there still sleep under the branches of the neem?) The film's emotional appeal for the expatriate, the N.R.I. or the nonresident Indian, lies in its evocation of an abandoned past life in India: a village India of peasant simplicity, of innocent childhoods, and of family spectacles centered around weddings and festivals. At the same time as the films conjure a pastoral India, they also strain, paradoxically enough, to reveal an India that, at least in its urban quarters, is also wholly Westernized. This latter representation arguably is more for the consumption of the indigenous middle-class viewers. As far as the diasporic audience is concerned, however, the Bombay films present an imagined homeland that is everything the inhospitable West is not.

In a broadly shared myth, at least among first-generation immigrants, India remains the space of wholesome purity. And films are accepted as documentary reports on the encroachment of the West. Numerous Bollywood films in the seventies— Manoj Kumar's *Purab aur Paschim* and Dev Anand's *Hare Rama Hare Krishna* being two early examples—had vigorously portrayed the East-West divide in the familiar binary terms. But it was not till the mid-1990s, perhaps as a result of increasing migration from India, especially of Punjabi migrants whose homes were torn by a raging armed conflict between the state and separatist militants, that a new wave of films emerged that spelled out what we might call a diasporic aesthetic. The best exemplar of this genre would be *Dilwale Dulhania Le Jayenge* from the mid-1990s, a film that opens with the shot of an affluent Indian migrant, a Punjabi in fact, feeding pigeons in London's Trafalgar Square. We hear the voice-over: "I have lived here for twenty-two years . . . I have walked these streets . . . and each day these streets ask me my name . . . you, Chaudhury Baldev Singh, where have you come from, why have you come here?" We recognize the voice. The rich baritone belongs to the veteran Indian actor Amrish Puri, who has seemingly signed a contract to play the wealthy N.R.I. in each Hindi movie. And yet, as diasporics, we also recognize our own voice there. "Half a life has gone by, and yet this land remains strange to me. I am a stranger here. Like me, these pigeons too have no home, but when will I be able to fly like them? Someday, surely, I too will return to my India, to my Punjab."

This is a dated dream. Travel between home and abroad, even among working-class migrants, is a more common feature than Baldev Singh's soliloquy suggests. It returns us to the prior history of now-forgotten indentureship or the earlier phases of more recent migration. In this narration, where it is framed as an impossible gesture, the return to the homeland is given an epic form. The migrant becomes Odysseus. He becomes Ram returning from exile to Ayodhya after fourteen years. He, and it is always a he, returns a hero.

Two years ago, in a small Florida town, I went to watch Subhash Ghai's *Taal* because I had read in the Indian newspapers that it had grossed $591,289 in North America in its first three days. An estimated 100,000 people, the report said, were expected to watch *Taal* during its first week in the United States. There was an introduction here to the strength of the growing Indian diaspora. But the film itself, as well as the reaction of the audience, told me something about how such films projected a sense of India to the diaspora. The film presented its heroine with rural roots, but she also discovers, almost reluctantly, the urban realities. In its repeated representation of MTV-inspired youth, corporate affluence, and high-tech toys like digital cameras, *Taal* showed how Bollywood only wants to display its closeness to Hollywood. When I came out of the theater, I asked the man sitting next to me what the film had meant to him, and he replied that the film had showed him "the effect of Western civilization on Indian culture." It suddenly seemed that diasporic spectatorship had signed a contract to see the West as urban, and as tainted with modernity, while India continued to be fixed in the imaginary as rural, bound to fixed locations of home and heart.

Let's take another Subhash Ghai film, *Pardes*, which was marketed with the slogan "American Dream, Indian Soul." The opening frames of the film declare "Long Live India on Fiftieth Anniversary of Independence." (*Pardes* was released in 1997.) The film, like Kapoor's *Aa Ab Laut Chalein*, promoted the familiar opposition of East and West. In fact, *Pardes* even had a song that could serve as the national anthem for nostalgia-filled diasporic Indians: "London dekha, Paris dekha, aur dekha Japan / Michael dekha, Elvis dekha, sab dekha meri jaan / Saare jag mein kahin nahin hai doosra Hindustan" (I saw London, I saw Paris, and I saw Japan / I saw Michael, I saw Elvis, I saw it all, my dear / But there is nothing in the world that is like India).

Imagine viewers in India who have never caught a plane abroad. When they see such films, even when they are drowned in the titillation of watching commodity culture on full display, they are also consoled for having never made the wrong decision of crossing the seven seas. While the captains of the film industry as well as the stars get rich—and have the freedom to be international jet-setters, if not also owners of a penthouse in

Manhattan like the mega-star Amitabh Bachchan—the ordinary *desi* is reassured for having been a prudent nationalist who has never left home. Here one cannot be contented with noting the hypocrisy of a film that relies on dollars from abroad but decides that it must promote the virtues of never venturing abroad. Rather, in the context of the rise of right-wing ultranationalism in recent years, one must ask what is the price one has to pay for nostalgia. It seems these days one can't ask for an inch of nostalgia without getting a mile of nationalism in return. And this is an ideology determined to use the national flag to put a cover over all the rents in the social fabric. You might be toiling twelve hours each day for minimum wages in New Jersey, or feel utterly poor walking the streets of London; you might even return to your dingy flats and mistreat your wives and your children, but you can take pride in the fact that you are an N.R.I. and your home is India!

This grand portrayal of N.R.I. nostalgia is emblematized by the presentation of a single image: the desirable Indian woman as an icon of docility and traditional charm, one manufactured on celluloid as an updated image of the mythical Sita. In every recent Hindi movie I have seen about Indians living abroad, it is the film's heroine who epitomizes and, indeed, becomes the bearer of the traditional culture that is always equated with everything Indian.

The heroine in *Pardes*, played by Mahima Chowdhury, is even named Ganga. She is supposed to be pure like the eternal river. Once again it is the actor Amrish Puri, playing the man who will become Ganga's father-in-law, who says: "Aaj Ganga jaisi hee betiyan hamari ek matr ummeed hain" (Today, it is daughters like Ganga who are our only hope). But what is the nature of this hope? And why do these words sound so much like the matrimonial ads in Indian newspapers—even the ones published for *desi* subscribers in North America—that are looking for "a fair and beautiful girl from respectable family, convent educated with traditional Indian values"? For many Indians living abroad, and to a lesser extent for many of their compatriots in India, heroines like Ganga are forced to provide a bulwark against the shock of the new culture. For the N.R.I., the world outside has utterly changed; they want the world inside their homes to remain familiar. There is nothing, of course, as familiar as the conventional. So women in these films, and often in real life, end up carrying the double burden—of daily labor and of national tradition—the Indian woman as a coolie for convention.

In the novels written in English by Indian writers, those dichotomies that govern the affective economy of Bollywood films are mercifully absent. India is not seen as a haven of innocence and America as a den of vice. However, in a novel that appeared early in the current wave of acclaimed Indian writing, Bharati Mukherjee's *Jasmine*, the relationship is reversed in almost a similar simpleminded way. In *Jasmine*, it is India that is nearly exclusively the site of patriarchal oppression, terrorism, pestilence, superstition; and America serves as a place where the protagonist is able to creatively free herself from the past. Thus, the structural difference that is ordained by Bollywood is also retained in the novel; it is just that the labels are switched.

Written as a renarration of *Jane Eyre* from a postcolonial position, *Jasmine* was the first Indian novel to deal primarily with the theme of Indian migration to America. The peasant life in Punjab that it constructs in the book is one imagined by a cosmopolitan, and the life of a domestic that it portrays in the United States is, for the most part, also unconvincing. I do not think it is simply a matter of the writer's class position and distance from the subject. Rather, I believe Mukherjee's novel suffers because it was a first. Although written as late as 1989, it reminds us of a previous era in which the realities of Indian immigrant life had still not found root in the American scene. The shape of the sentences does not yet carry the impress of other writings by Indians; they all struggle to describe a new reality that seems forever to be spoken in an alien tongue. As a result the book inhabits a landscape that seems empty of the by now familiar markers, and even its more imaginative leaps are reduced to editorial, sociological statements. The narrator discovers, for instance, that the Punjabi professor is actually not a professor of engineering at all. Professorji is an importer of human hair. Each day, he sits hidden in a basement measuring and labeling the length and thickness of each separate hair. The narrator informs us: "Junk hair he sold to wigmakers. Fine hair to instrument makers. Eventually, scientific instruments and the U.S. Defense Department. It was no exaggeration to say that the security of the free world, in some small way, depended on the hair of Indian village women." The writer, Mukherjee, is not loath to carry out some measurements of her own, letting each bit of reality fit nicely with her sense of the world.

As it happens, in *Jasmine*, the Professorji's wife is a consumer of Bollywood films in New York City. Mukherjee writes: "Every night, Nirmala brought home a new Hindi film for the VCR. Showings began promptly at nine o'clock, just after an enormous dinner, and lasted till midnight. They were Bombay's 'B' efforts at best, commercial failures and quite a few flops." Earlier in the novel, Mukherjee's narrator had gone to the cinema to watch a Hindi film, *Mr. India*. Mukherjee got the name of the male actor wrong, but, more important, the film's name is a ham-handed reference to the fact that the occasion is also an attempt to help the narrator meet her future husband.

The arranged marriage is a tired trope of Bollywood; it makes for dull reading when it is recycled as a part of Indian fiction in English.

However, I am happy to report that in a recent novel by another Indian writer based in the United States, the appearance of a Hindi film serves a more complex, and yet much more simple and touching, function. In the novel *The Death of Vishnu*, written by Manil Suri, the reader meets a young couple in Bombay for whom, on their marriage night, it was the talk about an old Hindi film called *Mughal-e-Azam* that had unlocked their silence. The man's name is Vinod; his wife's name is Sheetal. Strangers meeting for the first time on their marriage night are not really strangers because they have experienced this night in Bollywood films. Their gestures on the marriage bed—the hero reaching out to lift the embroidered cloth covering the heroine's head, her head bowed, the eyes shut under their arch of painted dots—are also familiar through their repetition on the silver screen.

Inevitably, of course, Vinod and Sheetal meet with tragedy. Their marriage and lives are suddenly unraveled when Sheetal is found to be suffering from cancer. She wants to live, however, and she wants to do this by entering the *Guinness Book of World Records*. In her heroic effort to get into the book of records, Sheetal now decides to commit to memory each line of dialogue of a Bollywood film called *Jeevan*, which means "Life." Sheetal's struggle to enter the world of Bollywood films and to touch the heart of "Mr William Warby, Associate Editor, *Guinness Book of World Records*" is a moving story that both relies on the melodrama of Bombay films and gives it a new face. Sheetal writes to Warby at the *Guinness Book of World Records* and gets a letter that is matted and framed and hung above her bed. The letter thanked Sheetal for her attempt to have "a new category for memorization of the dialogue of a movie" but also expressed regret that "we do not anticipate adding this category at this time." The letter was accompanied by a flyer for a new edition of the book. Although Sheetal is devastated, she takes heart from the suggestion that the category for memorization of movie dialogues might be added at a later time. When she dies, Vinod sends the petition once again to Guinness. He gets an almost identical reply, signed once more by William Warby.

Everything that separates Sheetal from what she wants before she dies cannot be reduced to a statement about the superiority of either the East or the West. Even though Suri's novel is often uneven and it struggles with the vestiges of those realities that had so constrained Mukherjee's writings, it is alert to the realities of cultural travel. Suri does not offer pat cultural judgment. Bollywood must be in the *Guinness Book of World Records* for making the most movies. In his novel, Suri takes the two different kinds of excess represented by those two cultural forms and stages a meeting that reveals the asymmetries of our divided worlds. Sheetal and William Warby: They participate in a strange and unusual dialogue, stranger perhaps than an arranged marriage.

3

In New York City, where the Mahatma is modeling for Apple, and where I recall the peasants of Gorakhpur with their fertile mythmaking about Gandhi baba, actors from Bombay appear on the screen dressed like peasants, uttering platitudes about the village home, the green and yellow fields of mustard, the purity of their daughters, the *gaon ki betiyaan*, with their lissome forms outfitted in suitably expensive boutique wear; in this New York City, I can seek solace in my own myth of eternal return or I can ask myself what there is to do instead of singing songs about the home that I left behind.

I am not demanding that I or anybody else turn our back on our past. Rather, the point is to ascertain what our narratives of travel are going to be. Against the mythologies of the Hindi films that offer paeans to the glory of the abandoned nation, apart also from more sophisticated fictions of writers who unfurl the magical realist drama of diasporic lives, what I would like to know more about are the day-to-day struggles, successes, failures, and confusions of the ones who leave home to seek better fortune elsewhere. And, equally crucial, what I want to see are accounts of what is suffered as well as celebrated in the most ordinary of ways by those who do not leave, those who stay behind, whether because they want to or simply because it cannot be otherwise.

Have you ever been on flights that come to Bombay via Dubai or Abu Dhabi? Has your luggage gone around the carousels in the baggage claim area with large cartons strapped together with tape? Have you traveled on flights where the flight attendants and even some passengers have smirked at the accents and demeanor of the less-well-heeled travelers? What if we were to replace all the hypocritical, self-mythologizing accounts of expatriate fiction, and its more vulgar version in Bollywood cinema that provides a nationalist fantasy, with imaginative maps of toil and tales of small, unnoticed triumphs?

Against generalities, we need individual stories. A few weeks ago, a writer-friend in Calcutta wrote me a letter asking me if I knew anything about the case of an Indian student who had been found dead at a nearby university. My friend's family had known the young man since he was a boy. I made inquiries and discovered that the young man, whose name was Anirban, had drowned in the river that ran past his university. The college newspaper said that the Indian student had died on his birthday. The cause of Anirban's death remained a mystery, and, unfortunately, the police had accepted it as such and closed the case.

Many Indians, some of them students and some others who had been former colleagues of Anirban's, wrote letters in the press saying that the police needed to investigate what exactly had caused their friend's death. Anirban had been healthy and also busy and engaged in his work. How had he ended up in the river one night? I was saddened by the news I was reading about a person who had, after all, been a stranger to me. And I found myself feeling sadder still as I read the detail about the university chaplain seeking the help of a Bengali professor to convey the news of Anirban's death to his mother in Calcutta. What had the chaplain said? What words had the Bengali professor added to what the chaplain had said? What were the words that she had held back? I ask these questions not because I am a writer, though I think this has something to do with it, but because this provides me a way to imagine the realities of an immigrant's life and the way it is joined to other lives in the homeland that he has left behind. These questions are the only way I have to measure the distance that death had added to the enormous divide that already existed between Anirban's two homes.

As I read about Anirban's mother in Calcutta, my mind went back to a moment one night in Delhi, long before I left India for America. Our family had bought a black-and-white TV in the early 1980s. I watched television religiously. One night, they showed a short TV film made by the great Bengali director, Mrinal Sen. The film was called *Aparajit*. The film was about an old couple, played with great restraint and vulnerability by the National School of Drama veterans Manohar Singh and Surekha Sikri. The pair is waiting for a phone call from their son in Chicago. He went there five years ago to get his doctoral degree. The call is awaited at a neighbor's house. The son is to call because it is his birthday.

Twice the phone rings, but it is not the son. The neighbor lady in whose house the old couple is sitting, waiting for the call, says that they have gotten four or five wrong-number calls that morning.

The phone call doesn't come. At night, the mother takes out a bundle of letters from her drawer. She asks her husband to read one of them. He looks at the letter and protests. He says, "The same one. You've read it nearly a hundred times, it's two years old." His wife says, "Read it. I love it. It never grows stale for me. Please read."

The letter that the husband, the character played by Manohar Singh with a white shawl wrapped around him, begins to read is a moving one. Midway through the letter, we begin hearing it in the son's voice. The effect is heightened. It is as if we ourselves were receiving news from a distance that now, for a moment, has been bridged.

The film's director, Mrinal Sen, had quoted from an actual letter that his own son had written to his mother, Sen's wife. I want to end by quoting the letter as it was used in the script for *Aparajit* because, caught up in its sentences, is a familiar drama of return. It relies on a promise, but it is already aware that dreams live on broken promises. Sen's film was also a tribute to the solidarity of an aged couple. It is not the immigrant but the ones who stay behind who are the true unvanquished. There is a more individual, and personal, story here too, I think. Each year, I travel to the town in India where my parents live. I am able to spend only a few days with them. And then I return to America. It seems to me that I recognize in this letter with a degree of startling intimacy the routine of crumbling resolve, and the course of desires, quite naked and unprotected by guilt. And I want, like Sen, to believe that my parents, old and set in their ways, anxious, and forever bickering, find in each other the strength that their children do not provide. Here, then, is that letter:

Ma, do you remember I had taken you to see a film once? It was Satyajit Ray's The Unvanquished. *You had wept a lot. You had said: Apu—the son—why is he so cruel? Why did he have to leave his mother and go to Calcutta to study? He wouldn't visit his mother on vacations even. Instead he tells his friends that he has sent some money to her and "managed her." Then you had turned to me: "Will you behave the same way—like Apu? Then it's going to be exactly like the film—on your return you'll find me no longer—I'll be dead and gone. You won't even see my dead face. . . ." Yesterday, a few of us had gone to the Chicago University Film Club, to see the film again.* The Unvanquished. *This time I cried. I cried a lot. After returning we had a heated discussion till the early hours of the morning. My friends who would like to settle down here—some have already secured jobs—argued that mothers shouldn't expect so much—shouldn't the sons think of their own future?—mothers shouldn't be selfish and tie their sons to their apron strings, and it's really unfair of them to take revenge by dying. . . . Ma, I don't agree with them. I shall return. Definitely. As soon as I finish my work here. I shan't wait a day longer.*

The Indian writer Rabindranath Tagore flew in a plane in 1932. He had awoken at three-thirty in the dark morning and was in the air at four. Tagore was traveling in what was then called Persia; at half past eight the plane reached Bushire. "Now comes an age in which man has lifted the burdens of earth into the air," the writer noted in his travel diary. The achievement of flight did not always promise freedom for Tagore. On the contrary, he felt that the airplane was not in harmony with the wind. It roared like an animal in rage. A plane in flight suggested very strongly that human conflict had been raised from the level of the mundane world into the heavenly skies above.

Tagore had been awarded the Nobel Prize in literature in 1913 for his book of poems, *Gitanjali*. The thought that the earth lost its hold on man when he flew into the sky was not the result of poetic fancy. A few paragraphs later in his travelogue, Tagore had supplied the context for his thoughts. "A British air force is stationed at Baghdad," he wrote. "Its Christian chaplain informs me that they are engaged in bombing operations on some Sheikh villages."

The fields, ponds, and rivers of his childhood bound Tagore to the earth and its beauty. To fly was to lose this contact with the earth. Only the sense of sight remained for the one who was in the air, and it gave man the disease of aloofness. For Tagore, the man in the plane raining bombs below could not even in good faith ask himself who is kin and who is a stranger: he has put himself in a place from where he is unable to be aware of the difference and to judge accordingly. "The men, women and children done to death there," wrote Tagore, "meet their fate by a decree from the stratosphere of British imperialism—which finds it easy to shower death because of its distance from its individual victims." At the same time, the invention of the airplane impressed Tagore. He saw in the race of the inventors qualities of character like perseverance and courage. The sight of his four Dutch pilots ("immensely built, the personification of energy . . . their rude, overflowing health, bequeathed by generations brought up on nourishing food") evoked admiration and the thought that his own compatriots had been deprived of food and exhausted by toil.

This picture has now changed. The descendants of those who were, in Tagore's time, the subject peoples have now for long been flying planes. They also travel in planes. This situation also incites ambivalence. The travelers are often workers migrating long distances in search of work. In fact, such travel remains a part of the fantasy in the minds of the poor. There are many in the poorer countries of the world for whom the plane in flight represents the journey that, when undertaken in the future, will take them to the promised land. In airports all over the world, one can see the migrant workers from countries like Tagore's India, waiting to be taken to another place to work.

Flight

On the morning of September 11 last year, nineteen men, in their appearance not different at all from the others who stand in the visa lines outside the embassies and consulates of rich nations in cities like Calcutta and Cairo, Karachi and Khartoum, hijacked four American jets filled with fuel and people. The suicidal acts of the hijackers also gave a perverse twist to the old story of the difficult travel to the land of plenty and promise. According to reports that were published in the days following the attacks, it was revealed that the hijackers believed that their deaths promised them entry into the garden of heaven and the ministrations of seventy virgins. We can persist with Tagore's vision of the fiery bird raining death, but his universe is already lost, the simple oppositions between the earth and the sky rendered obsolete. Those who had been chained to the earth have also learned to claw their way into the air and wreak havoc from on high. There are new stories of travel, and now terror touches all.

Salman Rushdie's novel *The Satanic Verses* opens with an explosion in the air. A jet is blown apart while in flight, and two actors tumble out, "like titbits of tobacco from a broken old cigar." The two men, Gibreel Farishta and Saladin Chamcha, were passengers in the jumbo jet *Bostan*, Flight AI-420. In the night air around them "floated the debris of the soul, broken memories, sloughed-off selves, severed mother-tongues, violated privacies, untranslatable jokes, extinguished futures, lost loves, the forgotten meaning of hollow, booming words, *land, belonging, home.*" Rushdie's fictional midair explosion was based on an actual event. On June 28, 1985, Flight AI-182 burst into flames off the coast of Ireland. The plane had taken off from Toronto and Montreal; it was headed for New Delhi and Bombay via London. All 331 people on board were killed. The plane's destruction was widely believed to be the work of Sikh extremists who wanted to avenge the Indian army's assault on the Holy Temple in Amritsar. Two Indo-Canadian Sikhs were arrested by the police and charged with first-degree murder. Flight AI-182 had indeed been packed with migrants. Rushdie's catalog of the debris from the destroyed airliner furnishes a valuable, and touching, inventory of the baggage—the load of everyday experience—that immigrants carry with them. And the play of magic realism allows the writer to introduce, amid the destruction, the miracle of rebirth. Gibreel Farishta and Saladin Chamcha survive death, and are transformed. This is an allegory of migration. Loss renews life. As Gibreel Farishta croons, even as he falls from 29,002 feet, "To be born again, first you have to die."

The sweet dream of reinvention is a radical one, but reality turns out to be more intractable. Rushdie's story of the passenger floating down to a part of London is not nearly as surprising as the actual, unheralded fall from the sky of a secret passenger at the edge of the same city. According to a July 2001 report in the *Guardian*, a body was discovered in a parking lot of a department store in west London. A workman in nearby Heathrow airport had seen a figure in jeans and a black T-shirt suddenly "plummeting from the sky like a stone." Where was the home of this dead man who was lying in a pool formed from his own split brains? The report said that the man who had fallen to earth was Mohammed Ayaz, a twenty-one-year-old stowaway who had made a desperate attempt to escape the harsh life of a peasant in his village in Pakistan on the Afghan border. The previous night, when a British Airways jet turned around to begin taxing at Bahrain airport in preparation for takeoff, Ayaz had apparently sprinted through the dark and climbed into the huge chambers above the wheels of the Boeing. It could not have been an easy task to find one's way into the wheel bay. The report said: "It involves climbing 14 ft up one of the aircraft's 12 enormous wheels, then finding somewhere to crouch or cling as the plane makes its way to the end of the runway and starts its deafening engines." At that point, the plane would have accelerated to 180 mph.

Ayaz would not have known this, though one cannot be sure, but the undercarriage compartment "has no oxygen, no heating and no pressure." Within minutes, the temperature around Ayaz would have dropped below freezing. The report that I have been quoting had furnished, at this point, its own sense of journalistic pathos: "At 18,000 ft, minutes later, while passengers only a few feet away were being served gin and tonic and settling down to watch in-flight movies, Ayaz would have begun to hallucinate from lack of oxygen." The report had then added plainly: "At 30,000 ft the temperature is minus 56 degrees." When, many hours later, the plane was still a few miles away from Heathrow, the captain would have lowered the wheels of the aircraft. It was at that time, when the plane was likely to have been between 2,000 and 3,000 feet, that Mohammed Ayaz's lifeless body must have been delivered into the morning air.

For seven months prior to his death, Ayaz had been working as a laborer in Dubai. His family is poor, finding a meager livelihood from farming wheat, barley, corn, and onions. The agent who had secured a way for Ayaz to go to the Gulf had demanded money in addition to the cost of travel and visa. The family had had to borrow heavily. The money that Ayaz was going to earn would allow him to repay the debts in two years. But things didn't turn out the way Ayaz had expected. In Dubai, Ayaz's employer took away his passport. The salary he received was less than one-fourth of what the agent had promised. Ayaz was able to make barely enough to buy food. Ayaz did not tell his family of his plan to cross into Bahrain or his attempt to make his way to England. Ayaz's brother, Gul Bihar, told the reporter: "He always spoke about going to work in America or England. But they don't give visas to poor people like us."

The report in the *Guardian* had been sent to me in the mail by a friend. I was standing outside my house when the mailman brought the letter one morning, and I read the newspaper clipping while standing on my steps. As I began reading the first few paragraphs, I thought of the opening lines from Rushdie's *Satanic Verses* quoted above. Those lines were what first came to mind. But in seconds, the mood had slipped. The pain and despair that surrounded me as I read the report took me away from the pages of celebrated fiction. In much that I have written in the past few years, I have tried to understand how Indian writing has populated the literary landscape familiar to Western readers with people who look and speak differently and who have their histories in another part of the world. The presentation of this record by Indian writers has been a great, imaginative achievement. But a dead stowaway? So much that appears in Indian fiction today, particularly in its magical realist versions, appears banal if not also meretricious, when compared to the fragmentary account that emerges from a news story of a poor youth's struggle to cross the borders that divide the rich from the poor. The textbook of "multicultural literature" carries no words of testimony of a young man narrating what flashed through his head as he went running in the dark behind a giant airplane that was about to pick up speed on the runway. It suddenly strikes me that Mohammed Ayaz could not have foreseen his death—and that seems to me to be more and more a triumph of his imagination.

The article in the *Guardian* also said that Ayaz was not the first to fall down from the sky. In October 1996, the body of a nineteen-year-old from Delhi, Vijay Saini, had dropped out of a plane at almost the same spot. Saini's corpse lay undiscovered for three days. (Vijay Saini's brother, Pradeep, according to the report, is the only person believed to have survived such a journey. The article said that the man was found at Heathrow "in a disorientated state shortly after a flight from Delhi landed.") Then, two years later, a couple drinking in a pub in nearby Marlborough had seen another man tumble out of the sky. That body was never discovered. The police believe that it might have fallen in a reservoir. "The undercarriage is always lowered at the same point, that is why they are falling at the same place," an official told the *Guardian*. "But it's an almost uncanny coincidence—these people fly right across the world in this way from different places, and they all end up in a car park in Richmond. If there are any more bodies to fall, that's where they will fall." The West rushes up to meet the migrant, not as the promised land but, instead, a parking lot that becomes for him a desolate, temporary graveyard.

On September 11, bodies fell from the top floors of the north tower of the World Trade Center. One writer, watching from the street below, wrote "it looked like a desperate ballet: some seemed to be flying, their arms sweeping gracefully as they picked up speed. Others tumbled and some just dropped, rigid, all the way down." As I reflect on that ghastly scene, months after it occurred, I find myself mentally moving Mohammed Ayaz from a parking lot in west London to the Twin Towers. He could have been one among the many migrant workers, dishwashers, messengers, cleaners, and restaurant help who perished on that day. But it doesn't work. I see him again and again in the wheel bay of the airplane. That thought won't go away. I also realize that I am perturbed by the thought that the hijackings and the mayhem that followed should erase from public consciousness the presence of the other illegal passenger, the humble stowaway, and stretching behind him, the memory of a whole history of dispossession. The sad truth is that the stowaway is not alone. Hidden behind that figure are the untold millions in countries like India or Pakistan who dream of a different future. Often, these young men and women have been turned into migrants in their own land because of poverty, or famines, or wars waged by others in the fields where their families have toiled for generations. How removed is the pathos of the stowaway from the rage of the hijacker?

The body falling out of the sky is the other and silent half of the story of international travel and tourism. We are reminded that not everyone crosses borders alive, despite the cheerful acceptance of globalization by many governments of the world. Standing near his son's unmarked grave, a mound of brown earth ringed by stones and covered with a plastic sheet, Mohammed Ayaz's father said, "My son was as strong as four men but he died in search of bread."

I can try to imagine the dreams that come to the stowaway when he begins to drift into sleep despite the cold and the noise in his shuddering cage. But these would be speculations. The stowaway will not share his secrets with the writer. It is impossible for me to know if the stowaway is nostalgic for the fields in his village and the familiar sunshine on the wall of his house. He had wanted to leave them behind. The plane is carrying him into the future. He tells himself that he can bear hunger for a long time. He is a quick learner. Once he has his feet on the ground he will find a way to earn money soon. These are the thoughts that I surround the stowaway with, as if he were, in reality, trapped inside the darkness in my head. It is because I am telling myself over and over that he does not feel any pain. He feels light-headed. He is not fleeing anything anymore. He is flying.

Flight

Shastriji was my neighbor. His apartment was on Westcott. I live on Forster Avenue, and Westcott is the next street on the way to the university. I think Shastriji came here in 1984, but I cannot be sure. When I met Shastriji six months ago, I liked going to his apartment. It was like visiting a friend's house in Bihar. He always asked me if I'd like to have tea, but I never came away without eating dinner.

Our first meeting was in the library. I was sitting in the periodicals section. I had seen him looking at me. He was a middle-aged man, slightly heavy, wearing a blue denim shirt tucked into his khaki pants. With his good clothes and small paunch, he looked respectable. I had never seen him before. When I saw him walking toward me, I knew he wanted the *Outlook* I was reading. He came and stood near me.

When I looked up, he smiled sheepishly. He didn't ask me to give him the magazine. He only said: "Excuse me, is it the latest one?"

I didn't know if it was or not. I showed him the cover with Sonia Gandhi on it. She was wearing a nice sari, but it seemed she had grown older in just two years.

Shastriji said: "I have already read that. They still haven't got the new one."

I said, "Maybe there is a postal strike in India."

He grinned, showing his teeth. "These days all the magazines are sent by computer. And then printed in New Jersey or Chicago. So, that wouldn't affect it." I didn't know this. He extended his hand and introduced himself. I did the same. He heard my name and asked, "You are from U.P.?"

"No, Bihar."

This time he grinned more broadly. His gums were dark, like his skin. This darkness made his eyes and teeth more striking.

Shastriji said, "I am too."

He asked, "From Patna?"

I nodded.

"Let's go have tea," he said.

In the university cafeteria, there were five types of coffee, and only one kind of tea. The girl behind the counter had a ring pierced through her right eyebrow. When she gave us the tea, she put the tea bag in hot water, dumped some sugar, and then poured the milk immediately over it. As a result, the tea remained very light and watery. Shastriji grinned again. He did not seem at all self-conscious about his dark gums and the peeling skin on his fingers. I liked him.

After Shastriji said a few things about Patna, I guessed he was about ten years older than I, somewhere around forty. He lived with his wife and two children, a son and a daughter. He was about to complete his M.A. in South Asian Studies. He had earlier taught for a short period in Allahabad after getting an M.A. in English. I asked him if his wife worked. He said, "Arre, ladies. . . ." And he looked at me, as if I understood everything. Although I didn't, I wanted to, and I said "Yes . . . yes."

Shastriji did not look worried when I told him I had managed to come on an exchange-student visa arranged for me by the secretary of the Education Department. I told him that, of course, I was interested in seeing if there was any scope of staying longer. He kept nodding vigorously while I talked, even though his eyes wandered away sometimes.

When women passed our table, he would suddenly jerk his head up and look them straight in the eye. A couple of times, the women would slow down, thinking he knew them or was going to say something. I found this intriguing rather than irritating.

We got up after having finished our tea. He took my phone number and then he said he would call me. I could drink real tea in his home, he said. I shook hands with him.

"What is your father's name?" Shastriji asked me before letting go of my hand. I answered him.

Then, he said, "And your mother's family is from Patna too? What is your mother's title?"

In America, they always say "last name." When I heard Shastriji use the word "title," it took me back home. Later on, however, I got the feeling that he had wanted to find out about my caste, but I cannot be certain of this.

Shastriji's father had been the postmaster in Patna. I must have heard his name when I lived at home. Every morning my father read out the names of all the officials in the news stories printed in the Patna edition of *Hindustan Times*.

"B. K. Singh has been transferred again."

"K. N. Das has been moved back to Supply."

"Rameshwar babu is still holding on. *Bahut* stubborn *aadmi hai.*"

The decision against the *Times of India* was taken in our household because the regional editor is a Bengali. The editor of *Hindustan Times* is from our own caste. It is true that we do not know him personally, but my uncle said the editor might even be related to us.

By the time two cups of tea had been drunk, and the whole newspaper read, my father was ready to proclaim: "It is useless to talk about this, this is only what can happen in Laloo's raj. . . ." When I left India, Laloo Yadav was still the chief minister of Bihar. Now, his wife is in that office; Laloo is in and out of prison these days.

I am sure I had heard the name of Shastriji's father on some of those mornings. It used to annoy me to hear my father go on and on with his list, but it is now one of the things I miss about home.

I have been living in this country for the past two years. Everyone tells me that the first years are the ones during which you have to struggle the most. I think that is natural. I did not see a bright future for myself in Bihar. Some people said to me that I should go to Delhi. But everyone was leaving for Delhi. Even the servants wanted to go there. I heard our servant Mantu one day talking about Palika Bazaar.

So I stayed behind. When the chance came to go to America, I took it. And I have been happy here. It is not very cold, except in winter. Three months after my arrival, I bought a coat for sixty-five dollars and also boots and gloves. Cooking is a bit of a problem, but you can buy rice that is ready in a minute.

It is called Minute-Rice. I think my English has improved. I'm less worried about money now.

I had come home that evening and was cutting cauliflower for my dinner when the phone rang. My roommate was Esra, an African man. I let him pick up the phone because he got most of the calls, but he said it was for me.

It was Shastriji. He said, "Were you cooking?"

"No, no, I was just washing my face," I said. I might have lied because I thought I would not be invited to his apartment if I said I was cooking.

Shastriji said, "Why don't you come over for tea?"

"Right now?" I said.

He said, "Yes, yes. It is only two minutes away. The kettle is already on the stove."

I had hoped the invitation would be for dinner. It was already seven in the evening. "Okay," I said.

"*Theek hai,*" he said. And added, "No formality."

Shastriji's wife and children were waiting behind the door. I was introduced to them.

Shastriji's wife was perhaps my age. She was tall and a little thin. Her face was pretty. She was dressed in a simple cotton sari but she had put on lipstick to look more presentable. Her name was Madhu. She folded her hands in greeting and said, "I have seen you walking to the university several times." From the way she spoke, it was clear that she was also from Bihar.

I learned the names of the children, Manav and Chitra. Chitra had pink butterflies clipped to her hair and she clung to her mother's sari. The boy said, "Uncle, do you want to see my website?" Shastriji laughed and shooed him off. I kept standing. Madhu went to get the tea. The kitchen was at the other end of the room. This was a graduate student apartment owned by the university. A large dining table took up much of the space.

Shastriji gestured toward the small sofa nearby. "Sit down," he said. He himself sat on the carpet, his legs folded under him. There was a pile of newspapers behind him. I was impressed that he bought papers here. The *New York Times* cost a whole dollar, and I picked it up only in the university cafeteria when people left it on the table.

I said, "The newspapers in America are thicker than the Patna phone directory."

Shastriji laughed. He said, "People don't talk to each other here. That is why they need such thick papers."

When Madhu brought the tea, Shastriji said, "Your bhabhi wanted to meet you."

She smiled and said, "He did not even ask you whether you were married!"

I had been to three Indian homes since coming to America. At each place, I was asked this question in the first ten minutes; I was happy I had identified a national trait. I said, "My mother is worried that I will marry a white girl here."

Madhu said, "Do you know Atul?" I did not know whom she was talking about. Shastriji said, "He's from Benares. Nice boy. Statistics."

Madhu said, "He has got a black girlfriend. Cynthia. *Baap re baap*, think of what his mother will say." I had seen an Indian with a black woman on campus; last year, they had also come together for the Diwali festival on the College Green. Now I knew who they were.

Later, when Shastriji and I were talking, Madhu came and asked me, "Do you like vegetarian or non-vegetarian?" I turned to Shastriji. I said, "I was just about to start cooking when you called."

Epilogue: Indian Restaurant

"No, no. You eat here," he said.

"I had taken the chicken out from the fridge," I lied again. "I should go. Some other time."

They were both persistent in a nice way and I stayed for dinner. Madhu went to the far end, where the stove was and began cooking.

Shastriji lit a cigarette and said, "Do you take anything alcoholic?"

He sounded a bit uncomfortable asking the question. So I said, "Sometimes."

He got up and said without any fuss, "Let's have some whiskey." I kept sitting while Shastriji padded across, barefoot, to his fridge. In front of me was a framed poster of a Festival of India exhibition in Chicago. Madhu was frying onions. She had placed a pressure cooker on the second stove.

When Shastriji brought a bottle of Johnny Walker and two glasses with ice, I said, "I haven't had a chance to go to many bars yet."

"No need to," he said. While he unscrewed the bottle, the cigarette was clutched between his lips. The smoke made him screw up his eyes. Madhu came into the part of the room where we were sitting, picked a pair of shoes from the floor, then climbed the stairs without saying anything to us.

"Why should we go to bars?" Shastriji asked. But he didn't answer the question. I stayed silent.

I took my glass and said, "Cheers."

He said, "To Bihar." And laughed.

I was hungry and the first sip of the whiskey cut into my stomach like sharp glass. But it felt good. I began feeling light-headed. There was music playing on the stereo in the corner, and Shastriji hit the repeat button when the Mastt-Mastt song from *Mohra* reached its end.

Shastriji said, "Do you go to coffeehouses? There's a great culture here of coffeehouses. . . . But I don't like bars. I like drinking at home."

"Yes," I said.

A little later we had dinner. There was chola and mutton, with raita on the side. Madhu also made puris. I had not eaten a puri for at least a year. I ate the food greedily, but so did Shastriji. I did not feel very bad about my gluttony. Madhu joined us when we were finishing up. She asked me a few questions about my sisters. After dinner, Shastriji stretched his legs out on the carpet and lit another cigarette.

We decided to have another drink. The kids could be heard in the room upstairs. I heard Madhu's voice talking to them. What would I call her? Madhu or bhabhi? She was attractive but a little withdrawn. I think she was lonely.

"Why would you want to go to bars?" Shastriji asked. The drink was making him repeat himself, but I didn't mind.

"For the experience," I said.

Some time passed. Then, as if I still needed to explain something, I added, "I would like to have a drink in a proper bar. To be served cocktails."

Shastriji nodded and then I became conscious that the music had stopped a while ago.

"When I was in Patna," he spoke in the silence, raising his right arm above him, "when the barber came . . . after shaving me, he would take his razor and shave my armpits."

Shastriji dropped his arm and said, "You can't get that kind of service here. So, why go to bars? Eat well and drink well at home, and be happy."

We had Halloween in November. I dressed up as Dracula for Manav and Chitra. They liked it when I laughed loudly and showed my fangs. Both of the kids wore small plastic masks. I noticed that even when children are wearing Halloween masks, you can so easily read the fear in their eyes and shapeless mouths.

I took Manav and Chitra trick-or-treating to every door in our neighborhood. Madhu had dressed Chitra in a pink *lehenga* with gold embroidery; she thought an Indian dress worked fine as a Halloween costume. When people gave candy to Chitra, they said things like, "Oh, look! An Indian princess."

Two days after Halloween, I got a call at home from Shastriji. Madhu's father had died. She got the news that morning from India. "Massive heart attack," Shastriji said on the phone. Madhu's father had been a well-to-do farmer in Purnea and ran a small publishing business. I went over to Westcott at once. Madhu had wiped all the makeup from her face and was wearing her long black hair loose. Her eyes looked unnaturally large. She had been crying.

I did not know what to say when I was in front of her. Shastriji smoked cigarettes and lowered his voice whenever Madhu came downstairs.

He told me that the Indian Students Association was going to invite Naseeruddin Shah to visit our campus. The actor was on a tour of the United States. This was exciting news. Shastriji was not very optimistic. He thought that the Indians who held office in the association were stupid and elitist.

He said, "English-speaking Doon School types. Rambo *ke aulaad hain.* They wouldn't know Naseeruddin Shah even if he was their father."

Madhu came down once again. She looked at me and asked me if I was very busy. I said no. She said, "Can you get some of your friends to come for dinner next Saturday? It will be for Babuji, for the peace of his soul. I should feed six of you."

I said, "Sure."

Shastriji and Madhu were Brahmins. I was not. In their family in Patna, I am certain that it was unmarried Brahmin youth who would have been fed after a ceremony. But how were they going to get so many Brahmins here? Both of them had clearly discussed this already and it was OK with them. I didn't mind. I got five others—only two of them Indian—to come with me for dinner. Half of them were American students from my own sociology department, eager to eat Indian food; the others were *desi* students I had met during the orientation week at International House.

We gathered in front of Willard Building and then walked to Shastriji's place. The apartment always smelled of food, but today the smell was especially welcoming. On the stereo, Bhimsen Joshi was singing *bhajans*. Shastriji wore a white *kurta* over his jeans. He looked freshly bathed.

Madhu had made fish because her father liked it. There was basmati rice and potato cutlets. Madhu said she looked for curd but the yogurt they sold here was nothing like the curds that her father loved. So she was giving us spoonfuls of sour cream from its plastic container. It was very rich and went well with the food. She served us gulab jamun at the end.

Shastriji didn't join us for dinner. While the guests were having their gulab jamun, he sat down at the table with a heaped plate of food. I went and sat next to him. He asked me, "*Mazaa aaya?*"

I had liked the food, so I nodded. Sometimes, at Shastriji's house, I surprised myself by my appetite. I now wanted some whiskey, but I did not know whether it would be appropriate. Did Madhu's father like whiskey? Shastriji said he had to take a driving test the next day. While chewing on the food, he asked me if I could come with him.

Epilogue: Indian Restaurant

At the driving license office, they wanted Shastriji to take a written test first. We needed to consult a manual for that purpose. I didn't have a license, although I used to have one in India. Shastriji had never driven before. I decided to take the test with him.

Both of us stood in front of computer terminals and touched the screen to answer yes or no to questions. The questions were from the manual. "If there are two yellow lines in the middle of the street, is it permitted to cross the line?" Shastriji bit his lip and often refused to make up his mind about the right response. Now and again, he would ask me for the answer in Hindi. I helped him. He did not know what "double parking" meant. This required a more detailed explanation. I looked around and began answering, but stopped when I saw a blonde who was wearing thick glasses looking at us.

I passed; Shastriji failed. He tried again the following week and did well. We had to return for the driving test. This test was more difficult. Shastriji had only driven around in a parking lot with his Chilean friend, Ricardo. The examiner was a tall, black man wearing dark glasses. He was very dignified and didn't waste any words. In his right hand, he carried a clipboard. Shastriji became nervous and started speaking to him in Hindi. The examiner turned to look at me but didn't say a word.

It was impossible to know what he was thinking. I looked at Shastriji and spoke to him in Hindi. I asked him, "Shall we let it be today?"

Shastriji quickly said, "Yes, let's go."

He looked back at the examiner and said to him in English, "Thank you." Neither of us got the license. Shastriji came out of the building and lit his cigarette. He laughed loudly. He said, "*Saala*, America *mein bahut tamaasha hai.*"

I thought of the examiner. Shastriji had said, "Damn, there is a lot of show in America." I thought of the tall man's gravitas. He had been so silent; I wondered what he thought of us.

As if to prove a point, I returned by myself for the test later, after two or three weeks had passed. I got the license in the mail a week before Christmas. Madhu said that when they had found a good secondhand car, I was to take her to the mall for holiday shopping. I said yes. We had just finished eating in Shastriji's home.

Madhu laughed when I told her about Shastriji asking me questions in Hindi during the written test. Shastriji didn't seem to mind my revealing all this. He chuckled quietly from time to time as he listened to me telling Madhu our story. I didn't tell Madhu the part about his becoming nervous and beginning to speak to the examiner in Hindi.

Shastriji got up and went to the kitchen sink. Madhu said to him that he wasn't to wash any dishes. "There'll be no one worse than me if you do that," she said to him in Hindi. It was clear to me that she loved him very much.

Shastriji filled a glass with water. Then he looked at me and said, "You should get married. You will not even have the freedom to drink water then." Madhu kept smiling. I remember thinking then that it was not only her love—she was also more patient with him than others were.

A few days later, I passed the Insomnia Coffee House and saw Shastriji inside sitting with an elderly man. The man had curly gray hair on the sides of his head. He gave me a limp hand when I was introduced to him. I noticed that Shastriji was not at ease and kept speaking to me in English. I left a few minutes later.

Shastriji called me on the phone that night. That man was his department head. Shastriji was having some problems with his thesis supervisor. I asked him what the problem was and he replied vaguely, "*Arre*, politics." I began to hear from one or two *desis* that Shastriji did not do much writing. His teaching evaluations were also low. His situation in the university was turning precarious. The most effort Shastriji made toward getting a degree was to invite a faculty member for dinner at his house. A German graduate student in my department who was older than I twisted his mouth and said, "Your friend Shastri is going to have problems with any supervisor who doesn't like Indian food."

A month later, the accident took place. I think it gave Shastriji an excuse to go back to India. I have not heard from him since he left; my father wrote in a letter that he had run into Shastriji at a wedding and that he looked well. I often wonder about Shastriji and ask myself if he had really failed in America. Wasn't there a part of him that could be happy only back in India, in Bihar? He had gone home.

All the others who succeeded in this country did so only by changing. They became someone else. Shastriji, for better or worse, never changed. I don't know why he hasn't written to me. Perhaps that too is a sign of his not having changed. But, sometimes, I wonder whether Madhu blames me for the accident. I want her to write to me someday.

Shastriji bought the old Volvo from someone in his department four days after New Year's. It was after he had already bought his car that Shastriji succeeded in getting his license. It was freezing cold during those days. The first day we only talked on the phone. On the second day, however, Shastriji called again. He had a plan. The university hadn't reopened, so I too had nothing to do. I walked over to his house. He said, "Let's take a drive in the parking lot."

We stood on the road with our hands in our coat pockets and inspected the car. It was old but looked OK. The blue paint had faded and some parts of the car looked rusty. The tires would need to be changed. Then we got in. Shastriji said that the steering wheel was a little unresponsive. But the heater worked and it was comfortable in the car. We took it around the neighborhood and then the parking lot, where during the academic season all the buses idled.

On the way back, Shastriji double-parked in front of the corner grocery store run by a Lebanese named Joe. Leaving me in the car, Shastriji hurried in to get his pack of Marlboros. When he came back, he said, "*Achha,* if you leave your emergency lights on when you double-park, will the police still give you a ticket?"

I said I didn't know and I took a cigarette from Shastriji. It felt good to smoke in that cold. Shastriji said, "There is only one advantage to driving: we won't need to walk in the cold to the grocery store anymore." I looked at the peeling skin around his fingers as he clutched the steering wheel.

The car wasn't used much. Shastriji drove it to the grocery store with Madhu and once, when I was there, to the mall to buy two sweaters and a new blender. Shastriji drove rather slowly, and people, as they sped by, sometimes looked back at us.

Shastriji did not care. While driving, he kept looking at me in the rearview mirror as he spoke. Our talking made Madhu uncomfortable. As a rule, she sat next to Shastriji in the front. She kept saying, "Keep your eyes on the road."

But Shastriji was not one for listening to such advice. I was only rarely bothered by this; being with Shastriji meant not giving the rest of the world much heed. It was as if we were back in Bihar. In the car that day, Shastriji was telling me about a man in his department who had gone to India as a hippie.

His name was Larry Drieker. Shastriji spelled his name for me, the ringed index finger of his right hand rising above the steering wheel. He said, "Wherever Larry Drieker went in India, he found out that Indians everywhere called him Lorry Driver. All over the country, *Kashmir se Kanya Kumari tak.* . . ." Shastriji and I laughed.

I had noticed that I laughed a lot at Shastriji's stories, even when they were not very funny. When I spent time at their apartment, I would try to be spirited and full of stories. Madhu loved my tales, particularly when they involved details about how young American women behaved. I think, somewhere in my heart, I felt I needed to earn the food I ate so greedily at their table.

In February, Shastriji wanted to travel to Chicago. His passport was to be renewed at the Indian consulate. Perhaps he had already decided that they were going back to India. When they mentioned the trip to Chicago, they talked of going to India only for a visit. Madhu was excited. It seemed to me that a visit would erase the ache she had felt when she couldn't go home after her father's sudden death.

Madhu said, "You have not seen Chicago. Come with us." I said yes readily.

Shastriji said, "Chalo, chalo. We will eat good Indian food on Devon Street."

In spite of the cold, we went to the shores of Lake Michigan after our visit to the Indian consulate. The water was a freezing expanse of blue and white. After a minute, we ducked back in the Volvo. An Indian taxi driver, with *paan* in his mouth, gave us directions to Devon Street. He called it Diwan Street.

It was two o'clock when we sat down for lunch. We ate hurriedly and we ate too much. Shastriji said, "Let's drink some beer for proper digestion." Madhu shook her head, but I was ready.

While we were drinking, Shastriji asked Madhu to go to the Gujarati store across the street and buy paan. When she was gone, he called the waiter. He said, "Please pack ten naans and two tandoori chicken. Please pack it quickly." On the way back, the car smelled of onion and the chicken. Madhu complained about the smell. Shastriji said, "At dinner-time tonight, you will be thanking me." Shastriji and I were sitting in the front; I was driving. When I looked at him, Shastriji laughed. The paan had turned his teeth red and they glistened under his dark gums.

We were still an hour away from home when a light freezing rain began to fall. The sun hadn't gone down and the light lit up the valley to our left. The children were getting drowsy and irritable in the back. Madhu said to them, "Look." She was pointing at a rainbow. It arched over the valley. A few cars passed with their lights on, spraying our windscreen with water. Shastriji began telling me about his old grandmother in Bhagalpur.

I cannot now remember what he was saying. All I remember is his starting to talk about his grandmother standing on the roof of her house and a rainbow above the Ganga. In the rain, the car skidded first into the lane on the left. I must have braked very hard when the car went out of control because under me I suddenly felt the car spin around with a shriek. I thought we were going to hit the rails in the middle of the highway.

Instead, in that long moment of spinning and shrieking, the car seemed to float on water. I heard Madhu's voice behind me but I don't know what she was saying. Then a pickup van hit us smack on the side and came to a stop. The car spun on impact and, for a split second, it must have appeared as if we had parked next to the van. Within that second, however, the truck that had been following the pickup van had hit us from behind.

This time the car sped toward the rails on the right side. Glass rained on me. For some absurd reason, I thought of the glass getting into the packages of tandoori chicken at the back. When we stopped, I tried feebly to open the car door. I said, "Shastriji." I heard nothing from my side. The children were screaming, it seemed, in my ear. That noise mixed with the loud sound coming from inside me. I was having trouble breathing. Not much time had passed but it seemed that it was already evening.

And then, out of nowhere, I saw in front of me the face of my elder sister in Patna. There were tears falling from her eyes. I stayed with that face till I thought I heard the wailing sounds of the sirens, which meant that the police, or perhaps the ambulance, had arrived.

When I saw them again, Shastriji was in the hospital. Madhu was in shock. Shastriji had to remain under close watch for four days because the cut on his head had worried the doctors. Madhu and the children had small bruises and cuts. I had broken a rib where my chest hit the steering wheel. The car would not be driven again.

Madhu's brother-in-law, Rakesh, a software engineer and industrialist in Delhi, happened to be in London for a fortnight. He came over to the United States for a weekend visit when he heard the news. Rakesh was a quiet man who spoke very elegant Hindi. One night we were together at the hospital and he took me to a Chinese restaurant for dinner; he sipped his beer methodically and spoke in English about the benefits of liberalization. He said things like, "If things keep going this way, in ten years there is no saying where India will be. India, not China, will be the sleeping giant that has at long last woken up."

Before Rakesh left, we brought Shastriji home from the hospital.

A couple of nights later, I was sitting with Shastriji watching the late-night news on the TV. Shastriji turned to me and said that he was thinking of quitting smoking. I thought that this was a great idea. When Madhu came down after putting the children to sleep, I said to her, "Boss is thinking of quitting smoking."

Madhu came near us and said to me, "You should go home." I thought she was worried that I was overstraining myself; I said I was alright but would leave soon. She said, "No, I meant India." I became quiet, and nodded. I was surprised by her abruptness. Then, she said, "We should too." I didn't ask her why. I thought back to the time when her father had died. I began remembering that Shastriji and I had talked about Naseeruddin Shah. Naseeruddin had fallen sick in Boston and was unable to come to our campus. At least Naseeruddin was now back in India.

I said, "Rakesh has the kind of money that makes living in America look like a stupid idea."

Madhu kept that calm expression of hers and said, "Money is never the reason why anyone says they are happy."

I could see that Madhu had changed. I remembered the evening I had taken her in their car to the mall for what Madhu had called "holiday shopping." She must have picked up the phrase from the ads on radio or television. After we had finished buying the things she needed, Madhu asked me in Hindi, "Will you eat something?" I suddenly liked the idea of going to a restaurant alone with her. I said, "You eat, I'll have a beer."

There was a T.G.I. Friday inside the mall. We went in and ordered some nachos with cheese. The beer was cheap. I was telling Madhu stories about being at a graduate student party one weekend. A woman named Eloise asked me to dance with her. I liked Eloise. I thought she was pretty. But she also made me nervous. I didn't know how to dance. Awkwardly, I shuffled my feet and swayed my upper body to the music, as Eloise made encouraging noises. Madhu said, "What happened after that?" I shrugged. Nothing had happened but I wanted to tease Madhu with the thought that something might have transpired that evening between Eloise and me. I wanted her to think I was someone that women liked. She smiled. Madhu's smile always reached her eyes. I felt this was the best part about talking to her.

We went on talking and I ordered another beer. Then the snow started to fall. The sight made us happy; it was as if we were back in India and the rain had begun to fall at the end of summer. I said this to Madhu and she began to talk of the rain in Purnea, how she would turn up her face to the clouds and feel the raindrops on her skin. I wanted to talk to Madhu about her childhood, but it was beginning to get late. In another half an hour it would be dark, and driving would be difficult.

When we stepped out of the mall into the open, the sight of all the snow made me suddenly feel cold. Impulsively, I drew closer to Madhu and she surprised me by taking my arm. My first thought was that I hadn't ever touched her. And then it struck me that we must appear to others right now as lovers. It might have been the beer I had drunk, but I remember feeling very content with the pressure of Madhu's body at my side, her black hair so close to my mouth. Half an hour later, we were home with Shastriji and the children.

That evening seems very distant now. Madhu was talking of going home and her voice betrayed an edge that I did not understand. I also began hearing from other people that Shastriji was going back to India. And then, Shastriji began to interrupt our own conversations to ask me whether I was coming back to Patna with them. He would say, "I will have a badminton court made in my garden. There we can play even in the winter."

I didn't find out whether Shastriji ever received his degree. There was no reason for me to ask him directly. It would have been rude. I heard Madhu saying to her Malaysian neighbor, "I am very happy that I came to this country. I am very happy that I am going back."

I decided I would ask Madhu more about this. But as the day of their departure neared, there were more and more chores to do. I did everything I could to help them, buying boxes from U-Haul with my own money, and using them to pack all the children's toys and books in them. One night, Shastriji was playing a tape of S. D. Burman's music. I began talking about the actress Nutan, and how my mother used to like her. The film *Bandini* had been released when my mother was a young bride. She was alone in the village with her in-laws, away from her friends and family, and would sing the songs she had heard on the radio. When I said this, Madhu began to sob. Shastriji suddenly became serious. His face wore a pained expression. He did not even look at me. I could not even ask Madhu what was wrong. Our conversation had touched on some hurt or regret, and Shastriji seemed to be aware of it. All at once, I too wanted to go home to Patna.

I often return to that moment when I remember them. It seems I have remained stuck there, while they have gone on to some place that I now know nothing about. I am still at the university. Next year, I will probably apply for admission to a doctoral program in Chicago. Only five weeks have passed since Shastriji left. Maybe Madhu will write me a letter. It is entirely possible Shastriji has mentioned this to Madhu a couple of times already. I can see him saying to her while drinking tea, "This is not nice. We should write him a letter. Why don't you write him a letter. . . ?"

I was thinking of Shastriji when I was at Xanadu Café today. One afternoon, soon after Shastriji had bought the car, we were both sitting there. He was smoking and nodding his head the way he used to do while listening to me. He looked at the people walking in and out. It was so cold outside that the glass walls of the cafe had misted over. It seemed to me that with every word I spoke my breath froze on the glass.

Shastriji interrupted me and said, "Let's go to Shalimar. We'll digest some samosas. *Mazaa aayega.*" Shastriji often said "digest" instead of "eating" and made the whole act appear very slow and leisurely.

I followed him out. As soon as I stepped out, I regretted it. The cold instantly entered my bones. Shastriji was unfazed. Unlike me, he never wore gloves. He lit a cigarette. I said, "Why are we doing this for a wretched samosa?"

He said, "Jab tak rahega samosa mein aloo, Tab tak rahega Bihar mein Laloo." Till we have in our samosas aloo, In Bihar we shall always have Laloo.

The restaurant was a good ten minutes away. At last, we got there. The owner was a Pakistani, Javed. He welcomed us with a smile. He took Shastriji's hand in both his hands. When we sat down, Shastriji laughed and repeated, "Jab tak rahega samosa mein aloo, Tab tak rahega Bihar mein Laloo."

While we were waiting, Atul and his black girlfriend, whose name I didn't remember, walked in. Shastriji looked up and saw them. He grinned his black-gummed grin and waved them over to us.

Atul said, "Hello." I was introduced to him. He shook my hand.

Shastriji said, "Hello Cynthia, long time no see." She smiled and leaning forward kissed him on the right cheek. I was introduced to Cynthia. She said, "Very nice to meet you."

I was meeting Cynthia for the first time. She was beautiful and even her voice was a part of her allure. Cynthia spoke to Shastriji, "So, how come you are here?"

Shastriji chuckled. When he laughed in an embarrassed way, his laugh struggled in his paunch. His laughter was a delaying tactic. Soon, he had an answer. He said, "We are celebrating the end of a politician called Laloo Yadav."

Cynthia looked puzzled. She glanced at Atul. Shastriji proceeded to explain the slogan he had been reciting: as long as there was aloo or potato in the samosa, in Bihar we would have Laloo. He said, "But, in this restaurant, you get samosas with meat in it. So, we're celebrating Laloo's cultural demise."

Everyone smiled politely. We sipped our tea and waited for the samosas. When the food came, Shastriji continued in a philosophical vein. He bit into a samosa and said, "We have come to America and made something new. Look at you two, for example."

Atul and Cynthia smiled. Then Cynthia turned her face to me. At this distance, you felt you could drown in her eyes. She said, "Are you from India? Or Pakistan?"

Before I could answer, Shastriji said, "What is the difference?"

Often, when I was in Shastriji's company, I was able to relax and just be myself. I think we both knew who we were when we were with each other. I didn't need to hide from him the fact that I didn't have an impressive record behind me or a future that was calling out to me; I was a youngish man from Bihar, single and somewhat aimless, stranded in this new land

Epilogue: Indian Restaurant

called America. Shastriji reminded me of my uncles. They put off things till tomorrow, and they knew that in some way tomorrow never comes. But in front of strangers, Shastriji could affect a deep gravity. This was a part of his charm, and it dawned on me later that this might have been the main reason why I spent so much time with him.

Shastriji had asked Cynthia that last question with a fine seriousness. He continued to smile faintly. Cynthia raised her lovely, plucked eyebrows. She said, "What is the difference? I don't know. You tell me."

Shastriji looked at her for a long moment and then, still smiling, began reciting the famous lines of Ali Sardar Jafri: "Tum aao gulshan-e-Lahore se chaman bardosh / Hum aayen subh-e-Banaras ki roshnee le kar. . ." He repeated the two lines because he could not recall what came next. Then, Shastriji mumbled a few words and said, "Aur iske baad yeh poochein ki kaun dushman hai?"

The words that Shastriji had remembered were delivered with a fine intensity. Cynthia had looked at Atul when Shastriji mentioned Benares. That was where Atul was from. She now asked Shastriji, "What does it mean?"

This was the woman whom Shastriji as well as his wife were in some ways opposed to, and perhaps even looked down upon, because of the color of her skin. But I don't think Shastriji was the least bit conscious of his prejudice now. I cannot say whether it was a part of something new, or whether it was a return to an older, more dignified part of Shastriji's past. What I understood very clearly was that he had another sense of himself, and also of Cynthia, as he looked at her and smiled.

Shastriji nodded and took another drag from his cigarette. Then, once again affecting his noble charm, he translated Sardar Jafri's words for her in a very conversational way. He first looked at the restaurant owner, Javed, in the corner and then pointed to Cynthia. He said: "You come to me laden with the flowers from the gardens of Lahore. I will come bearing the light of the morning of Benares. . . . There is a line that I am forgetting. . . . After that, together we can ask, who is the enemy?"

There was a pause during which Shastriji drew on the cigarette. Cynthia was smiling. She waited a moment. Then, she said, "That's so beautiful."

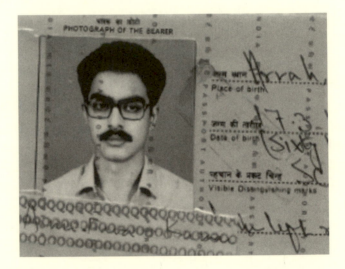

ACKNOWLEDGMENTS

I want to thank the NEH, Yale, and the Institute for the Arts and the Humanities at Penn State, for the expected reasons; Dan Cottom, for being there from the start; Pankaj Mishra, for his example and his encouragement; Raza Mir, Lis Harris, Amir Khan, Gulzar, Namvar Singh, and Hap Veeser, for their gifts; Shoma Chaudhury, for giving me a column and, on occasion, money; Rob Nixon and Amit Chaudhuri for being as good readers as they are writers; Hanif Kureishi for being Hanif Kureishi; William Germano for his enthusiasm; David Davidar and Kamini Mahadevan for their welcome help; Zahid Ebrahim, Jaya Sarma, Laura Schere, Rakesh Chandra, Jeff Nealon, and Arun Agrawal, for being in my life; the members of my family in Patna, Virginia, Karachi, and Toronto, for their support; Sonam, Satya, and Mishu, for their magic; and Mona, my love and fellow traveler, for her laughter.

Page 3. Sonam, my little nephew, was showing me his colorful new paper mask. It was summer, and the sun had already set. In this photograph, Sonam is standing outside the house in Patna where my parents used to live when I left India for America.

Page 12. My elder sister was working as a doctor in a hospital in the small town of Darbhanga, in Bihar, in the mid-1990s. I met this boy there. He had fallen from a tree and broken his hip, and also his arm and leg. His parents sat beside him. They had brought him some days back to the hospital from their village, but it was already too late. The doctors had to amputate the boy's right arm because the gangrene had begun to spread.

Page 20. On a recent visit to Patna, I found a vehicle parked near my old school. It would be used to transport the electricity generator for the wedding bands. All the signs in the picture—including one that says "Do Not Disturb" in the right-hand corner—are a little off. The painted image of the man with the tie interested me for the same reason. He is trying to don the modern look: he bears a certain resemblance to the image in my first passport. See p. 258.

Page 63. This policeman was sitting with the rest of his patrol at a bus stop in New Delhi. This photograph is more than a decade old. Now, it is more common to see automatic machine guns in the hands of such policemen.

Page 72. In Patna, on the banks of the Ganga, I came across two laborers. They were loading sand on a tractor trailer. It is not only in Patna that one might meet laborers from other parts of Bihar; they do this work in faraway cities like Delhi, Bombay, and Calcutta, as well.

Page 74. The two old women, both Bangladeshi Hindu refugees, were sitting on the floor of the unreserved train compartment. They were on their way to Mughalsarai. I remember the train journey for another reason: I was on my way to the Buxar prison, to interview a peasant activist who had been denied trial for three years.

Page 84. My grandmother—interrupted in her prayers, the beads hiding in her hands—is sitting in my uncle's crumbling house in Bettiah, about an hour's journey by car from our village. When my grandmother died, my link with the village broke.

Page 98. The poet Alokdhanwa read for me in his flat in our hometown. It was in Patna again that I heard Alok reading recently. He was reciting "Girls in Flight" when the youth at the back of the gathering began to giggle and whistle at the mention of illicit romance. Alok stopped reading and looked at the leering men. He said, "Try to understand a bit. How barbaric is this society . . . that even after death a woman is known only by her husband's name."

Page 123. Two friends of mine took a cigarette break during their dance rehearsal at the Desh-Pardesh festival in Toronto. Young South Asians show up in droves for *desi* cultural events in places like Toronto, Los Angeles, and New York City.

Page 123. A South Asian man stood in front of a poster of Madhubala, the heartthrob from the Bollywood cinema of the 1950s. I took this picture on Girard Street in Toronto. A few years later I got married to a Pakistani woman in that city, and it was from the shops on this same street that my clothes were bought for the wedding.

Page 127. On Friday afternoons, the crowd of worshippers at the New Market mosque in Patna spills out into the streets. Tufani, who was cutting my hair, hurried through his job quickly, and I followed him out to take a picture as he joined the line of the faithful.

Page 128. The priests in Deogarh, Bihar, can tell you your family history if you give them the name of your village and an ancestor. I spent many a New Year's Day at this temple. My father would take the whole family there. We ate only after we had offered prayers. The day was special and I looked forward to eating chicken.

Page 179. Punjabi cabbies at La Guardia airport in August, 1997. I had just arrived in the city to take pictures at the India

About the Pictures

Day Parade. It was the fiftieth anniversary of Indian independence. This was the first picture I took after landing in New
York City.

Page 181. This is how a British joke goes: "Why don't Asians
play football?" "Because every time they get a corner, they
open a shop." The grocery stores in the East Village, near Sixth
Street, are the American equivalent of the stereotypical symbol
of British Asians—the cornershop.

Page 199. "Make Whitey Pay." The young man in the picture had picked up his ornament during the 2001 carnival in
Trinidad. He had arrived in New York City just in time for the
India Day Parade. A member of the NYPD was happy to pose
with the sign.

Page 209. I took this picture in a snack store in Jersey City.
In such places, I love the cheap food, the formica tables, and
the bad lighting. The previous evening I had attended a cultural
festival organized by the progressive South Asian youth. A sign
on the food table said, "Eat Samosa. Fight Racism. $1"

Page 217. Immigration help in Jersey City. Our lives are so
often reduced to pieces of paper: a visa, a passport, a green card.
But we also hold paper worthless. For the Indians in the diaspora, the sense of national identity is constructed not from sections of the Constitution, but from the small consumer items
we buy in the *desi* grocery stores, things like Chyawanprash or
Multani Matti or Lijjat Papad.

Page 258. The photograph from my first passport, which was
issued in April 1986. I would travel in a plane for the first time.

PAPER

There is a short story I like: see A. K. Ramanujan's "Annayya's Anthropology," trans. by Narayan Hegde, in Ramachandra Sharma, ed., *From Cauvery to Godavari: Modern Kannada Short Stories*. New Delhi: Penguin, 1991, 44–53.

The PL 480 library program: see Maureen L. P. Patterson, ed., *South Asian Library Resources in North America: A Survey Prepared for the Boston Conference, 1974*. London: Inter Documentation Company, 1975, 11–12.

The environmental scientist Vandana Shiva: see Vandana Shiva, *The Violence of the Green Revolution*. Dehra Dun, India: Research Foundation for Science and Ecology, 1989, 5–11.

This lesson about the worldliness of books: see Raj Kamal Jha, *The Blue Bedspread*. New Delhi: Picador India, 1999, 176–80.

In that wonderful memoir: see C. L. R. James, *Beyond a Boundary*. Durham, N.C.: Duke University Press, 1993, 113.

In a short story by a Hindi writer: see Uday Prakash, *Paul Gomra Ka Scooter.* New Delhi: Radhakrishan Prakashan, 1997, 38–39.

GOING BACK

On the last page of *Miguel Street:* see V. S. Naipaul, *Miguel Street.* New York: Vanguard Press, 1959, 222.

At that time, I hadn't read: see V. S. Naipaul, *The Enigma of Arrival.* New York: Vintage, 1987, 156.

He had been told that if he ate meat: see M. K. Gandhi, *The Story of My Experiments With Truth.* Ahmedabad, India: Navjivan, 1927, 13–18.

Who is an N.R.I.?: see Pankaj Mishra, *Butter Chicken in Ludhiana: Travels in Small Town India.* New Delhi: Penguin, 1995, 88–89.

Naipaul had once impressed: see Paul Theroux, *Sir Vidia's Shadow.* New York: Houghton Mifflin, 1998, 346.

A well-known Indian critic: see Meenakshi Mukherjee, *The Perishable Empire.* New Delhi: Oxford University Press, 2000, 168–69.

In the novel, the writer Amit Chatterjee: see Vikram Seth, *A Suitable Boy.* New York: HarperCollins Publishers, 1994. First published 1993, 1369.

In a long essay published recently: see V. S. Naipaul, *Reading and Writing: A Personal Account.* New York: New York Review of Books, 2000, 15–16.

There is an account of Naipaul: see Theroux, *Sir Vidia's Shadow,* 326.

The headline read: see Sanjoy Hazarika, "Street Dramatist in India Slain Over Play." *New York Times,* January 4, 1989. See also Qamar Azad Hashmi, *The Fifth Flame: The Story of*

Safdar Hashmi, trans. by Madhu Prasad and Sohail Hashmi. New Delhi: Penguin, 1997.

The business of "nostalgia economics": see Salman Rushdie, *The Ground Beneath Her Feet*. New York: Henry Holt, 1999, 179.

BOMBAY

The year after Arundhati Roy won fame: see Arundhati Roy, *The God of Small Things*. New York: Random House, 1997. See also Roy, "The End of Imagination," in Roy, *The Cost of Living*. New York: Modern Library, 1999, 123, 196.

The Srikrishna Report states: see V. Krishna Ananth, "Action Needed on Srikrishna Report." *The Hindu*, November 9, 1999.

U. R. Ananthamurthy once wrote: see U. R. Ananthamurthy, "A Horse for the Sun," trans. from Kannada by Manu Shetty and A. K. Ramanujan, in Amit Chaudhuri, ed., *The Picador Book of Modern Indian Writing*. New Delhi: Picador, 2001, 239–65.

A visit to the village Khetolai: see Amitav Ghosh, *Countdown*. New Delhi: Ravi Dayal, 1999, 5–18, 88, 95–106.

Ramana's paper: see M. V. Ramana, *Bombing Bombay?* Cambridge: International Physicians for the Prevention of Nuclear War, 1999.

After the Taliban fled: see *New York Times*, November 15, 2001, A1.

In the lane behind my house: see Arundhati Roy, "The Ladies Have Feelings, So . . . Shall We Leave It to the Experts," in Arundhati Roy, *Power Politics*. Cambridge: South End Press, 2001. All other quotes, unless otherwise indicated, are from the same book.

The French sociologist: see Pierre Bourdieu, *Acts of Resistance*. Trans. by Richard Nice. New York: New Press, 1998, 39.

Writer is the midwife: see Arundhati Roy, "The Progressive Interview," with David Barsamian, *The Progressive*, April 2001, 33–39.

A Scottish newspaper: see James Hamilton, "How Arundhati Roy Took Back the Power in India," *Sunday Herald*, January 20, 2002.

A silver coin: see Liz Mathew, "Booker winner takes up Narmada cause," *India Abroad*, July 2, 1999.

Transforming experience into awareness: see Pankaj Mishra, "There is no shared literary culture in India," Rediff.com, http://www.rediff.com/chat/pankchat.htm.

Chevalier des Arts et des Lettres: see Shoma Chaudhury, "I, Good Globalization?," Tehelka.com, http://www.tehelka.com/channels/literary/2001/apr/27/lr042701roy.htm.

Rogue literary gene: see Tarun J. Tejpal, "New gold-rush in the east," in *Guardian*, August 14, 1999.

People get so angry with me: see Arundhati Roy, "The Progressive Interview," with David Barsamian, *The Progressive*, April 2001, 33–39.

Golden Rice: see Vandana Shiva, "Global Brahmanism," Interviewer Rebecca Gordon, *Colorlines*, Summer 2000, 30–32.

IN THE LIGHT OF SMALL TOWNS

Arundhati Roy: see Arundhati Roy, *The God of Small Things*, 122, 120, 26, and 14. Later references in the chapter to 257 and 259.

A video parlor: see Upamanyu Chatterjee, *English, August*. London: Faber and Faber, 1988, 208.

Older forms of globalization: see Mukul Kesavan, *Looking Through Glass*. Delhi: Ravi Dayal, 1995, 108.

India's "shabby borrowed modernity": see Pankaj Mishra, *Butter Chicken in Ludhiana: Travels in Small Town India*, 68, 10–11, 112–13. See also Mishra, *The Romantics*. New York: Random House, 2000, 3, 157–65, 91.

R. K. Narayan's Malgudi: see Ashis Nandy, *An Ambiguous Journey to the City*. New Delhi: Oxford University Press, 2001, 19, 26.

He wrote in his memoirs: see R. K. Narayan, *My Days*. First published in 1973. New York: Viking, 1974, 79–80. See also 66 and 115.

I could have profitably: see R. K. Narayan, *The Man-Eater of Malgudi*. First published 1961. New York: Penguin, 1983.

The delightful story: see R. K. Narayan, "A Horse and Two Goats," in R. K. Narayan, *A Horse and Two Goats*. New York,Viking, 1970, 5–26.

Scratch a relic: see Amit Chaudhuri, "A Bottle of Ink, a Pen and a Blotter," *London Review of Books* 23, no. 15, August 9, 2001.

An editorial in the *Statesman:* see Amit Chaudhuri, *A New World*. New York: Picador, 2000, 113. Later reference to 55.

Bengal-Bihar truck rumbling by: see Raj Kamal Jha, *The Blue Bedspread*, 57.

Bhaiyas from UP: see Ardashir Vakil, *Beach Boy*, 132.

The Bombay slum dwellers: see Rohinton Mistry, *A Fine Balance*. New York: Vintage, 1997, 311.

The others who are cosmopolitans: see Vikram Chandra, "The Cult of Authenticity," *Boston Review* no. 25, 1 (2000): 42–49.

All the toughest jobs: see Vikram Seth, *A Suitable Boy*, 1216.

To be translated into Hindi: see Harish Trivedi, "Epilogue/Epitaph," in *The Fiction of St Stephen's*, Aditya Bhattacharjea and Lola Chatterji, eds. Delhi: Ravi Dayal, 2000, 220–21.

The politician Piloo Doodhwala: see Salman Rushdie, *The Ground Beneath Her Feet*. New York: Henry Holt, 1999, 115.

Crude and witless buffoonery: see Pankaj Mishra, "The Emperor's New Clothes," *New Statesman*, April 9, 1999.

WINTER IN THE HINTERLAND

In Bihar both paucity and plenty: see Arvind N. Das, *The Republic of Bihar*. New Delhi: Penguin, 1992, 8.

The British Council library: see "Bihar runs on the mercy of God," Rediff.com, June, 2001.

Slave of MS.H6: see Amitav Ghosh, *In An Antique Land*. London: Granta Books, 1992.

Alok writes in Hindi: see Alokdhanwa, *Duniya Roz Banti Hai*. New Delhi: Rajkamal Prakashan, 1998. For my translation of Alokdhanwa's poems, see Amitava Kumar, "The Poet's Corpse in the Capitalist's Fish Tank," *Critical Inquiry* 23 (Summer 1997): 894–909. [A brief glossary of terms used in the poems: "daroga": head constable; "Laila": the heroine of the famous folktale about the two doomed lovers Laila and Majnu; "para": a small earthen bowl; "dupatta": a woman's scarf; "santoor": a musical instrument with fine strings that are touched by metal sticks.]

One such publication: see *Prasang*, nos. 7–8 (May–Oct. 1990): 1. For Alokdhanwa's poetry in that issue, see also 26–32.

A piece of criticism that was published in a small magazine: see Maheshwar, "*Sahitya Mein Mahilain*" (Women in Literature), *Samkaleen Janmat*, Aug. 1–15, 1994, 34–35.

LONDON

A section entitled "Prologue to an Autobiography": see V. S. Naipaul. *Finding the Center.* New York: Knopf, 1984, 1–72.

My friend fed me stories: see Amit Chaudhuri, *Afternoon Raga,* in Amit Chaudhuri, *Freedom Song.* New York: Knopf, 1999.

I began reading: see V. S. Naipaul, *A House for Mr Biswas.* New York: Knopf, 1961.

The collection of family letters: see V. S. Naipaul, *Between Father and Son.* Gillon Aitken, ed. New York: Knopf, 2000.

The themes of the letters: see Pankaj Mishra, "The House for Mr Naipaul," *New York Review of Books,* January 20, 2000.

In an interview: see Geoffrey Wheatcroft, "V. S. Naipaul: Scourge of the liberals," in *The Independent* (London), August 4, 2001.

Mr Burnett had been drawn from: see V. S. Naipaul. *Finding the Center.* All quotations from Naipaul, unless otherwise indicated, are from this book.

When asked by Elizabeth Hardwick: see Elizabeth Hardwick, "Meeting V. S. Naipaul," *New York Times Book Review,* May 13, 1979, 1, 36.

A portrait of Emperor Shah Jahan: see Stephen Schiff, "The Ultimate Exile," *The New Yorker,* May 23, 1994, 60–71.

PURE CHUTNEY

Now that you have come: see the documentary, *Pure Chutney* (scriptwriter, Amitava Kumar; director, Sanjeev Chatterjee; produced by Amitava Kumar and Sanjeev Chatterjee, 1998).

To be an Indian from Trinidad: see V. S. Naipaul, "East Indian," *The Reporter,* June 17, 1965. Reprinted in V. S.

Naipaul, *The Overcrowded Barracoon.* New York: Knopf, 1973, 30–38.

Dean Mohamed (1759–1851): see Michael H. Fisher, *The First Indian Author in English.* Delhi: Oxford University Press, 1996.

Gandhi's writings: see M. K. Gandhi, *An Autobiography or The Story of My Experiments With Truth.* Trans. by Mahadev Desai. Ahmedabad, India: Navajivan, 1927.

One of India's major post-independence novels: see Qurratulain Hyder, *River of Fire.* New Delhi: Kali for Women, 1998.

In a memoir: see Mulk Raj Anand, *Conversations in Bloomsbury.* New Delhi: Arnold Heinemann, 1981.

No tradition or model: see Pankaj Mishra, "A Spirit of Their Own," *New York Review of Books,* May 20, 1999.

Gibreel Farishta's decision: see Salman Rushdie, *The Satanic Verses.* New York: Viking, 1988.

Four maps: see Martin Rowson, "Literary London," *Granta* 65, 103–11.

A travelogue about a visit: see Hanif Kureishi, "Bradford," *Granta* 20, 147–70.

An Indian girl growing up: see Meera Syal, *Anita and Me.* New York: New Press, 1996.

Syal's second novel: see Meera Syal, *Life Isn't All Ha Ha Hee Hee.* Originally published 1999. New York: New Press, 2000.

MY HANIF KUREISHI LIFE

I have a newspaper clipping: see Joydeep Gupta, "Cultural Politics Dissected," in *The Statesman,* February 13, 1987, 3.

Raj revival: see Salman Rushdie, "Outside the Whale," first published in *Granta* 11 (1983), and reprinted in Salman

Rushdie, *Imaginary Homelands*. New York: Granta Books, 1991.

Forster's days: see E. M. Forster, "Kanaya," in E. M. Forster, *The Hill of Devi and Other Indian Writings*. London: Edward Arnold, 1983, 310–24.

In a letter to his friend: see P. N. Furbank, *E. M. Forster: A Life*. Oxford: Oxford University Press, 1979, 106.

In New York City: see Glenn Collins, "A Screenwriter Returns to the Themes of Race and Class in London," *New York Times*, May 24, 1990, B3.

My name is Karim Amir: see Hanif Kureishi, *The Buddha of Suburbia*. London: Faber and Faber, 1990, 3. Later references to 149, 40, and 216.

A kiss rarely carried: see J. R. Ackerley, *Hindoo Holiday*. First published 1932. New York: New York Review of Books, 2000, 240.

Sex and bureaucracy: see Upamanyu Chatterjee, *English, August*. The references to the book are drawn from 127–28, 10, and 1. See also Upamanyu Chatterjee, *Mammaries of the Welfare State*. New Delhi: Viking, 2000.

When I reminded Kureishi of this line: see Amitava Kumar, "A Bang and a Whimper: A Conversation with Hanif Kureishi," *Transition*, vol. 10, no. 4, 114–31.

I like to write about sex: see David Nicholson, "My Beautiful Britain," in *Films and Filming*, January 1988, 9–10.

Sex in *East Is East*: see Stuart Klawans, "On Tyson vs. Downey," *The Nation*, May 15, 2000, 34–36.

NEW YORK

According to INS figures: see Lavina Melwani, "Yesterdays," *Little India*, March 1999, 28–34.

India was far, far away: see Mira Kamdar, *Motiba's Tattoos.* New York: Public Affairs, 2000, 236.

While the astronauts: see Jhumpa Lahiri, *The Interpreter of Maladies.* New York: Houghton Mifflin, 1999, 198.

Azhar founded the jihadi outfit: see, "Jaish-e-Mohammad says jihad will go on against India," *Indian Express,* October 13, 2001.

Face number 33: see "100 Lives. This Is Who We Were," *Washington Post,* January 1, 2000, Section M. See M 4 and also M6–7.

Seasoned translators: See Pico Iyer, *The Global Soul.* New York: Knopf, 2000, 18–20.

Simultaneous translations: see Jhumpa Lahiri, "To Heaven Without Dying," *Feed Magazine,* July 24, 2000.

Sakina's Restaurant: see Philip Gourevitch, "A Husband for Dil," *The New Yorker,* February 22 and March 1, 1999, 78–102.

Misery often makes me: see Akhil Sharma, *An Obedient Father.* New York: Farrar, Straus and Giroux, 2000, 65. See also 54, 92.

I am as good a writer: see Landon Thomas Jr., "Akhil and Mohsin Get Paid," *Financial Observer,* April 23, 2001, 25 and 28.

DIGITAL CITY

When an American calls: see Beth Duff-Brown, "U.S. Dials 1-800-Bangalore," Associated Press, August 3, 2001.

The tech version of burger flipping: see Chidanand Rajghatta, "Curry Fever," *India Abroad,* October 26, 2001, M10–11.

An ancient civilization: see Arundhati Roy, *Power Politics,* 83.

Among the highest-income ethnic groups: see Ashwin Mahesh, "Brown Man's Burden," *India Abroad*, August 3, 2001, 19.

There were 788 Silicon Valley hi-tech companies: see Kuhu Singh, "Techie-la Sunrise," *Indian Express*, July 20, 2001, 18.

The defining character: see Jeff Goodell, "The Venture Capitalist in My Bedroom," *New York Times Magazine*, May 28, 2000, 32–59.

Silicon Valley Indian immigrants: see Melanie Warner, "The Indians of Silicon Valley," *Fortune*, May 15, 2000.

A labor-intensive workplace: see Andrew Ross, "Jobs in Cyberspace," in *Real Love: In Pursuit of Cultural Justice*. New York: New York University Press, 1998, 12.

Foreigners should go home: see Carrie Johnson, "Anger in Downtown Turns Against Foreign-Born Workers," *Washington Post*, September 9, 2001, L1–2.

Temp workers in Silicon Valley: see Raj Jayadev, "Silicon Valley's Underbelly: Overworked, Underpaid, Essential," *San Francisco Chronicle*, January 20, 2002.

The role of "bodyshops": see Amarnath Vedachalam, "The Bloodsuckers," *Little India*, September, 1998.

In a short story: see Vikram Chandra, "Artha," in Vikram Chandra, *Love and Longing in Bombay*. New York: Little, Brown, 1997, 166–67.

High-tech braceros: see William Branigin, "White-Collar Visas: Importing Needed Skills or Cheap Labor?" *Washington Post*, October 21, 1995, A01.

The Immigration and Naturalization Service: see Sujeet Rajan, "Double Whammy," *Indian Express*, October 26, 2001, 14–15.

Battered spouses: see Lakshmi Chaudhry, "World of Pain," *Village Voice*, October 4–10, 2000.

A South Asian women's group: see Linda Ocasio, "In a New Land, Support from Knowing Sources," *New York Times*, November 17, 1999.

Narika: see Aruna Chakravorty, "Indian Brides in US Need to Learn Survival Skills," in *Indian Express*, November 17, 2000, 7.

Artists from aggrieved communities: see George Lipsitz, *Dangerous Crossroads*. New York: Verso, 1994, 34–37.

Bhangra remixes: see Marc Ferris, "A Spicy Mix," *Newsday*, January 7, 2001.

Planet 28: see Somini Sengupta, "To Be Young, Indian and Hip," *New York Times*, June 30, 1996, Section 13, 1.

DJ Siraiki: see Vivek Bald, "Appropriating Technology," interviewers Alondra Nelson and Thuy Linh N. Tu, in *Technicolor*, Alondra Nelson and Thuy Linh N. Tu, eds. New York: New York University Press, 2001, 88–99.

TRAVELING LIGHT

"Think different": see Salman Rushdie, "Mohandas Gandhi," *Time Magazine*, special issue on 100 most important people in history. Undated.

From New York to New Delhi: see Nayantara Sahgal, "With Pride and Prejudice," in *Mirrorwork*, Salman Rushdie and Elizabeth West, eds. New York: Henry Holt, 1997, 5–24.

Gandhi Hall: see Upamanyu Chatterjee, *English, August*, 21.

That suave cosmopolitan: see Vikram Chandra, "The Cult of Authenticity," *Boston Review*, February/March 2000, 49.

Peasants in Gorakhpur: see Shahid Amin, "Gandhi as Mahatma: Gorakhpur District, Eastern UP, 1921–2," in *Subaltern Studies III*, Ranajit Guha, ed. Delhi: Oxford University Press, 1984, 1–61.

An early novel: see Bharati Mukherjee, *Jasmine*. New York: Grove, 1989, 151–52, 144–45, and 69.

A recent novel: see Manil Suri, *The Death of Vishnu*. New York: Norton, 2001, 185–210.

FLIGHT

In a plane in 1932: see Rabindranath Tagore, "Persia, April 13, 1932," in Rabindranath Tagore, *Rabindranath Tagore: An Anthology*. Krishna Dutta and Andrew Robinson, eds. New York: St. Martin's Press, 1997, 126–29.

A jet is blown apart: see Salman Rushdie, *The Satanic Verses*.

A body was discovered in a parking lot: see, Esther Addley and Rory McCarthy, "The Man Who Fell to Earth," *Guardian*, July 18, 2001, G2, 1–3.

It looked like a desperate ballet: see Michael Specter, "The Twisted Sky," *The New Yorker On-Line*, September 12, 2001.

INDEX